THE WOLFSONIAN–
FLORIDA INTERNATIONAL UNIVERSITY

The Journal of Decorative and Propaganda

SOUVENIRS
AND OBJECTS OF REMEMBRANCE

THEME ISSUE

The Wolfsonian

Issue 27, Souvenirs and Objects of Remembrance Theme Issue
The Journal of Decorative and Propaganda Arts,
published by The Wolfsonian–Florida International University.
ISBN 978-1-930776-19-7
ISSN 0888-7314

Editorial Offices:
The Journal of Decorative and Propaganda Arts
The Wolfsonian–Florida International University
1001 Washington Avenue
Miami Beach, Florida 33139
Telephone: (305) 535-2613
Fax: (305) 531-2133
Email: dapa@thewolf.fiu.edu
www.wolfsonian.org

Distributed by Penn State University Press,
www.psupress.org.

For information on the availability of back issues,
contact The Wolfsonian–FIU Museum Shop,
(305) 535-2680, museumshop@thewolf.fiu.edu.

Cover: Postcard, Germany, 1917. Collection of Mike Robinson.

Support for Issue 27 has come from the
American Art Foundation, Leonard A. Lauder, President.

Printed in Spain by Grafos S.A.

THE WOLFSONIAN–
FLORIDA INTERNATIONAL UNIVERSITY

The Journal of Decorative and Propaganda Arts

27

SOUVENIRS
AND OBJECTS OF REMEMBRANCE

THEME ISSUE

FOREWORD

Sharon Misdea
Deputy Director for Collections and Curatorial Affairs
The Wolfsonian–Florida International University

The collection of The Wolfsonian–Florida International University focuses on the century that ended with the Second World War, a time of social and political upheaval and accelerating technological change. It is not surprising, given this historical context, that many of the museum's holdings point toward the future, an outlook expressed by such objects as a model for the Trylon and Perisphere at the 1939 New York World's Fair and Hugh Ferriss's visionary renderings of *The Metropolis of Tomorrow*. What is striking about the collection, however, is how much of it looks back. Commemorative medallions, murals depicting historical scenes, photograph albums, or even the application of "Revival" styles in decorative arts and architecture, all give fixed form to understandings of the past and to fleeting, malleable memories. Precisely for that reason, they play a critical role in modern cultures where, as Karl Marx put it, "all that is solid melts into air."

With this issue of the *Journal of Decorative and Propaganda Arts*, The Wolfsonian gives full attention to this capacity of objects to depict or evoke the past. Taken together, the ten essays collected here affirm the power of The Wolfsonian's approach to visual and material culture, one that finds meaning in all human-made objects as artifacts that reveal important dimensions of the societies that produced them. Souvenirs and objects of remembrance, it turns out, include the kinds of things one would expect, such as commemorative ceramics, photograph albums, devotional prints sold at pilgrimage sites, and postcards from international expositions.

But they also include handmade toys, the intricate marquetry of a tabletop, cotton headscarves, and an irradiated dime. By juxtaposing these and many other types of objects, the contents of this issue echo the juxtapositions of objects that visitors typically find in The Wolfsonian's galleries.

Such an approach is made possible only by a commitment to interdisciplinarity. The authors of these essays come from a range of scholarly fields—including history; art, decorative art, design, and photography history; and tourism studies—and bring to bear insights derived from other fields as well. Equally diverse is the geographic scope of the essays' focus, which includes the United States, Japan, India, the Netherlands, Great Britain, France, and Austria.

Congratulations and thanks for setting the ambitious intellectual agenda for this issue, as well as offering advice that helped shape the individual essays, go to Marta Zarzycka, assistant professor of Gender Studies and Photography Studies, Utrecht University, who served as guest editor. Throughout, she has demonstrated a strong commitment to the success of the project, as well as patience and good humor in working with The Wolfsonian's team. Jon Mogul, assistant director for research and academic programs at The Wolfsonian, served as senior editor. I thank Jon for guiding the project from beginning to end and for his extensive editorial contributions, while serving as a valued member of the museum's senior management team. Kara Pickman's expert copy editing and proofreading were invaluable in the last stages of the project.

The production of this issue represented a happy reunion of sorts, as it gave us a chance to work with Tim Hossler, The Wolfsonian's former art director who now teaches visual communications at the University of Kansas. Thanks to Tim's great design work, and to Marlene Tosca, the museum's current art director, the issue's visual content is a match for its editorial content. The Wolfsonian's photographers, David Almeida and Lynton Gardiner, also contributed their time and expertise to the project.

Leonard A. Lauder has been a friend of the museum for many years and, even before the museum itself opened, a reader of the *Journal*. As one of the world's great collectors of postcards, he is well aware of how inexpensive, mass-produced "ephemera" can often serve profoundly important purposes once transformed into keepsakes, something for individuals to preserve and cherish. It is very fitting, then, that this issue is made possible by his generous financial support. I cannot thank him enough.

The animating vision behind the *Journal* remains that of Mitchell Wolfson, Jr. As founder of both the *Journal* and The Wolfsonian, he has been a champion of scholarship that uncovers the astonishing variety of meanings and purposes—remembrance being just one among them—attached to the things that people make. The intellectual generosity of his vision, one that can accommodate everything from devotional prints to irradiated dimes, is what inspires our work, including this publication.

INTRODUCTION: SOUVENIRS AND OBJECTS OF REMEMBRANCE

Marta Zarzycka
Guest Editor

Jonathan Mogul
Senior Editor

Memories are constructs of the mind and, as such, notoriously subject to changing, fading, and vanishing entirely. It is the very malleability and ephemerality of memory that make physical objects, with their quality of (relative) physical stability, so important for processes of remembrance. The scholar Peter Stallybrass wrote movingly about the experience of delivering a paper while wearing a jacket given to him by the widow of a deceased close friend. In the middle of his talk, he was suddenly overcome by the sense that his friend had returned: "He was there in the wrinkles of the elbows, wrinkles which in the technical jargon of sewing are called 'memory'; he was there in the stains at the very bottom of the jacket; he was there in the smell of the armpits."[1] While keepsakes such as a piece of clothing or a travel souvenir enable us to recall people or life episodes that carry intimate meaning, other sorts of objects, especially large monuments, are focal points for collective rituals of remembrance of traumatic or triumphant episodes in local, national, and global history.

Among the most important dimensions of the "social life of things"[2] is their acquisition of meanings from human uses, transactions, attributions, and emotional attachments, all of which enable them to mediate between the lived present and the remembered past. The relationship between object and memory can be either accidental or intentional. Some things, like a family photograph album, are created in order to serve the purposes of memory; others, like a decades-old toy encountered by chance during a visit to a childhood home, may unexpectedly evoke one's personal past. In his introduction to the book *Material Memories: Design and Evocation*, Marius Kwint identified three forms this relationship can take: objects can "furnish recollection," becoming an important part of the mental picture of the past; they can "stimulate remembering" (as in the case of the jacket described by Stallybrass); and they can "form records" that expand the limited capacities of our minds for holding information about the past.[3]

Although the significance of objects for personal and collective memory is not in any way a phenomenon of recent times, objects of remembrance have proliferated since the eighteenth century, speaking to a widely felt desire for tangible markers of both fleeting personal experiences and significant public events. As Kwint writes, the characteristically modern idea that time moves in a linear direction and that the past is irretrievable makes the stability possessed by objects all the more meaningful in terms of memory.[4] At the same time, new production processes and technologies and the expansion of national and international markets have made such objects more widely and cheaply available than ever before.

The ten essays in this issue of the *Journal of Decorative and Propaganda Arts* investigate objects of remembrance as they are embedded in broad processes of modernity. They address such phenomena as European and Japanese colonial expansion (and resistance), world war and political upheaval, the growth of travel and tourism, technological change, and the expansion of commodity culture. They include examples from Asia, Europe, and the United States, and run the social gamut from religious pilgrims in colonial India, to Viennese designers and their wealthy patrons, to middle-class Americans in the mid-twentieth century.

Although the essays address diverse contexts and social and cultural practices, there are several themes that tie them together. First is the idea that the contest between forgetting and remembering that is a central part of public life in the modern world takes place not only through politicians' speeches, history books, and commemorative events, but also on the level of everyday objects. While essays by Paul Bijl and Peter Clericuzio show how people mobilize objects to assert historical claims against a dominant discourse that would prefer to forget them, those by Elizabeth Heath, Mike Robinson, and Kari Shepherdson-Scott address how objects—photograph albums, postcards, a photography book—play a role in the cultural aphasia that is part and parcel of nostalgic remembering. A second common theme of many of the essays is the importance of commodity culture in forming modern memory. From the cheap commercial lithographs sold at a Hindu shrine in Imma Ramos's essay or the world's fair souvenirs described by Ethan Robey, to the matchbooks given away by hotels and restaurants discussed by Anna Jozefacka, modern processes of remembrance are powerfully shaped by mass-produced objects made available through market exchange. Finally, the importance of objects for forming (partially) memory-based class, national, and other collective identities—whether the middle-class camera owners discussed by Makeda Best, the wealthy purchasers of Wiener Werkstätte toys in Megan Brandow-Faller's essay, the colonial elites described by Heath and Shepherdson-Scott, or the colonial or post-colonial subjects addressed by Bijl and Ramos—is a theme that runs throughout the collected essays.

Souvenirs, as tangible markers of a particular experience or place, are the class of objects most directly linked to remembrance. Imma Ramos's essay, which opens the issue, is a reminder that today's souvenir industry has a centuries-old lineage connected to religious pilgrimage. The essay's focus, however, is the role pilgrimage souvenirs play in modern political life, as much as in religious practice. Ramos writes about the watercolor paintings and mass-produced chromolithographs sold to nineteenth-century pilgrims at the Kalighat temple in Calcutta, one of many shrines to the goddess Sati scattered across India. Featuring depictions of the god Shiva carrying Sati's lifeless body following her self-sacrificial death, these souvenirs were not only a means for pilgrims to extend the religious experience of Sati worship upon their return home, but also acquired a "political electricity" as the body of Sati came to stand for India itself in the rhetoric of anticolonial nationalism that flourished toward the end of the century. The next essay, by Ethan Robey, switches attention to souvenirs of secular, rather than religious, pilgrimage. The proliferation of world's fairs starting in the second half of the nineteenth century was an important spur to the growth of mass production of memorabilia. Robey writes about the postcards, ceramics, textiles, and other items that memorialized the spectacular displays of electrical power at early twentieth-century American fairs. Much like irradiated dimes available later in the century at displays promoting nuclear energy, these souvenirs looked forward—toward visions of technological modernity—even as they looked backward to the individual's experience visiting a fair; they were "reminders of something that would be, as much as something that was," in Robey's words.

Perhaps the quintessential modern object of remembrance is the photograph. Makeda Best's essay focuses on the design of the Kodak No. 1 camera, which from its 1888 introduction was marketed by the Eastman Company as a device linked to remembrance. She shows how Eastman's camera and the advertising that accompanied it engaged nonvisual, "proximal" senses of touch and bodily motion in the process of recording scenes for memory. The camera was, in Best's words, an "active sensory interface between the user and the world." The next three authors examine photographs themselves, paying particular attention to their various material manifestations as memory objects—pasted into albums, printed on postcards, or published in an expensive art book. Elizabeth Heath writes about the photograph albums compiled by British officials and travelers in nineteenth-century India. Comparing albums made by disparate individuals, she finds striking similarities in terms of the scenes they record and argues that they emerged from, and also reinforced, a collective narrative about the British role in India. Like colonial travelers in India, German soldiers during the First World War carried cameras with them as they marched east and west. They were at liberty to take snapshots with their portable cameras and often sent the film to laboratories that printed the photographs onto the backs of postcards. By examining these so-called real photographic postcards, Mike Robinson shows how soldiers often mimicked the memory-recording practices they might have learned as tourists before the war, emphasizing moments of camaraderie, playfulness, or homelike comfort amid the trauma and destruction of war. The last essay in this group, by Kari Shepherdson-Scott, is about a 1958 book by the Japanese art photographer Fuchikami Hakuyō. Compiled from photographs taken in the Japanese puppet state of Manchukuo during the 1930s and 1940s, the book offered a nostalgic, aestheticized view of the Japanese colonial enterprise on the Asian continent, wiped clean of violence and suffering—a visual manifestation of the "process of remembering and forgetting the Japanese experience in northeast Asia" in the postwar period.

Essays by Peter Clericuzio and Megan Brandow-Faller concentrate on how memory can inflect the design of objects. In the case of the French designers who are the subjects of Clericuzio's essay, this inflection was explicit and intentional. He writes about designers and architects who strove to resurrect the "lost provinces" of Alsace and Lorraine, annexed by Germany from France during the Franco-Prussian War, in French national consciousness. They did so by incorporating ornamental elements that evoked the regions' historical traditions in their designs for furniture, glassware, buildings, and exposition pavilions. Brandow-Faller's essay about early twentieth-century Viennese toy design is concerned with personal rather than collective memory. She writes that the toys produced by designers in the Wiener Werkstätte's orbit expressed nostalgia for the playthings of their own childhoods, products of a supposedly authentic vernacular culture uncorrupted by modern commercialism. Such toys, Brandow-Faller argues, were designed to appeal to adult memories of childhood at least as much as to the desires of children.

The last two essays in the issue emphasize the meanings that users, rather than producers, give to objects. The matchbook, as Anna Jozefacka writes, was invented in the late nineteenth century as a utilitarian source of flame and soon acquired a complementary purpose as an advertising medium for restaurants, hotels, and other establishments. Jozefacka's interest lies in what people do with matchbooks besides light cigarettes. She compares the practices of hobbyist collectors, for whom the matchbooks are advertising ephemera that shed light on the visual culture of their times, with collections that treat matchbooks as personal memorabilia—accidental souvenirs—that offer a path of reminiscence through youthful experiences. Paul Bijl's essay, the last in the issue, concerns the *angisa*, a kind of headscarf worn by enslaved women in the former Dutch colony of Suriname, that is now a common feature at ceremonies dedicated to the remembrance of slavery in the Netherlands. Bijl argues that the women who wear *angisas* on those occasions are performing an act of memory that defies the powerful impulse in Dutch discourse to forget the history of slavery in the Dutch West Indies.

*****

When the present is separated from the past not just by time, but also by unbridgeable physical distance, the capacity of objects to conjure memories becomes especially meaningful. Edward Said wrote about the objects that Palestinians carried into exile:

> These intimate mementos of a past irrevocably lost circulate among us, like the genealogies and fables of a wandering singer of tales. Photographs, dresses, objects severed from their original locale, the rituals of speech and custom: much

> reproduced, enlarged, thematized, embroidered, and passed around, they are strands in the web of affiliations we Palestinians use to tie ourselves to our identity and to each other.[5]

Said's passage recognizes that tangible, portable things (like "albums, rosary beads, shawls, little boxes"), whatever private and idiosyncratic meanings they may have for individuals, also tie displaced people to one another and to the shared past that is the basis for forming community.[6] His words suggest, at the same time, the contingent, even poetic, relationships such objects bear to that same past. "[T]he genealogies and fables of a wandering singer of tales" are not to be understood as photographic records of what happened before.[7] Indeed, as several of the essays gathered here have shown, photographic records themselves, together with other kinds of souvenirs, offer a view of the past that is filtered through nostalgia, social and ethnic hierarchies, and powerful cultural narratives such as nationalism or technological optimism. Souvenirs are there to prompt remembrance; but what they show us is never a simple reflection of what they claim to represent.

NOTES

1. Peter Stallybrass, "Worn Worlds: Clothes, Mourning, and the Life of Things," *Yale Review* 81, no. 2 (April 1993): 36.
2. This phrase was coined by Arjun Appadurai for the title of the edited collection *The Social Life of Things: Commodities in Cultural Perspective* (Cambridge: Cambridge University Press, 1986).
3. Marius Kwint, "Introduction: The Physical Past," in *Material Memories: Design and Evocation*, ed. Marius Kwint, Christopher Breward, and Jeremy Aynsley (Oxford: Berg, 1999), 2.
4. Ibid., 9–10.
5. Edward Said, *After the Last Sky: Palestinian Lives* (New York: Columbia University Press, 1999), 14.
6. Ibid.
7. Ibid.

COPYRIGHT REGISTERED
महादेव
" মহাদেবঃ সতীদেহং স্কন্ধে নিধায় নৃত্যতি।
তদ্দেহং বিষ্ণুনা ছেত্তুং প্রিয়তেঽসৌ সুদর্শনঃ ॥"
MAHADEV
Designed & Published by The Calcutta Art Studio
মহাদেব
185 Bowbazar Street. Calcutta.

THE FRAGMENTATION OF SATI: CONSTRUCTING HINDU IDENTITY THROUGH PILGRIMAGE SOUVENIRS

Imma Ramos

Imma Ramos completed her doctorate at the University of Cambridge in the department of the History of Art. Her research concerns the role of cultural nationalism in India and the relationship between politics and religion in the visual arts from the nineteenth century until the present. Her thesis examines how the Bengali population reclaimed traditional Hindu practices during the British colonial period. In particular, it explores the reception of places of worship dedicated to the Hindu goddess Sati, known as Shakti Pithas.

In 1883, the Bengali playwright Girishchandra Ghosh staged the story of the martyr-goddess Sati for a Calcutta audience made up, according to one source, of fifteen hundred spectators.[1] That very year, the Calcutta Art Studio, which specialized in inexpensive lithographs, published a print depicting Sati's sacrifice (fig. 1). In the late nineteenth century, this particular image, along with others made by Kalighat *patuas* (village artists), began proliferating in Calcutta. They were intended as souvenirs for pilgrims to the city's Kalighat temple, which was said to enshrine Sati's sacred remnants.

This essay examines how these souvenirs contributed to resurrecting the myth of Sati's fragmented body as an icon of cultural crisis and national consciousness by visually articulating the rhetoric of sacrifice for one's country. The Sati myth had a profound resonance with Bengali audiences in the late nineteenth century as part of the broader development of Hindu nationalism among the Western-educated middle classes, or *bhadralok*, in Calcutta, the British imperial capital and epicenter of the colonial encounter.[2] In order to inspire patriotism and anticolonial sentiment among the indigenous population, many Hindu nationalists represented the nation as female in literature and in visual culture. The personification of India as a mother goddess, subjugated by foreign rulers, was a rhetorical device designed to encourage Hindus to adopt the role of her loyal children. Perhaps the most prominent manifestation of this gendered conception of the Indian nation was Bharat Mata (Mother India), a

fig. 1
Calcutta Art Studio, *Shiva and Sati*, hand-colored lithograph, 16 1/8 x 12 in. (41 x 30.5 cm), 1883. Collection of Mark and Elise Baron.

fig. 2
P. S. Ramachandra Rao, *The Splendour that Is India*, chromolithograph, P. Ethirajiah and Sons, Madras (printer), c. 1947. Priya Paul Collection of Popular Art.

goddess first invoked in an 1868 poem by Jyotirindranath Tagore.[3] Bharat Mata is usually portrayed as a woman dressed in a traditional sari, either wielding the flag of India or else directly superimposed on a cartographic outline of the country (fig. 2). This icon achieved such hegemonic status that it has obscured an important contemporary parallel in the Sati myth, rendered with remarkable consistency through images of the god Shiva carrying the body of his lifeless wife, Sati.

The Sati Myth and Kalighat Pilgrimage

The earliest known illustration of the Sati myth appeared around the turn of the nineteenth century in an anonymous miniature painting (fig. 3), but the myth itself dates back to before the tenth century. It is probable that the myth was not depicted for many centuries because it is a narrative of suffering, a theme not usually present in Hindu devotional iconography. According to versions of the story in the *Kalika* and *Devibhagavata Puranas*

fig. 3
Artist unknown, *Shiva Carrying Sati on His Trident*, watercolor and gold on paper, 11.5 x 16 in. (29.2 x 40.6 cm), Himachal Pradesh (Kangra), c. 1800. Los Angeles County Museum of Art.

(religious texts devoted to the veneration of the divine feminine, or Shakti, dated to around the tenth and eleventh centuries CE, respectively), Sati's father, King Daksha, did not invite her husband, Shiva, to his *yajna*, a ceremonial sacrifice during which oblations are poured into a ritual fire. Humiliated by this act of disrespect, Sati performed self-immolation. The distraught Shiva retrieved her body and began to dance with it in his arms across the cosmos. His grief risked the destruction of the world, so Vishnu, god of preservation, threw his discus and cut Sati's body into pieces, which were scattered across the undivided subcontinent.

From the seventh century CE onward, a network of Shakti Pithas (Seats of Power) was established to enshrine each piece of the goddess.[4] At many of the Shakti Pithas, particularly those in Bengal, the representation of Shiva carrying Sati functions as a visual reminder of their dedication to Sati's relics, as at Nalhati, home of Sati's vocal pipe (fig. 4). Before devotees reach Fullara Attahas temple in Birbhum, a gate commissioned in 2001 welcomes them; Sati and Shiva appear at the top, while fifty-one panels all around classify each body part and its location (figs. 5, 6).

The Shakti Pithas, however, are dedicated not only to Sati's relics, but to local goddesses as well. Many of these temples, in fact, were originally associated with various non-Vedic goddesses, and the Pithas may have been

fig. 4
Relief sculpture of Shiva carrying Sati at Nalhati temple (a Shakti Pitha in Birbhum, West Bengal), twentieth century. Author's photograph, 2012.

fig. 5
Gate at Fullara Attahas temple (a Shakti Pitha in Birbhum, West Bengal), c. 2001. Author's photograph, 2012.

conceived as a way to legitimize and integrate these local goddesses into the Brahmin (orthodox Hindu) pantheon.[5] These shrines thus articulate the paradox that the goddess is both formless (cosmic and unified, as Sati) and form-bound (in her manifestation as a local goddess).[6] Since Sati's "relics" are often either concealed from view or take the form of a rough, uncarved stone, devotees frequently focus their devotion on the *murti* (divinely embodied icon) of the local goddess.

Today it is commonly accepted that there are fifty-one Pithas, as listed in the authoritative *Mahapithanirupana* (1690–1720), a sacred text dedicated to the sites. Kalighat was acknowledged as a Shakti Pitha from at least the fifteenth century, when the ascetic Chowranga Giri received a vision of the goddess Kali telling him that the toes of Sati were buried on that spot. The present temple was built in 1809 and follows the *atchala* (eight-roof) hut pattern, a traditional Bengali design. The building consists of one large room, the inner sanctum, surrounded by an elevated, circumambulatory balcony. The Kali *murti* is in full view as devotees circle around it. The *murti* was created in the nineteenth century to contain Sati's toes. It consists primarily of a face with a large, golden tongue (held in place by an upper row of golden teeth), four hands, and feet. The prominence of the latter is an apt reference to Sati's toes, as well as an indication of the pilgrims' desire to touch the feet of the goddess. Sati's toes, in the form of a stone, are said to be kept inside a box below the *murti.*

Kalighat temple is a significant site of pilgrimage. The Sanskrit word for a place of pilgrimage is *tirtha*, which derives from the root *tr*, meaning to "cross over"—that is, to make a transition to the divine. However, Kalighat

fig. 6
Panels around Fullara Attahas gate, c. 2001, representing Sati's dismembered body parts. Author's photograph, 2012.

and other sites dedicated to Sati's remains are known as Pithas, or "seats," stressing the rootedness of the goddess, whose power is firmly grounded in the earth itself. The hundreds of pilgrimage sites across India created a network that was hugely significant in the construction of a Hindu cultural identity. As Sister Nivedita, a Scots-Irish writer and disciple of Swami Vivekananda, pointed out in "An Indian Pilgrimage" (1904):

> All over India, away from her ancient high roads, and thrown like a network across her proudest Himalayas, are little thread-like paths like this—ways made indeed by the feet of men, but worn far deeper by the weight of impelling ideas than by the footprints of the toil-stained crowds.... Assuredly, a deep and conscious love of place pervades the whole of the Indian scheme. It has never been called patriotism, only because it has never been defined by boundaries of contrast; but the home, the village, the soil, and, in a larger sense, the rivers, the mountains, and the country as a whole, are the objects of an almost passionate adoration.... In its essence, the institution [of pilgrimage] is so entirely an expression of love for the Motherland.[7]

The Pithas, which linked together all the corners of India, expressed a worldview in which the earth was considered sacred and the goddess embodied herself in earthly form. Together, they formed a powerful pilgrimage network that affirmed the notion that the subcontinent itself was a goddess. This deification of the earth is ancient and pervasive in the Hindu tradition: Prithvi Mata (Earth Mother) is the primordial goddess of the *Rgveda* (a collection of Vedic Sanskrit verse, composed roughly between 1700 and 1100 BCE), while Bhudevi (Mother Earth) appears in the *Vishnu Purana* (a sacred text dedicated to the god Vishnu, dated approximately to the fourth century BCE).

The social dimension of pilgrimage was also significant in nationalist discourse. Victor Turner's interpretation of pilgrimage in terms of *communitas* is relevant here; according to him, pilgrimage could temporarily dissolve social hierarchies by creating a sense of communal belonging. Turner suggests that pilgrimages are "both instruments and indicators of a sort of mystical regionalism as well as of a mystical nationalism."[8] As Sister Nivedita noted: "the [Shakti] Pithas not only make a cultural impact but also a social impact," referring to their accessibility to pilgrims regardless of caste, creed, and sex.[9] Crucially, she pointed out, "railways have in modern times opened up the country, and created the possibility of a geographical sense amongst classes who in older days could not have aspired to travel far or often."[10]

When pilgrims reach Kalighat temple today, they carry out rites that enable them to achieve a state of communion with the divine. Clockwise circumambulation around the sacred *murti* is a habitual observance. They approach the goddess for the granting of health, procreation, longevity, protection from danger, and enlightenment.[11] To experience *darshan*, or "sacred vision," of the *murti* is the ultimate objective of pilgrimage, involving seeing and being seen by the deity in a reciprocal act of "visual communion."[12] Sight in this case is not passive, but an active form of sensual tactility, an imprint made by the eyes onto the object of worship.

fig. 7
Artist unknown, *Kali Murti*, watercolor on paper, 17 1/2 x 11 in. (44.5 x 27.9 cm), c. 1865. © Victoria and Albert Museum, London.

fig. 8 (opposite)
Artist unknown, *Shiva and Sati*, watercolor on paper, 18 x 11 1/8 in. (45.6 x 28.2 cm), c. 1885. © Victoria and Albert Museum, London.

Kalighat *Pats* and the Souvenir Trade

For pilgrims in the nineteenth century, souvenirs such as the paintings and prints of Sati sold at Kalighat temple extended and preserved the religious experience at Calcutta's most famous site of worship. One could have the experience of *darshan* not only of the temple *murti*, but also of the souvenir itself, which retained the religious potency of the site and reminded devotees of its association with Sati. Christopher Pinney coined the term *corpothetics* to denote this experience in the case of Hindu popular prints in particular, entailing a religious "desire to fuse image and beholder."[13] Unlike the temple *murti*, which was formally installed in a fixed position and whose worship was mediated by priests, these affordable, portable souvenirs could be placed anywhere by individuals wishing to have direct contact with their chosen deity. In the course of a pilgrimage, devotees took home such mementos so that the benefits of their visit could continue to be enjoyed.

One form that Kalighat souvenirs took in the second half of the nineteenth century was watercolor paintings known as *pats*. These peaked in popularity from the 1850s to the 1880s.[14] They were made by former village scroll painters who used to travel from place to place singing stories from the Hindu epics depicted on the paintings during village gatherings and festivals.[15] Migration to Calcutta was encouraged by the availability there of industrial products such as mill-made paper and watercolors, and by a high demand for souvenirs that came when the introduction of railways increased the flow of pilgrims (as well as traders and tourists). By 1871, Calcutta had become connected with the national railway network linking it with Varanasi, Bombay, Allahabad, and Agra. Other minor lines connected the city with more rural areas of Bengal.[16]

In 1932, Mukul Dey nostalgically described the souvenir trade around Kalighat temple during his "younger days" two decades earlier:

> The lanes and bye-lanes leading to the temple courtyard were full of small shops dealing with everything interesting to the pilgrims. . . . There were. . .pictures in colours as well as in lines, hung up in almost all the shops. . . . The *patuas* would naturally sell a good lot of these pictures every year and I remember to have seen

> many in my younger days, at least 30 or 40 shops in those bye-lanes to deal exclusively in these pictures and I remember the *patuas* drawing the pictures in their "shop-studios". . . . [They] would draw paintings and sell them before standing crowds of buyers.[17]

The *patuas* adapted their skills to provide cheap pictures for the pilgrims to Kalighat temple, rendering single iconic scenes or characters instead of the sequential narrative required of scroll paintings. Each painting measured about forty-five by twenty-eight centimeters and was inexpensive, costing one anna, or one-sixteenth of a rupee. These shops offered watercolor souvenirs that portrayed a variety of subjects, including the temple's Kali *murti* (fig. 7), but one of the chief subjects of the Kalighat *pats* was the Sati myth (figs. 8–10).

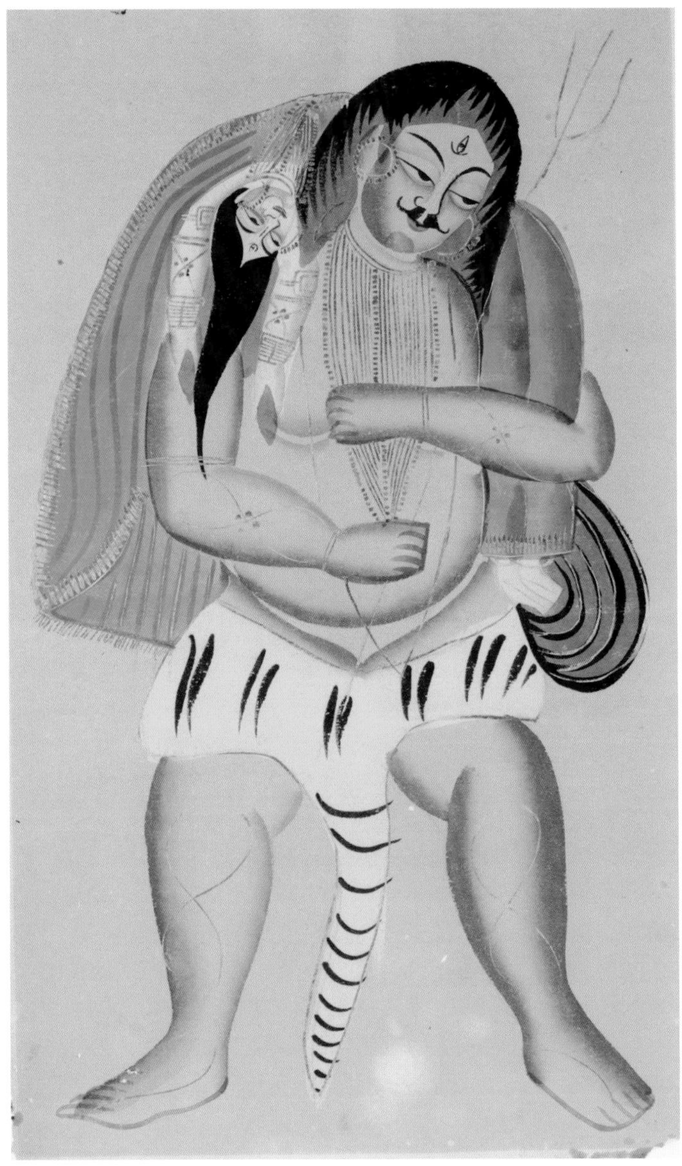

The requirement that the paintings be made quickly to cater to this high demand was undoubtedly a crucial determinant of the Kalighat style, with its vigor and bold simplicity. The resulting basic pictorial vocabulary focused on key narrative elements, boiling the story down to its bare essentials. For example, in the case of the Sati myth, the key element apart from the figures of Shiva and Sati is often Vishnu's *chakra* (discus) hovering beside or above them, poised as if about to dismember Sati's corpse (fig. 9). The discus functions as a reminder that Sati's body was distributed across the country, crucial to the story in the context of the larger network of pilgrimage sites. The *pats* emphasize Shiva's virility by means of the tiger skin around his waist, a phallic tail hanging suggestively below his torso. This image of an ascetic yet very masculine Shiva was in marked contrast with the contemporaneous stereotype of the *bhadralok babu*, a submissive Bengali servant of the British colonial administration—also a subject for depiction in *pats* (fig. 11). As Dey commented, "These 'shop-studios' in those days were more or less news

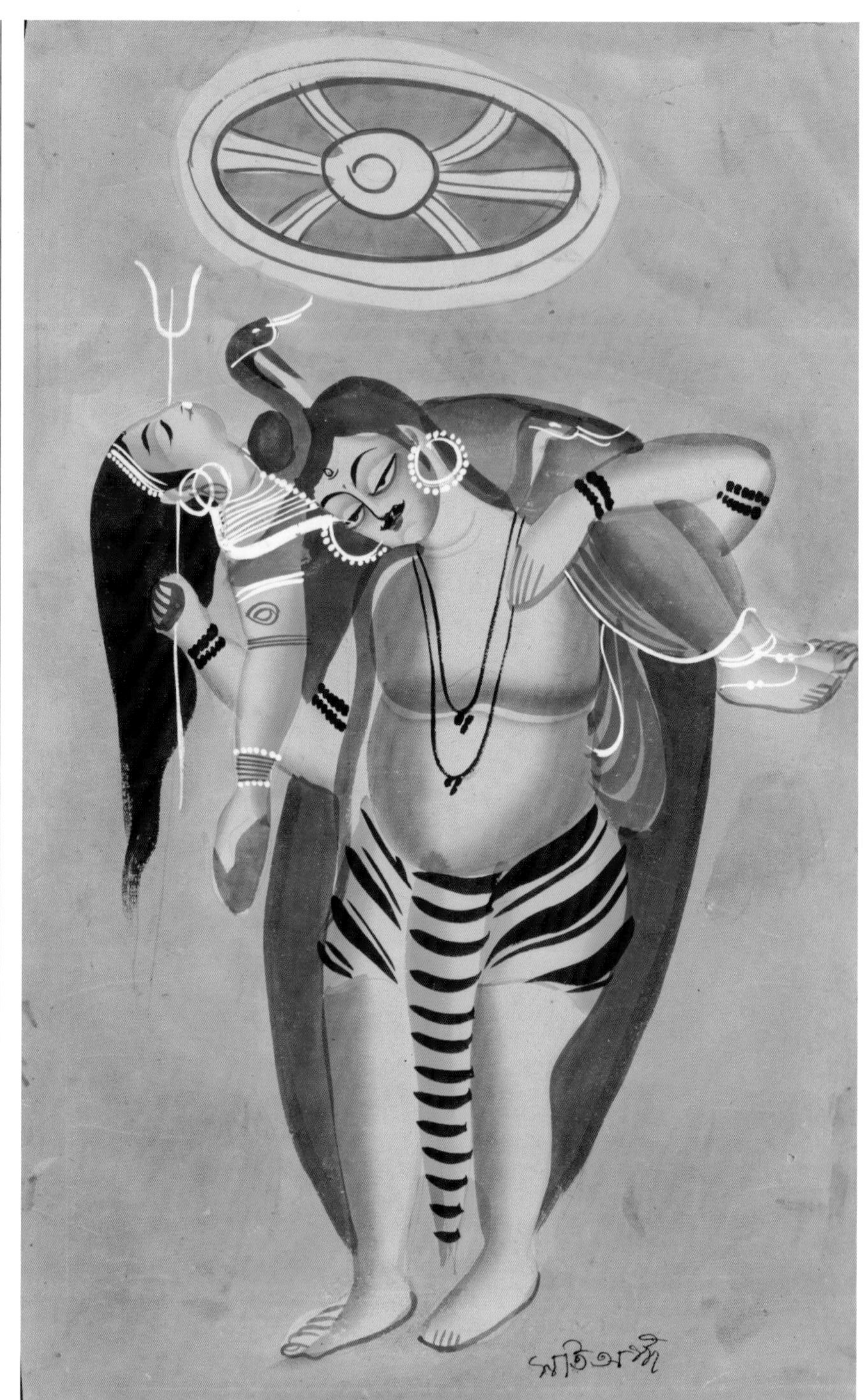

fig. 9
Artist unknown,
Shiva and Sati, watercolor on paper, approximately 17 $^{3}/_{4}$ x 11 in. (45 x 28 cm), c. 1885. © Victoria and Albert Museum, London.

fig. 10 (opposite)
Artist unknown,
Shiva and Sati, watercolor on paper, approximately 17 $^{3}/_{4}$ x 11 in. (45 x 28 cm), c. 1890. © Victoria and Albert Museum, London.

bureaus of the country, where not only the pictures of mythological subjects were drawn but caricatures and satirical sketches would be drawn dealing with the topics of the day."[18]

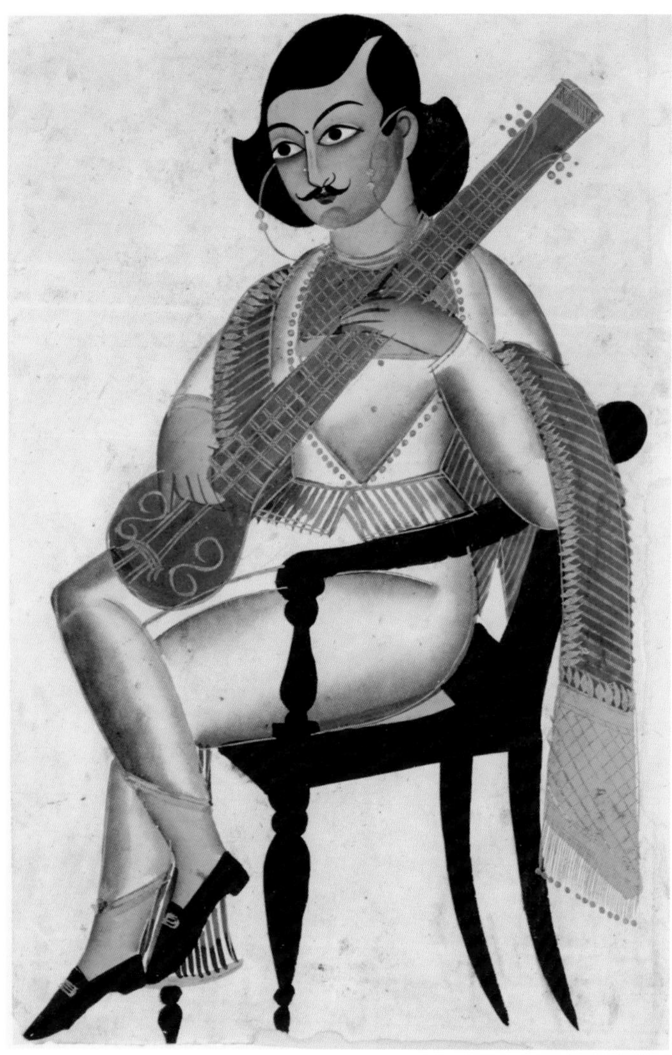

Usually the pilgrimage souvenirs would adorn the household prayer room or drawing room. Dey, writing about Kalighat paintings, noted that:

> As pilgrims know no caste or difference in wealth, naturally these pictures would be taken, liked and hung by peoples of all classes and communities from the big Rajas and *zamindars* down to the most ordinary villagers and children.... They would brighten up—some of them—the drawing-rooms of people of all sorts; they would add a touch of colour and joy in the humble hut of the tiller of the soil; and the village grocer or the "panwalla" round the corner of a city street would find no better and no cheaper decoration than these pictures.[19]

fig. 11
Artist unknown, *Babu*, watercolor on paper, 17 1/4 x 11 3/8 in. (43.8 x 28.9 cm), 1870–85. © Victoria and Albert Museum, London.

Political Electricity

In portraying the Sati myth, pilgrimage souvenirs like the Kalighat *pats* were taking on a subject fraught with both spiritual and political meaning. According to Hindu belief, the Shakti Pithas were animated by Sati's divine presence. Through her dismemberment, the *shakti* (power) in her body was distributed across the subcontinent, stressing her relationship to the earth. Bengali writers, artists, and intellectuals responded to the myth by reformulating and resurrecting her into a more powerful body, India itself. The nineteenth-century increase in the story's popularity suggested to some nationalists that the concept of the subcontinent representing the body of the goddess was a manifestation of a precolonial sense of national unity. They thus contested claims by such figures as the British administrator Sir John Strachey that "there is not, and never was an India"[20]; or by a European schoolteacher who told the future Bengali nationalist writer Bhudev Mukhopadhyay that patriotism was unknown to Hindus. For Bhudev, the Sati myth showed that "the entire motherland with its fifty-two places of pilgrimage is in truth the person of the deity."[21] Sister Nivedita similarly singled out the Pithas: "In the story of Sati. . .who can miss the significance of the fifty-two places in which fragments of the smitten body fell? . . . No foreigner can understand the crowding of associations. . . . Nor is the historic element lacking, in this unconscious worship of country."[22]

Diana Eck has pointed out that "recognition of India as a sacred landscape, woven together north and south, east and west, by the paths of pilgrims, has created a powerful sense of India as Bharat Mata—Mother India."[23] This conception of India is made even more explicit by the Pithas that enshrine Sati's remnants. As Sati's fragmented body is multiplied and distributed across the subcontinent, so is her power. For Bhudev and Sister Nivedita, the Pithas formed a network of sites that transformed each individual act of devotion into a collective reverence for India itself.

The political salience of the Sati myth became highly evident in the response of revolutionary nationalists to the British Partition of Bengal in 1905—a literal dismemberment or fragmentation of the nation by the colonial power. Aurobindo Ghosh, one of the leaders of the Swadeshi (self-sufficiency) movement that arose at this time to contest British power, published a rousing 1908 article for the English-language newspaper *Bande Mataram* titled "The Parable of Sati." In it, he reinterpreted the story in terms of the contemporary political struggle in India, with Sati representing the Indian nation, and Shiva India's destiny. For now their union had been frustrated:

> Sati had left her old body and men said she was dead. But she was not dead, only withdrawn from the eyes of men, and the gods clove the body of Sati into pieces so that it was scattered all over India.... For Sati will be born again, on the high mountains of mighty endeavour, colossal aspiration, unparalleled self-sacrifice she will be born again, in a better and more beautiful body, and by terrible *tapasyā* [asceticism] she will meet Mahadeva [Shiva] once more and be wedded to him in nobler fashion, with kinder auguries, for a happier and greater future.... Sati shall wed Mahadeva, that the national life of India shall meet and possess its divine and mighty destiny.[24]

The political reinterpretation and adaptation of the Sati myth that emerged in the late nineteenth century made it suitable for nationalist, anticolonial discourse, thus nurturing modern nation-formation in India. Bruce Lincoln's theory of myth is useful in this context; to him, myth is a narrative device that serves to resolve anxieties in a changing or threatened world. Under conditions of political fragmentation and colonial rule, Hindu nationalists sought an empowered identity by forging a

fig. 12
Detail of fig. 3. Artist unknown, *Shiva Carrying Sati on his Trident*, watercolor and gold on paper, 11 1/2 x 16 in. (29.2 x 40.6 cm), Himachal Pradesh (Kangra), c. 1800. Los Angeles County Museum of Art.

remembered national unity through mythology. Applying Walter Benjamin's concept, one could say that the representation of Shiva carrying Sati is an example of a "dialectical image," one that synthesizes contemporary politics and religious myth.[25] As a dialectical image, the myth assumed revolutionary potential by appealing to indigenous tradition: "[The] shock of this recognition [can] jolt the dreaming collective into a political awakening. The presentation of the historical object within a charged force field of past and present, which produces political electricity. . .is the dialectical image."[26]

While the image of Sati was not a "historical object," but a devotional one, the appeal to tradition still applied. A pilgrimage souvenir depicting Shiva carrying the body of Sati functioned as a metaphor for the need to protect and fight for Mother India during the troubling colonial period. This "political electricity" is visually articulated by invoking pathos, mourning, and sacrifice. It is worthwhile, in this regard, to compare the late nineteenth-century *pats* to the earliest known visual rendering of the Sati myth, made around 1800 in Kangra in the Punjab Hills (fig. 3). Despite her status as a goddess, Sati's body is represented in this miniature painting as mortal in its vulnerability: held aloft by Shiva's trident, she is charred and burned after immolation, the smoke rising from her figure (fig. 12). The hem of her sari obscures her face, emphasizing her corpselike anonymity. In contrast, by the late nineteenth century, she is idealized and immaculate. In the Kalighat *pats*, her traditional Bengali sari and numerous ornaments are untarnished; her long black hair cascades elegantly across Shiva's figure and her unblemished face often reveals a half-smile (fig. 10). In the context of the colonial period and the re-envisioning of Sati as nationalist icon, there is a strong suggestion that her martyred body appears not to suffer at all, but instead willingly sacrifices itself for the nation. This reading of the souvenir images was, of course, not part of the original myth, which described her sacrifice as one she performed for her husband. However, by the nineteenth century, writers such as Aurobindo had taken inspiration from the narrative and lent it contemporary relevance by interpreting the distribution of her body across the country as a sacrifice for the nation.

Commemorating Sacrifice in Souvenir Prints

Although they remained popular until the early twentieth century, Kalighat *pats* were gradually superseded as pilgrimage souvenirs by the introduction of modern printing technology imported to Calcutta by the British. The first printed souvenirs were woodcuts, followed by metal engravings. Lithographic prints became popular starting in the 1870s, and were produced famously by the Calcutta Art Studio, established in 1878 by Sri Annadaprasad Bagchi along with four students who took over a year later when he became headmaster of the Government School of Art,

Calcutta. The studio, reflecting the patriotic motivations of its founders, began by producing monochrome lithographic portraits of major cultural nationalists including Bankim Chandra Chatterjee and Swami Vivekananda (fig. 13). The turning point in the production of popular prints came in the 1880s with the development of chromolithographs offering a range of bright colors and subtle shading. The studio's most successful prints among pilgrims were chromolithographs of Hindu deities and mythological scenes.[27] Among these prints was a ferocious image of Kali, which had an explicitly anti-British nationalist agenda (fig. 14). Pinney notes that one colonial official, Herbert Hope Risley, anxiously described this image of Kali as garlanded with seemingly European heads, a prediction of the fall of the British Empire. Indeed, it was anxiety about this print in particular that seems to have precipitated the drafting of the 1910 Press Act, which would rigorously control picture production and circulation in the first half of the twentieth century.[28]

Originally the Calcutta Art Studio issued these prints in bound folios, a European convention aimed at connoisseurs. However, due to high demand for their use in domestic ritual by Hindus, they soon changed to single prints designed as pilgrimage souvenirs. Like Kalighat *pats*, Calcutta Art Studio prints were affordable to people of all classes who wished to decorate the walls of their homes or places of work. Mukul Dey was critical of popular prints, comparing them unfavourably to the *pats*: "In place of these hand-drawn and hand-painted pictures, garish and evil-smelling lithographs. . .quite appalling in their hideousness—have come. The old art is gone forever."[29] Though Calcutta Art Studio prints may have used the modern technology of chromolithography, they did not necessarily represent the decline of an artistic tradition or signify a commercialization and secularization of religious values. Their universal availability, in fact, signaled the democratization of religious practice, since everyone was able to have *darshan* of the readily available two-dimensional devotional images. Partha Mitter comments: "Mechanical reproduction, with endless repeatability as its chief characteristic, turned India into an 'iconic society.' It affected the elite as much as the underclass, by creating a common visual culture," an "imagined community" to take Benedict Anderson's expression.[30]

The Calcutta Art Studio's 1883 print of Sati (fig. 1) reinforced and refreshed collective memory of the sacred Shakti Pitha sites and their association with the motherland. This collectively shared interpretation of a mythological past helped cement nationalist sentiment and identity.[31] The creation and proliferation of these souvenirs (both paintings and prints), with their consistent and mass-produced religious iconography, contributed to the shaping of visual imagination on a national scale.

The Sati lithograph deserves closer examination for the purpose of illuminating the nature of the image of Sati in pilgrimage souvenirs, especially in comparison with one of the Calcutta Art Studio's earlier prints depicting the figure of Bharat Mata, Mother India. During the nineteenth century, the mythicized concept of motherhood was borrowed by nationalists from the prevalence of the Hindu mother cult, leading both to the reinterpretation of the Sati myth and to the conjuring of Bharat Mata, a new deity to personify and publicize their political cause.[31] The identity of the country was subsequently often expressed and represented in terms of devotion to this new goddess. After Bharat Mata was first mentioned in Jyotirindranath Tagore's 1868 poem ("Rise! O rise! Children of Bharat"), she was "invented" as a character in the form of a dispossessed mother in an 1873 play by Kiran Chandra Bandyopadhyay, in which her condition under foreign domination was described as bare, deprived, and unkempt. This vision of Mother India as impoverished was visualized during the 1870s by Calcutta Art Studio as *Bharat Bhiksha*, or India Begging (fig. 15). In the print, she appears as an elderly and haggard woman, her poverty indicated by her tattered widow's sari. Her expression is aggrieved, with furrowed brows and downturned mouth, and she holds prayer beads to her chest in an act of begging. Looting foreigners have robbed her of her former glory and she needs rescuing, apparently not by her own citizens, but by Queen Victoria to her right, the embodiment of Britannia and harbinger of Western progress in the eyes of many of the

fig. 13
Calcutta Art Studio, *Bankim Chandra Chatterjee*, lithograph, 16 1/8 x 12 in. (41 x 30.5 cm), c. 1880. Photo: courtesy Christopher Pinney.

fig. 14
Calcutta Art Studio, *Kali*, chromolithograph, 16 1/8 x 12 in. (41 x 30.5 cm), c. 1883. Collection of Mark and Elise Baron.

Bengali *bhadralok* of the time. She offers Victoria a child, a symbol of India's future. This is an ambiguous image of crisis, reflecting the *bhadralok*'s own predicament as torn between Mother India and Mother Victoria.[32] During this early period of cultural nationalism, the impact and embrace of Western influence tempered pride in indigenous culture.

From the 1890s onward, however, as anti-British nationalism grew, the image of Bharat Bhiksha alongside Victoria became a distant memory, replaced by a heroic Bharat Mata associated with India as map. The map of India began appearing in patriotic "bodyscapes" of Bharat Mata from at least 1907, but especially after the 1930s, when she was superimposed on it (fig. 2). The first temple devoted to her, which opened in Banaras in 1936, even featured a giant marble relief map of India.

The image of Sati in Kalighat souvenirs represents a transitional icon between Mother India imagined as impoverished and Mother India envisioned as heroic. Like the Calcutta Art Studio's figure of Bharat Bhiksha, the image of Sati and Shiva published about a decade later is infused with pathos, but there is no sign of pro-British sentiment (fig. 1). Instead, it absorbs the flavor of Bankim Chandra Chatterjee's nationalistic novel *Anandamath* (1882) by presenting India as a suffering goddess, here imagined as Sati, while calling on the nation's citizens (rather than Queen Victoria) to protect and restore her.[33] Again, the myth of her dismemberment and distribution of her body parts across the subcontinent lent itself to this conflation of Sati and Mother India. The emphasis on Sati's vulnerability was a response by the studio to a demand created by nationalist writers like Bankim to inspire men, who could identify with the heroic figure of Shiva portrayed as a *sannyasi*, or ascetic, to protect the motherland.[34]

The artists behind the Calcutta Art Studio's designs were trained at the Calcutta School of Art in a Western style of painting through the study of classical and Renaissance imagery, accessible through European prints. In the case of the studio's Sati print, attention must be drawn to Christian precedents, Pietà images in particular (fig. 16). There is an inscription at the bottom of the studio print of Sati in Bengali that reads: "Mahadev [Shiva] is carrying the body of Sati on his shoulders while dancing. Vishnu cuts her up with his *chakra*." As described in Puranic texts,[35] Shiva's dance is a dance of destruction, and Shiva is often represented in this guise as Nataraja (the Lord of Dance), surrounded by flames. However, the Art Studio's image of Shiva with Sati (like the *pat* watercolors) does not depict this dynamic, destructive Shiva. Instead, we are presented with an image of suffering, a veritable Pietà or Lamentation of Christ. In the case of the studio's print in particular, Shiva is shown as Virgin-like in his grief-stricken carrying of Sati. Not only does the print show stylistic resonance

fig. 15
Calcutta Art Studio, *Bharat Bhiksha*, lithograph, 16 1/8 x 12 in. (41 x 30.5 cm), c. 1878. Photo: courtesy Christopher Pinney.

fig. 16
Marcantonio Raimondi (after Michelangelo), *Pietà*, print on paper, c. 1547.

with European Pietà images, but in terms of content, it also absorbs the pathos of sacrifice for the greater good, directed toward nationalist ends. The Pietà print is an image of remembrance in its appeal to the faithful to recall Christ's sacrifice for humanity, while the Sati print accomplishes the same petition in its evocation of the deity's sacrifice for the nation through her corporeal relics. Sati has sacrificed her body, as Christ did, and like him, she is resurrected and reborn into a more powerful body: in her case, the subcontinent itself. Both the Pietà and Sati images are icons of commemoration taking inspiration and strength from this pathos of sacrifice.

fig. 17
Artist unknown, *Sati, Shiva and Dismemberment*, print, c. 2000. Priya Paul Collection of Popular Art.

The Church Missionary Society collected Calcutta Art Studio lithographs for use in loan exhibitions in England. One anonymous missionary noted that they were modeled on Christian prototypes and argued that this emulation anticipated the death of Hinduism: "As authentic representations of their gods by Hindus they mark a fast fading phase in the religious history of the country—the period when by adopting Christian tactics—the people are trying to bolster up their own tottering faiths."[36] He could not have been more wrong: the influence of Christian iconography in fact nurtured Hindu nationalistic sentiment rather than weaken it. Astrid Erll's discussion of migrating images as vehicles of "transcultural memory" seems apt in this context. She defines the term as "the incessant wandering of carriers, media, contents, forms, and practices of memory," and notes "their continual 'travels' and ongoing transformations through time and space, across social, linguistic and political borders."[37] As an archetypal image of sacrifice and grief, the iconography of Pietà was disseminated through print to Bengal, a "carrier of memory" that had a strong influence on Kalighat *pats* and the Calcutta Art Studio prints alike.

The enduring appeal of the Sati and Shiva image of pathos displayed in the Kalighat souvenirs would lead to its iconographic consistency right up until the present day in the form of contemporary prints (fig. 17), sculptures (fig. 4), and monuments (fig. 5). It is evident in an extraordinary example of propaganda that places the Sati image of pathos in an overtly political context—an election billboard in Hyderabad from December 1984, the year of Prime Minister Indira Gandhi's assassination (fig. 18). The billboard was one of many street hoardings set up by Indira's Congress Party to promote her son Rajiv as the next leader. It shows her dead body across an anthropomorphized map of India, which appears to be holding her the way Shiva holds Sati. Blood from her wounds drips down the map while tears flow from the map's face. Inscribed across these hoardings are words from her last speech: "When my life is gone, every drop of my blood will strengthen the nation," suggesting that, like Sati, Indira will be reconstituted into the more powerful body of the nation itself. The scholar Sumathi Ramaswamy writes that the image represents the potential demise of Mother India after Indira's death.[38] Instead, if we see in the map of India the figure of Shiva, it is rather India's grief that threatens a kind of apocalypse, just as Shiva's own grief threatened the destruction of the world, and the martyrdom of Indira is equated with Sati's own martyrdom.

Conclusion

In late nineteenth-century Bengal, Hindu nationalists harnessed the power of myth for the purpose of national regeneration, and made mythological characters symbols of sociopolitical realities. Souvenirs of Sati offered pilgrims a way to extend, relive, and remember their experience at the Kalighat temple by bringing an image of Sati (India) back with them to their homes. Through souvenirs, the network of physical sites became a network of printed and painted images that was broadly dispersed across Bengal and the rest of India. Sati came to represent a nation in need of saving, while Shiva represented its citizens (or India's destiny), and the Pithas symbolized the nation's fragments. A souvenir of Sati sold at Kalighat was an image of remembrance, reminding devotees that the temple represented one piece of a vast network of sites that stretched across the subcontinent and together made up the body of the goddess, and of the nation.

fig. 18
Election billboard, Hyderabad, 1984. Text reads: "When my life is gone, every drop of my blood will strengthen the nation." Photo: Raghu Rai.

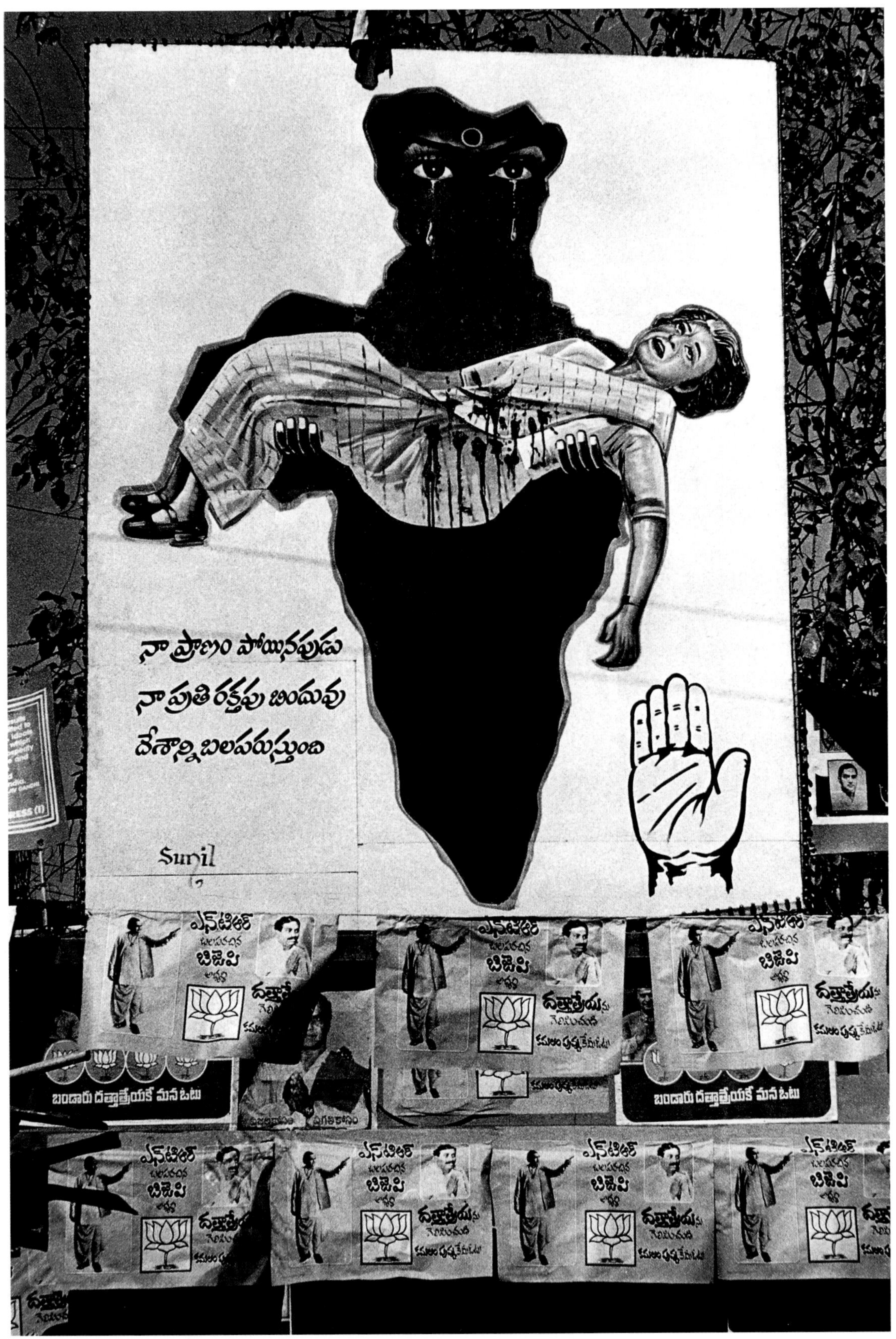
నా ప్రాణం పోయినపుడు
నా ప్రతి రక్తపు బిందువు
దేశాన్ని బలపరుస్తుంది
Sunil
బిజెపి
బండారు దత్తాత్రేయకే మన ఓటు
బండారు దత్తాత్రేయకే మన ఓటు

NOTES

1. Chittaranjan Ghosh, *Desh* (April 1993): 25; Sushil Kumar Mukherjee, *The Story of the Calcutta Theatres, 1753–1980* (Calcutta: K.P. Bagchi, 1982), 64; Binodini Dasi, *My Story and My Life as an Actress* (New Delhi: Kali for Women, 1998), 124.
2. The Bengali *bhadralok* were a largely Western-educated middle class that arose during the colonial period (approximately 1757 to 1947). From the 1850s onward, their typical occupations lay in colonial government service.
3. Sumathi Ramaswamy has analyzed the cultural and visual phenomenon of Bharat Mata in *Goddess and the Nation: Mapping Mother India* (Durham, NC: Duke University Press, 2010); and in her articles "Maps and Mother Goddesses in Modern India," *Imago Mundi* 53 (2001): 97–114; and "Visualising India's Geo-Body," *Contributions to Indian Sociology* 36, nos. 1–2 (2002): 151–89.
4. The most extensive work on the Shakti Pithas has been done by Dinesh Chandra Sircar in a short but comprehensive overview based on a selection of Tantric texts: "The Śākta Pīthas," *Journal of the Royal Asiatic Society of Bengal, Letters*, 14 (1948): 1–108. The earliest reference to the Pitha temples is in the *Hevajra Tantra* (seventh century CE).
5. Kunal Chakrabarti, *Religious Process: The Purānas and the Making of a Regional Tradition* (Oxford: Oxford University Press, 2001), 172.
6. Tracy Pintchman examines this idea of the goddess as one and many, regional and universal, in *Seeking Mahādevī: Constructing the Identities of the Hindu Great Goddess* (Albany: State University of New York Press, 2001); John Stratton Hawley and Donna Marie Wulff, eds., examine the concept of Devi, the great goddess, and the ways various Hindu goddesses are related to her in *Devī: Goddesses of India* (Berkeley: University of California Press, 1996).
7. Sister Nivedita, *The Web of Indian Life* (London: William Heinemann, 1904), 1–5.
8. Victor Turner, *Dramas, Fields and Metaphors: Symbolic Action in Human Society* (Ithaca, NY: Cornell University Press, 1974), 212.
9. Quoted from Parimal Kumar Datta, *Tantra: Its Relevance to Modern Times* (Kolkata: Punthi Pustak, 2009), 6.
10. Nivedita, *The Web of Indian Life*, 5.
11. E. Alan Morinis, *Pilgrimage in the Hindu Tradition: A Case Study of West Bengal* (Oxford: Oxford University Press, 1984), 24.
12. Diana Eck, *Darśan: Seeing the Divine Image in India* (New York: Columbia University Press, 1998).
13. Christopher Pinney, *Photos of the Gods: The Printed Image and Political Struggle in India* (London: Reaktion, 2004), 194.
14. It was only after 1925 that critics began to take Kalighat painting as an art form seriously, beginning with Ajit Ghose's 1926 critical essay, "Old Bengal Paintings," in *Rupam* 27–28 (1926). Since then, the most substantial contributions to the subject have been: William George Archer, *Kalighat Paintings: A Catalogue and Introduction* (London: Victoria and Albert Museum, 1971); and Jyotinda Jain, *Kalighat Painting: Images from a Changing World* (Ahmedabad, India: Mapin Publishing, 1999).
15. Jain, *Kalighat Painting*, 50.
16. Ibid., 40.
17. Mukul Dey, "Drawings and Paintings of Kalighat," *Advance* (1932).
18. Ibid.
19. Ibid.
20. John Strachey, *India* (London: Kegan Paul, 1888), 5–8.
21. Quoted from Tapan Raychaudhuri, *Europe Reconsidered: Perceptions of the West in Nineteenth-Century Bengal* (Oxford: Oxford University Press, 2002), 39. Note that Bhudev mentions fifty-two and not fifty-one Pithas. This is because there have been discrepancies regarding the names and number of the Pithas, ranging from four, to fifty-one, or even 108, and other variations besides, including fifty-two (as pointed out in the *Brihad-Nila Tantra*).
22. Nivedita, *The Web of Indian Life*, 3.
23. Diana Eck, "India's 'Tirthas': 'Crossings' in sacred geography," *History of Religions* 20, no. 4 (1981): 336.
24. Aurobindo Ghosh, "The Parable of Sati," *Bande Mataram*, April 29, 1908.
25. Hugh Urban discusses the dialectical image in relation to the Tantric goddess Kali, whom he describes as being transformed into a "source of anticolonial struggle" during the nineteenth century, in *Tantra: Sex, Secrecy Politics, and Power in the Study of Religion* (Berkeley: University of California Press, 2003), 87.
26. Susan Buck-Morss, *The Dialectics of Seeing: Walter Benjamin and the Arcades Project* (Cambridge, MA: MIT Press, 1989), 219.

27. Christopher Pinney's *Photos of the Gods* stands as a foundational work in establishing the social, religious, and political importance of such popular prints. Partha Mitter provides a crucial introduction to the Calcutta Art Studio in "Mechanical Reproduction and the World of the Colonial Artist," *Contributions to Indian Sociology* 36, nos. 1–2 (2002): 1–32.
28. Pinney, *Photos of the Gods*, 28.
29. Dey, "Drawings and Paintings."
30. Mitter, "Mechanical Reproduction," 1; Benedict Anderson, *Imagined Communities: Reflections on the Origin and Spread of Nationalism*, rev. ed. (1983; London: Verso, 2006).
31. The modern nation has often been gendered as feminine in the formation of nationalist rhetoric. Apart from Ramaswamy, see also: Charu Gupta, "The Icon of Mother in Late Colonial North India: 'Bharat Mata,' 'Matri Bhasha' and 'Gau Mata,'" *Economic and Political Weekly* 36, no. 45 (2001): 4291–99.
32. Ramaswamy (*Goddess and the Nation*) and Pinney (*Photos of the Gods*) have also briefly discussed this image. As Indira Chowdhury has suggested in her analysis of Bengali songs and plays of this period by the *bhadralok*, Queen Victoria appears as a rival mother capable of rescuing the nation: *The Frail Hero and Virile History: Gender and the Politics of Culture in Colonial Bengal* (Oxford: Oxford University Press, 1998).
33. Set in the context of the late eighteenth-century Sannyasi Rebellion, *Anandamath* became synonymous with the fight for Indian independence. For an English translation, with a critical introduction, see Julius Lipner, *Anandamath, or, The Sacred Brotherhood* (Oxford: Oxford University Press, 2005).
34. Shiva is described as a powerful *sannyasi* and *yogi* in Hindu mythological texts. The ideal of the *sannyasi* was envisioned through Bankim's own revolutionary ascetics in *Anandamath*.
35. Including the *Kalika* and *Devibhagavata Puranas*. For English translations, see: Karel Rijk van Kooij, *Worship of the Goddess According to the Kalikapurana: A Translation with Introduction* (Leiden: E. J. Brill, 1972), and Swami Vijayanand, *Srimad-Devibhagavatam: Text with English Translation* (Delhi: Chaukhamba Sanskrit Pratisthan, 2008).
36. Quoted in Pinney, *Photos of the Gods*, 30.
37. Astrid Erll, "Travelling Memory," *Parallax* 17, no. 4 (2011): 11.
38. Ramaswamy, "Maps, Mother/Goddesses," 846.

N.Y. WORLD'S FAIR 1964 · 1965
NEUTRON IRRADIATED DIME
LIBERTY

ATOMIC ENERGY COMMISSION
UNITED STATES OF AMERICA

SOUVENIRS OF THE INVISIBLE: DISPLAY OF ENERGY AT TWENTIETH-CENTURY WORLD'S FAIRS

Ethan Robey

Ethan Robey is assistant professor of the History of Decorative Arts and Design at Parsons School of Design, and Associate Director of the MA Program in the History of Design and Curatorial Studies run by Parsons and Cooper Hewitt Smithsonian Design Museum. His scholarship addresses issues of display, consumerism, and the social effects of technology in the nineteenth and twentieth centuries.

I am a casual collector of world's fair souvenirs, yet there is one item I have always been somewhat wary of acquiring: a neutron-irradiated dime (fig. 1). Irradiated dimes were a popular souvenir of the 1964–65 New York World's Fair, and many thousands were produced. They were made at Atomsville, U.S.A., a hands-on introduction to atomic science for children, run by the Atomic Energy Commission (AEC).[1] These dimes would have been kept by kids along with other meaningful trinkets, maybe carried around in their pockets or tucked in a desk drawer, a reminder not only of a day at the world's fair, but of the promise of nuclear energy as the power source for a future of technological marvels.

There is a dark fascination to such an item; the idea of children carrying around potentially radioactive coins now sounds a bit disconcerting. The dime memorializes not only personal experiences of the world's fair, but also a mid-century late modernist faith in technology that now seems somehow foreign. The AEC's exhibit at the New York World's Fair was a component of a multifaceted initiative, in operation since the late 1940s, to demystify and domesticate atomic power.

The irradiated dime in its plastic holder, imperceptibly transformed by neutron rays, was a physical marker of that invisible, intangible, but terrifyingly powerful force. As such, it has a parallel in early twentieth-century souvenirs of electric displays. Souvenirs of these displays also materialize an unseen force, but do so more in allegorical terms. Around

fig. 1
Neutron-irradiated dime in plastic enclosure from the New York World's Fair, 2 in. (5 cm) diameter, 1964–65. Author's collection.

the turn of the century, electricity was an ill-understood, awe-inspiring, and potentially deadly force, newly harnessed for practical uses. Like nuclear power, electricity was invisible, traveling unseen through conductive wires. Like the irradiated dimes, souvenirs of electric displays at world's fairs memorialize both the immediate experience of the spectacle of electric power and general social attitudes toward technology and the new power source. Electricity was a promising and real technology as well as a symbolic energy: a metaphor for progress itself.

In her classic rumination on the souvenir, poet and scholar Susan Stewart points out that souvenirs compress monuments into a purchasable form: a private marker of the public spectacle used to recall a personal experience. The souvenir, she says, "generates a narrative which reaches only 'behind,' spiraling in a continually inward movement rather than outward toward the future."[2] Yet mementos of technical marvels at world's fairs contain meanings in ways that many other souvenirs do not. For all that they may serve as personal reminders of an individual's visit to the fair, they also work on the level of public discourse. Souvenirs from the early electrical age and the nuclear age both embody promises of a world improved by the judicious application of new technologies. They point backward to a personal experience, but also forward to a better future: reminders of something that would be, as much as something that was.

Commoditizing Memories

Consider a small ceramic candy dish, a memento of the 1901 Pan-American Exposition in Buffalo, New York (fig. 2). Like many souvenir objects, the dish is a thing of no great utility. It is too small to hold much candy, and filling it would obscure the image anyway. The dish is decorated with a black-and-white transfer-printed drawing of the Electric Tower, the central structure of the fair, hand-painted in browns, blues, and pinks, to evoke an evening sky behind and a cascade of water in front of the tower. The label "Electric Tower" is also included to prevent any misidentification. As with any souvenir object, the inherent quality of production or usefulness is secondary to its role as a memento of a particular time and place.[3] A souvenir spoon is not meant to be eaten from, and a souvenir cup will likely never hold a drink (fig. 3).

If our little candy dish was once was a personal memento of a visit to the Pan-American Exposition, that meaning has been long lost. But a souvenir such as this was never solely about personal experience. It is a marker of affinity, celebrating the fairgrounds and the monumental tower and evoking all the public symbolism of the building. The exhibition, or at least a building such as the Electric Tower, does not celebrate individual artisanship as much as corporate innovation. The fairground was an expression of a widespread network of production and distribution,

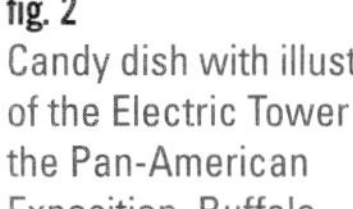

fig. 2
Candy dish with illustration of the Electric Tower from the Pan-American Exposition, Buffalo, porcelain, 4 ½ x 3 ¼ in. (11.4 x 8.25 cm), 1901. Author's collection.

fig. 3
A. C. Bosselman (designer), Pyro Photo Mfg. Co. (manufacturer), souvenir cup from the Pan-American Exposition, Buffalo, metal, 3 ½ x 2 ¼ in. (8.9 x 5.7 cm), c. 1901. The Wolfsonian–Florida International University, The Mitchell Wolfson, Jr. Collection, 85.9.43.

The Electric Tower, designed by John Galen Howard, is 409 feet high, and is the architectural centerpiece of the Exposition. It stands in the center of a great basin. The main body of the Tower, to a height of nearly 300 feet, is 80 feet square. The crown of the Tower is of diminishing proportions—first, four open pavilions at the corners, with loggias between, then a circular colonnade with winding stairway leading up to the cupola and lantern. Curved colonnades, 110 feet high, extend from the base of the Tower on the east and west sides, and form a semi-circular space, 200 feet across, upon the south side. In the southern face of the Tower is an arched niche, 75 feet high, from which gushes a veil-like cascade. All about the base of the Tower are other fountains and water effects. The water features and the Tower are brilliantly illuminated at night by means of invisible searchlights of great power. The Tower is used for searchlight signalling at night, the signals being answered from the great Observation Tower at Niagara Falls, 15 miles away. The Tower is also used for restaurant and observation purposes, and it is thickly studded with electric lights, in consonance with the general plan of brilliant illumination of all buildings.

making the cheap, mass-produced object particularly apt as an embodiment of the kind of consumerist modernity celebrated there. The dish was probably purchased at the fair, but it was definitely not produced there. On the reverse it is stamped "made in Germany." At the time, German manufacturers were world leaders in the mass production of inexpensive toys and household goods, so the mark would have indicated a low-status ceramic, not something to be prized for its intrinsic quality.[4] The mark also, of course, distances the dish from Buffalo and the fair. Either the blanks were imported from Germany and an American dealer added the decoration, or the dish was entirely made and decorated overseas. In either case, it is its iconographic connection to the exhibition, rather than any physical one, that makes the dish work as a souvenir.

Modern mass-produced souvenirs evolved somewhat in step with the world's fairs. Both were born of advances in production and transportation in the mid-nineteenth century.[5] Industrialization allowed great masses of goods to represent national prowess in the halls of exhibitions. It also made leisure travel available to more people, and gave ordinary travelers a chance to purchase cheap mementos of places or spectacles.[6] From the very first world's fair, London's 1851 Great Exhibition, a host of commemorative objects of every kind was available to visitors looking to affirm their connection with the unique event, the grandiose building, and the wonders it contained.[7] The fairs were temporary events, most only lasting from spring to fall, so a souvenir marked not only one's visit to a place but the date of the visit as well.

World's fairs in America were privately run, for-profit corporations, unlike European fairs, most of which were state-sponsored. Since the mid-nineteenth century, there had been official producers of guidebooks and other fair merchandise, but from about the 1890s onward, American world's fair corporations became ever more closely involved with the branding of their fairs and the propagation of images of them. The 1893 World's Columbian Exposition in Chicago had an official set of photographs and restricted visitors from taking their own on the grounds unless they had paid a hefty two-dollar fee. Images of fairgrounds and structures were copyrighted; memories were commoditized.

fig. 4
Illustration of the Electric Tower from the Pan-American Exposition, Buffalo, from Mark Bennitt, *The Pan-American Exposition and How to See It* (Buffalo: The Goff Company, 1901), n.p.

The image of the Electric Tower on the Pan-American Exposition candy dish is far from unique; other souvenirs show the very same view, even down to the group of visitors in the right foreground (fig. 4). This is no surprise of course, as the image was one of the official views—actually a rendering of the projected building done before the tower was completed—copyrighted by the fair corporation. The same image shows up in souvenir viewbooks, and in other media as well, including a version in woven silk, replicating even the scrollwork around the caption from the

copyrighted image (fig. 5). The silk ribbon, unlike the candy dish, was likely made at the fairgrounds itself, woven on an electric-powered Jacquard loom.[8]

Both the candy dish, produced in a German ceramics factory, and the silk ribbon, woven on a programmable automatic loom, derive some of their affective power from their status as multiples. They commemorate a structure that itself is meant to embody commercial and technological progress. Other souvenirs of symbolic palaces or towers of electricity are not even very effective at giving a sense of the structures' form. Many only include the image as a kind of symbol: a cursory representation, accompanied by a caption, to simply evoke the building by name. The purpose of these objects is not to inform a viewer about the particulars of the structure, but to mark the fact of the structure's existence and that the object itself was purchased nearby. For example, pennies elongated on rolling machines and impressed with rough images of fair structures appeared first at the 1893 Chicago world's fair and remained popular as souvenirs of expositions and other tourist attractions throughout the twentieth century (fig. 6). The penny refers to the fair in its imagery and text, but also remains a physical marker of its own moment of transformation, likely at a machine on the fairgrounds, from currency to memento. All these souvenirs can embody the memory of a unique personal experience, but they also signify, at least in part, their purchaser's willing participation in the project of the fair and its promise of social improvement by the expansion of industrialization, specifically the production, distribution, and application of electricity.

fig. 5
Jacquard-woven silk ribbon with illustration of the Electric Tower from the Pan-American Exposition, Buffalo, 5 ⅞ x 4 ⅝ in. (15 x 11.7 cm), c. 1901. Cooper Hewitt, Smithsonian Design Museum, 1962-149-14-b.

Representations of Electricity at World's Fairs

World's fairs were designed to give concrete form to abstract concepts such as social progress, national identity, and international economic competition. Decorated displays of the products of various industries grouped by national origin were more than showroom samples for individual firms; rather they carried symbolic significance as collective representations of national groups, expressed in object form. The fairgrounds themselves were cities of allegory, representing an ideal of progress in the solemnity and grandeur of their elaborate temporary "palaces" of manufactures, fine arts, agriculture, machines, and so on.

The nearly four-hundred-foot-high, neoclassical Electric Tower was the most prominent building on the fairgrounds of the 1901 Buffalo Pan-American Exposition, presiding over the symmetrical buildings of the Grand Court. Surrounded by personifications of American lakes and rivers and other allegorical sculptures, the tower was topped by a sixteen-foot-high, classically draped Goddess of Light holding a torch. At its base was a seventy-foot tiered cascade alluding to nearby Niagara Falls. The tower housed a restaurant and, for adventurous visitors, elevators up to a colonnaded observation platform.[9] The Electric Tower was not the exhibition hall for electric devices—that was the adjacent Electricity Building. Its main purpose was as a scaffold for a dazzling spectacle of electric illumination.

The Pan-American Exposition was explicitly organized around the theme of electricity. The force of the Niagara River had been tapped by hydroelectric power plants, most notably the one owned by the Niagara Falls Power Company (its successor company is now owned by the utility conglomerate National Grid), the first and largest alternating-current hydroelectric station in America. In 1901, the plant had ten Westinghouse generators, which provided electricity for all of western New York State; one of the generators, by itself, could provide all the electricity needed for the whole exposition. All the companies involved—the Niagara Falls Power Company, Westinghouse, its great rival General Electric, and many others—were represented by displays at the exposition. The Buffalo General Electric Company, which distributed the power from the plant to the exposition and engineered the lighting displays, constructed its transformers and other infrastructure as a public exhibit. The Niagara Falls Power Company presented a scale model of the power station, with a lighted electric sign fed with a current so strong that it is said that it gave off a noise like thunder. The Pan-American Exposition celebrated the new technology but also its passage from a natural force into a saleable, branded commodity. Indeed, electric power had already become fairly widespread in industrial applications by 1901; the focus especially on illumination at the Buffalo fair, as at several earlier expositions, was part of a campaign supported by electric companies to sell the general public on the idea of electricity for domestic uses.

fig. 6
Elongated penny with illustration of the Electric Tower from the Pan-American Exposition, Buffalo, 1 ¼ x ¾ in. (3 x 2 cm), c. 1901. Author's collection.

The first fairs to prominently feature electric devices were in the 1880s—what exactly electric power was, however, remained somewhat obscure to many fair visitors. Most people had only the vaguest ideas about how it was produced or how it worked, and the actual equipment of the production and distribution of electricity was stubbornly difficult to transform into spectacle. Large metal boxes offered no moving parts that a spectator could see and produced only a force traveling invisibly through copper wires. Few mementos of electric displays at world's fairs show the dynamos and transformers themselves; the majestic buildings are far more common. Displays of electric equipment tended to leave fair visitors feeling like they ought to be impressed, but not entirely sure about what. One visitor to the 1904 Louisiana Purchase Exposition in St. Louis reminded himself in a memoir that "the different electrical machines and motors were unintelligible to you. . . . There were a number of interesting experiments conducted in the Electricity Building. But as you did not understand them they served simply as a sort of intellectual amusement."[10] Most famously, the American historian Henry Adams found himself moved but uncomprehending in the presence of the dynamos at the 1900 Exposition Universelle in Paris. "I. . .go down to the Champ de Mars [the exhibition grounds] and sit by the hour over the great dynamos," he wrote to his close friend John Hay; "the charm of the show, to me, is that no one pretends to understand even in a remote degree what these weird things are that they call electricity, Roentgen rays and whatnot."[11]

If the machinery for the production and distribution of electric power remained inscrutable, its application, in the form of illumination, was an immediately graspable sensory delight and a favorite attraction of many turn-of-the-century fairs. The Electric Tower at Buffalo was bedecked with forty thousand incandescent light bulbs and housed an arc lamp searchlight that swept the fairgrounds, whose buildings were trimmed with another two hundred thousand bulbs (fig. 7). The lighting of the

fig. 7
B. W. Kilburn, "The great Search Light and Electric Tower, Pan American Exposition," stereo-view card, c. 1901. Photography Collection, Miriam and Ira D. Wallach Division of Art, Prints and Photographs, The New York Public Library, Astor, Lenox and Tilden Foundations.

fig. 8 (opposite)
Postcard, Electric Tower from the Pan-American Exposition, Buffalo, Niagara Envelope Manufactory, Buffalo, 1901. Yale University Library, Beinecke Rare Book and Manuscript Library, uncataloged acquisition 20051130-x.

tower at dusk became a kind of ritual. With a band playing "The Star-Spangled Banner," nature's dark night was transformed into the dawn's early light of the electric city. Audiences were hushed into a reverent silence by the majesty of the electric lights, an example of what historian David Nye labels the "technological sublime"—a translation of the awe and dread inspired by natural wonders into responses to man-made technological spectacles.[12] A popular record of the fair describes the nightly lighting of the Electric Tower as "indescribably brilliant," and notes that "the spectators were spellbound."[13] One visitor described the scene:

> Through some wonderful mechanism the light comes on by degrees, and this creates a novel effect. . . . There is a deep silence and all eyes are intent on the Electric Tower. In the splendid vertical panel there is a faint glow of light, like the first flush which a church spire catches from the dawn. This deepens from pink to red, and then grows into a luminous yellow, and the Exposition of beams and staff has vanished and in its place is a wondrous vision of dazzling wonders and minarets, domes, and pinnacles set in the midst of scintillating gardens—the triumph not of Aladdin's lamp, but of the masters of modern science over the nature-god Electricity.[14]

These sorts of light shows had been common features in world's fairs since the 1890s and were repeated again at the 1904 Louisiana Purchase Exposition in St. Louis. A souvenir book of that fair described the nighttime illumination of the fairgrounds as "a mighty bouquet of light blossoming out of the darkness," noting the way the buildings were transformed, visible more as "fiery outlines" than substance.[15]

Candy dishes and ceramic piggy banks could reference the building, but souvenir manufacturers, especially printers, explored new technologies of reproduction to replicate these electrical performances. The Niagara Envelope Manufactory, a licensed concessionaire at the 1901 fair, produced color lithographic postcards of paintings of the Electric Tower and the fairgrounds at night, in full radiance, with metallic glitter overprinted on the beams of light streaming from the building (figs. 8, 9). Printers also experimented with "hold to light" postcards. For example, a card from the 1904 St. Louis fair shows the Festival Hall, the fair's central pavilion, and the Cascades leading down into

fig. 9
Oversized postcard, Electric Tower from the Pan-American Exposition, Buffalo, Niagara Envelope Manufactory, Buffalo, 6 x 9 in. (15.25 x 23 cm), c. 1901. The Wolfsonian–Florida International University, The Mitchell Wolfson, Jr. Collection, XB1991.650.3.

fig. 10 (opposite)
Postcard, Cascade Gardens and Grand Basin from the Louisiana Purchase Exposition, Samuel Cupples Envelope Co., St. Louis, c. 1904. Author's collection.

the gondola-filled Grand Basin in front (fig. 10). The caption reminds its owner that the card is an "Official Souvenir" of the exposition, produced by Samuel Cupples, whose firm is careful to identify itself as the sole authorized publisher of world's fair stationery. The cards employ a die-cut printed image glued to a thin backing layer printed with multicolored dots, a technique pioneered by German printers in the 1890s. In reflected light, it is a daylight scene; with backlighting, the buildings glow with colored lights that are reflected onto the waters below. Such a souvenir not only illustrates the fairgrounds, but replicates, in its miniaturized fashion, the nightly performance of electric illumination, using whatever light source the owner has at home. As Stewart points out, the miniature transforms the exterior into the interior, public space into something that can be consumed in private.[16] The spectacle is contained, and mailed.

The experience of the world's fair was preserved not only in the standardized images of official souvenirs, but also in the many printed trade cards, pins, or other trinkets given away at particular manufacturers' booths. Capitalizing on visitors' desire to keep mementos of the fairs, manufacturers juxtaposed images of their products with the standard views of significant fair structures. Some visitors created extensive scrapbooks of the trade cards they collected, preserving a memory of the fair told through brand names. Beyond postcards and images affixed to souvenir objects, visitors could recall the wonder of electric lighting at the

HOLD CARD TO LIGHT.
OFFICIAL SOUVENIR
WORLD'S FAIR - ST. LOUIS 1904
Cascade Gardens and Grand Basin.

fig. 11
Souvenir advertisement, Louisiana Purchase Exposition, St. Louis, American Electrical Novelty and Mfg. Co., 5 7/8 x 3 in. (15 x 8 cm), 1904. The Wolfsonian–Florida International University, The Mitchell Wolfson, Jr. Collection, XB1991.501.

fair through printed pieces, such as a bulb-shaped brochure distributed by the American Electrical Novelty and Manufacturing Company, the predecessor of today's Eveready Battery Company (fig. 11). With an image of the Festival Hall and Cascades superimposed over the filaments of the bulb, the brochure was likely distributed in the Palace of Electricity, where the company displayed its batteries, handheld flashlights, and small lights in a booth lit by six hundred colored bulbs.[17]

Machine-made and Handmade Souvenirs

What is clear about all these souvenirs of electrical innovations is that their affective power to stand for social improvement was wrapped up in the precision and multiplicity of the object made possible by mass-production. By design, the objects themselves have little to distinguish one from another. Inasmuch as their materiality might refer back to their means of production, only mechanized processes are evoked. Mementos of other parts of turn-of-the-century world's fairs work differently. Along the Pike, the amusement zone of the 1904 St. Louis exposition, where many Middle Eastern, Asian, and African cultures were represented—usually as commercial ventures run by Western promoters—visitors could purchase all manner of traditionally made goods. The small shops, according to one account, were "full of real nice things to sell, rich Eastern woven goods, embroideries, cushions, curtains, rugs, lamps, jewels, ornaments, trinkets of all kinds, etc., etc."[18] Or they could visit the Philippine Reservation, a vast display devoted to America's newest colonial possession, and pick up some souvenirs, perhaps a set of miniature spears (fig. 12). The Philippine exhibit was a microcosm of the world's fair itself, with its own administration building and exhibit halls. Instead of national pavilions, representatives of the different ethnicities of

the Philippines lived on the grounds in "villages" constructed from wood and thatch. Guidebooks encouraged visitors to construct hierarchies of the Filipinos on display, from the "civilized" in Western dress and habits, to darker-skinned peoples, scandalously wearing little clothing at all. The Philippine display was constructed as a demonstration of progress, the redemption and gradual civilization of the islanders, equivalent, in a way, to a display of the processing of raw materials into finished consumer goods.

The spears, likely fashioned in the Moro Village,[19] are rough models of functional implements, their heads punched out of sheet metal and fitted onto bamboo shafts. Like other souvenirs, their small scale renders them purely decorative, but unlike the German factory-made ceramic dish or the machine-produced silk ribbon souvenirs of electricity, which pointed to a literally brighter future in their precise, mechanical anonymity, these handcrafted spears were consumable markers of a visitor's encounter with the past. Colonial sections of early twentieth-century fairs were positioned as contrasts, a measuring stick to show how far the dominant civilization had advanced, and demonstrations of the progress of its civilizing errand into the wilderness.[20] The souvenir's means of production itself marked the divide. An extreme image of this divide can be found in a cartoon from the Paris world's fair of 1900 (fig. 13). In it, a female visitor is examining souvenir trinkets at a stand in the Dahomey Village (an African nation with a reputation among the French at the time for cannibalism). "How much is this wallet?" the slightly perturbed-looking visitor asks. "Two Louis," the cheery Dahomean vendeuse replies, "but keep in mind it was made out of my sister's skin!"[21]

World's fair visitors were not attracted to the handmade cushions, curtains, and rugs just to prove themselves superior to the cultures that produced them, however; in the late nineteenth and early twentieth centuries, American culture was itself ambivalent about the spread of impersonal, mass-produced commodities. Trompe l'œil still life paintings of the 1890s, for example, tend to be stuffed with warmly worn consumer goods: if not human-skin wallets, at least precisely rendered dented brass instruments, well-thumbed books, and rusted guns with cracked

fig. 12
Miniature spears made by Filipino tribesmen in the Moro Village, from the Louisiana Purchase Exposition, St. Louis, wood and metal, 1904. Missouri History Museum, St. Louis, 1990 025 0001.

fig. 13
G. Ri (Victor Mousselet), "Les petits dialogues de l'Exposition de 1900 (au Dahomey)," in *L'Exposition comique*, September 13, 1900, n.p. Bibliothèque historique de la Ville de Paris.

handles—objects whose condition implied rich lives of use, adding a layer of individualization to them.[22] By contrast, the bits of Jacquard-woven silk stood for technological triumph most potently when they resembled every other bit of Jacquard-woven silk to come out of the fair's weaving machines, as close to the condition of industrial production as possible. These and other souvenirs of electrical displays of this era make no claim to being one of a kind; they gain no value from being worn, handled, cherished, or affectively passed on.

As anonymous, mass-produced objects, these tokens of electrical displays are dispassionate expressions of the inevitability of progress. Bought, taken home, and shown off, the dishes and decorations transformed the official rhetoric of progress into individual possessions. It is very probable that a souvenir of the Electric Tower from the 1901 exposition would be illuminated at home by gas light rather than electricity. Electric lighting was more expensive than gas in America until just before the First World War and, as a new technology, was both less trusted and less reliable than gas.[23]

For all that it represented progress, electricity was still a deadly force. To spectators, the lighting was pure marvel, but the engineers were always aware of the hazards. In order to achieve the gradual illumination of the Electric Tower at the Pan-American Exposition, for example, engineers had to construct a water rheostat. The system employed electric motors to raise and lower electric leads into vats of water to vary the amount of current passing through. It was incredibly dangerous—the amount of current made the water boil within seconds—and was done in a building raised on stilts on the edge of the exhibition grounds because of the risk of shock or fire.[24] Electricity and death shared a space in the public consciousness. Buffalo, so full of electric power from the Niagara generators, was a pioneering city in the use of that power for capital punishment.[25]

The transformation of energy into spectacle at turn-of-the-century world's fairs was, by design, an act of domestication, not just to demonstrate home uses for electric power, but also to symbolize modern industry's taming of the beast. The director in charge of electricity for the 1893 exposition in Chicago was proud that the fair "brought electricity to the people in the light of a servant not as an awful master," and that it had done so largely by the decorative halos of electric lighting "that brought exclamations of wonder and admiration" from visitors.[26] Thus the postcards, ceramic bibelots, silk ribbons, and other souvenirs of palaces and towers of electricity decorating turn-of-the-century parlors not only memorialized blazing spectacles of electric light, but also welcomed this mysterious and dangerous power into the domestic sphere as a form of beneficent technological progress.

Atomsville, U.S.A.

The irradiated dime (fig. 1), no less than the penny with the image of the Electric Tower, developed from a campaign to naturalize and domesticate a potentially deadly source of power. The 1960s souvenir comes from a very different era, with a different aesthetic, celebrating a different source of energy, yet it has much in common with the earlier souvenirs. Like electricity, atomic energy was power and danger balanced, a promise and a mystery. Whereas the potential threat of electricity in the late nineteenth century was evident, it was outweighed by the power's miraculous promise. Nuclear energy, on the other hand, had first come into the public consciousness in the form of a destructive force, and remained primarily associated with world-ending war. Practically right after the end of the Second World War, the United States government and its nuclear research facilities tried to counter that image and stress the benefits a nuclear-powered future might offer.

The irradiated dime is a souvenir of the AEC's Atomsville, U.S.A exhibit at the 1964–65 New York World's Fair. The souvenir was free: visitors provided their own dimes. The machine that irradiated them was a narrow, tabletop-sized device with transparent sides so visitors could watch their coins roll into a lead-lined box, where they were bombarded by radiation. The dimes were then pushed into a shielded chamber fitted with a Geiger counter that would register their radioactivity. An attendant, wearing protective gloves, would retrieve the dimes, pop them into cheery blue plastic holders imprinted with the orbiting electron logo of the AEC, and hand eager young fairgoers their souvenirs. From the sans serif typography to the boomerang curves of the AEC logo, the souvenir's aesthetic is steeped in dreams of a future perfected by technology.

The irradiated dime embodies atomic power primarily as a trace, a physical marker of the encounter with a beam of neutrons, a process that had to be taken on faith, as the transformation of the metal happens on an atomic level, impossible to perceive. Dimes were the coin of choice, because in the 1960s they were made of silver. When some atoms of the silver were hit by the emissions generated by the machine, they absorbed the extra neutron and changed into a radioactive isotope of silver, silver 110. Silver 110 is unstable and decays rapidly, giving off beta radiation, whose energy the Geiger counter detected, before transmuting into nonradioactive cadmium 110. The half-life of silver 110 is about twenty-two seconds, so within a few minutes all the irradiated atoms in the dime would have become cadmium.

The transformed dime was a small product of a larger campaign to promote nonmilitary uses of atomic energy. Shortly after 1945, the newly formed AEC and corporations such as Westinghouse and Union Carbide launched a coordinated campaign to promote public acceptance of atomic energy, presenting it in the best light possible and smoothing over concerns about its potential dangers, in the interest of promoting development of nuclear-powered generating plants. Later formalized as the "Atoms for Peace" initiative in 1954, the campaign began with traveling exhibits such as Man and the Atom in 1948, which included the dime-irradiating machine. These exhibits formed the nucleus of the nation's first museum of atomic power, established in 1949.[27] The museum, initially called the American Museum of Atomic Energy (known since 1978 as the American Museum of Science and Energy), was part of the laboratory at Oak Ridge, Tennessee, a city secretly built for the Manhattan Project.[28] The Oak Ridge museum featured innovative hands-on demonstrations of atomic principles, and touted applications of nuclear power in research and electricity generation. The machine that irradiated dimes was one of its most popular exhibits, and the dimes were given away by the thousands in aluminum and plastic holders imprinted with the name of the museum.

The AEC understood the messaging power of a world's fair and made plans to have a presence at the 1964 fair in New York. The original idea was to have a mobile nuclear fission reactor at the fair, but the AEC opted instead for two exhibits drawn from the museum at Oak Ridge, and so the dime irradiator came back to New York.[29]

Thus the world's fair dime is part of a larger family of irradiated dimes, all intended to be signifiers of the potential peaceful applications of nuclear power. The promise, or threat, of nuclear power cropped up all over the fair, whose very theme, "Peace through Understanding," hinted at the looming danger of the Cold War turning hot. Exhibits such as the fallout-proof Underground World Home were products of a nuclear age. Nuclear energy, however, was the power source of the future. General Motors' Futurama II, a series of dioramas of possible technologies, included a machine for building jungle roads, to be powered by an onboard nuclear reactor. The climactic exhibit in General Electric's Disney-designed Progressland was a nuclear fusion reaction. Visitors were treated to a bright flash and loud pop inside a transparent dome as enough energy was released to coax deuterium atoms to fuse and emit some nuclear energy. The reaction was spectacular (though highly inefficient, as orders of magnitude more energy had to be put into the system than it produced).

The AEC display was in the lower level of the Hall of Science, adjacent to NASA's display of rocket engines and missiles. Adult visitors were offered a display called "Radiation and Man," demonstrating natural and man-made nuclear radiation, radiation's effects on living tissues, explanations of nuclear half-life, and protection from radioactive fallout.[30] For children, there was Atomsville, U.S.A. (visitors over age fourteen were not allowed) (fig. 14). Parents could keep an eye on their kids through one-way mirrors

fig. 14
Children at the Atomsville, U.S.A. exhibit, New York World's Fair, 1964. Photo: Associated Press.

or the rather sophisticated surveillance technology of a bank of closed-circuit TV monitors. Atomsville, U.S.A. featured many of the popular hands-on exhibits from the Oak Ridge museum, including mechanical grippers that the children could use to manipulate blocks representing radioactive materials, and a large pinball-like display where visitors could shoot ping-pong balls representing neutrons into clusters of balls representing the nuclei of uranium atoms, starting a chain reaction of plastic balls. Young visitors could measure their weight in octillions of atoms, generate electricity on stationary bicycles, or manipulate the controls of a simulated pool-type nuclear reactor—with a bluish-white glowing core immersed in an open tank of water.[31]

A Souvenir of a Past Future

A neutron-irradiated dime was a fine souvenir of these displays. It is estimated that hundreds of thousands of dimes were irradiated at Oak Ridge and the New York World's Fair. After the fair, the machine was returned to the museum in Tennessee, which only stopped making the irradiated dimes in the 1970s, not out of safety concerns, but because dimes minted after 1965 no longer contained any silver.

Like souvenirs of electric displays from the early twentieth century, the dime in its holder reminds its owner not only of a particular visit to a world's fair but also of a larger promise of a better tomorrow made possible by new forms of energy, developed in corporate-supported research and development facilities. With the passage of time, though, dreams of the future slip into the past. The celebrations of electricity in the early twentieth century seem quaint in their adherence to classical style and allegory, and the energy itself is now so widely used that we usually do not give its presence in our homes a moment's thought. Atomic power, on the other hand, still implies something dangerous and unnatural, giving the souvenir dime an almost ghoulish appeal. If the multicolored sparkling Electric Tower of 1901 celebrated domestic electrification and the transformation of industry only just beginning, Atomsville, U.S.A. seems, from fifty years on, to have been something more like an end: a kind of technological optimism that would not survive intact the growing doubts about what, in the late 1960s, Lewis Mumford would call the "megamachine," a social organization built around the inevitability of industrialization.[32]

By the late 1970s, especially after the Three Mile Island nuclear power plant accident, the idea of distributing irradiated coins had already become a kind of horror story from the bad old days. A coin collector's newspaper column from 1980 doubtingly refers to official statements about the coins' safety, referring to the dimes as "free samples of radiation."[33] Now, after the Chernobyl and Fukushima disasters, as well as countless other demonstrations of the potential hazards of even peaceful uses of atomic energy, the irradiated dime seems ever more an artifact of another era. Perhaps because of that, because of the irrecoverable technological optimism embedded in the artifact itself, and because I finally came to understand the physics, I bought one after all.

NOTES

1. The AEC was superseded by the Department of Energy and the Nuclear Regulatory Commission in 1974.
2. Susan Stewart, *On Longing: Narratives of the Miniature, the Gigantic, the Souvenir, the Collection* (Baltimore: Johns Hopkins University Press, 1984), 135–37.
3. David L. Hume, *Tourism Art and Souvenirs: The Material Culture of Tourism* (New York: Routledge, Taylor & Francis Group, 2014), 3.
4. On the status of German-made ceramics in the early twentieth century, see, for example, Carl Bergmans, "Modern Ceramics of Art," *Journal of the American Ceramic Society* 9, no. 2 (February 1926): 161–62.
5. Jon B. Zachman, "The Legacy and Meaning of World's Fair Souvenirs," in *Fair Representations: World's Fairs and the Modern World*, ed. Robert Rydell, Nancy E. Gwinn, and James Burkhart Gilbert (Amsterdam: VU University Press, 1994), 200.
6. Nineteenth-century world's fairs differed from other early tourist destinations in that they were specifically constructed to be consumable events. Unlike a mountain, for example, made into an accessible, purchasable, contained experience by railroad stations, carriage trails, viewing platforms, and maybe a hotel on top, the world's fair had no pre-tourist "natural" state.
7. Zachman, "The Legacy and Meaning of World's Fair Souvenirs," 200.

8. These punch-card guided machines could weave intricate patterns automatically and were a familiar sight at world's fairs since the Great Exhibition in 1851. There were several Jacquard looms around the Pan-American fairgrounds producing woven souvenir picture ribbons, including one that could produce sixteen separate silk ribbons at once. Donald Murray, "The Automatic Age. Electrical Marvels and Mechanical Triumphs at the Pan-American Exposition," *Everybody's Magazine* 5, no. 26 (October 1901): 402.
9. John Galen Howard, "The Electric Tower," in *Art Hand-Book, Official Handbook of Architecture and Sculpture and Art Catalogue to the Pan-American Exposition* (Buffalo: David Gray, 1901), 34.
10. Edward V. P. Schneiderhahn, "World's Fair Memoir," in *"Indescribably Grand": Diaries and Letters from the 1904 World's Fair*, ed. Martha R. Clevenger (St. Louis: Missouri Historical Society, 1996), 34.
11. Adams to John Hay, November 7, 1900, in *Henry Adams: Selected Letters*, ed. Ernest Samuels (Cambridge, MA: Belknap Press, 1992), 395.
12. David E. Nye, "Electrifying Exhibitions, 1880–1939," in *Fair Representations*, 140–56. See also Nye, *American Technological Sublime* (Cambridge, MA: MIT Press, 1994).
13. Thomas Fleming, *Around the "Pan" with Uncle Hank* (New York: The Nut Shell Publishing Co., 1901), 50.
14. Mabel E. Barnes, "Peeps at the Pan-American" (manuscript), quoted in David E. Nye, *Electrifying America: Social Meanings of a New Technology, 1880–1940* (Cambridge, MA: MIT Press, 1990), 46.
15. Marshall Everett, *The Book of the Fair* (Philadelphia: P. W. Ziegler Co., 1904), 201–2.
16. Stewart, *On Longing*, 137–38.
17. *The St. Louis Electrical Handbook* (St. Louis: Published under the auspices of the American Institute of Electrical Engineers, 1904), 104–5.
18. Marietta Holley and Charles Grunwald, *Samantha at the St. Louis Exposition* (New York: G. W. Dillingham Company, 1904), 222.
19. For comparative images of real spears, see Herbert W. Krieger, *The Collection of Primitive Weapons and Armor of the Philippine Islands in the United States National Museum* (Washington, DC: Govt. Printing Office, 1926), 116.
20. Sharra L. Vostral, "Imperialism on Display: The Philippine Exhibition at the 1904 World's Fair," *Gateway Heritage* 13, no. 4 (Spring 1993): 18–19; Clevenger, *"Indescribably Grand"*, 20–22.
21. Cartoon by "G. Ri" (Victor Mousselet) in *L'Expositon comique*, September 13, 1900, reprinted in *Fair Representations*, 40.
22. David M. Lubin, *Picturing a Nation: Art and Social Change in Nineteenth-Century America* (New Haven, CT: Yale University Press, 1994), 281.
23. Marc Olivier, *Nostalgia and Technology: Embracing the New through Art and Design* (Provo, UT: Bingham Young University, 2005), 38.
24. Murray, "The Automatic Age," 390.
25. Craig Brandon, *The Electric Chair: An Unnatural American History* (Jefferson, NC: McFarland & Co, 1999), 20–21.
26. John Patrick Barrett, *Electricity at the Columbian Exposition* (Chicago: R. R. Donnelley & Sons, 1894), xi.
27. John Krige, "Atoms for Peace, Scientific Internationalism, and Scientific Intelligence," *Osiris* 21, no. 1 (2006): 162.
28. Arthur Molella, "Exhibiting Atomic Culture: The View from Oak Ridge," *History and Technology* 19, no. 3 (2003): 214.
29. The exhibition Man and the Atom had first been mounted in New York in the summer of 1948 as part of the city's celebration of the semi-centennial of the consolidation of the boroughs.
30. Barbara Tufty, "Fair View of Future," *The Science News-Letter* 85, no. 15 (April 11, 1964): 235; Lawrence R. Samuel, *The End of the Innocence: The 1964–1965 New York World's Fair* (Syracuse, NY: Syracuse University Press, 2007), 166.
31. Joan Cook, "Visitors to Atomsville have Energy to Burn," *New York Times*, May 12, 1965: 50; "Atomic Playground," *The Science News-Letter* 85, no. 25 (June 20, 1964): 386; Tufty, "Fair View of Future," 235; "It's A Small World's Fair, If You're Very Young," British Pathé newsreel, "News of the Day" series, June 26, 1964. Sort number UN 3902 B; Samuel, *The End of the Innocence*, 166–67.
32. Lewis Mumford, *The Myth of the Machine: The Pentagon of Power* (New York: Harcourt, Brace, Jovanovich, 1970), 300–02.
33. Ed Rochette, "Coin Roundup: Fallout in your pocket," *Frederick News* (Frederick County, Maryland), March 10, 1980: 5.

OUTING ADVERTISEMENTS. xlvii

Size:
3¼ x 3¾ x 6½ inches.

Weight:
1 lb., 10 oz.

PRICE, $25.00.

Loaded for 100 pictures, including Sole Leather Carrying Case with Strap.

Size of Picture:
2⅝ inches diameter.

ONE-HALF LENGTH.

THE KODAK CAMERA.

ANYBODY who can wind a watch can use the Kodak Camera. It is a magazine camera, and will make one hundred pictures without reloading. The operation of taking the picture is simply to point the camera and press a button. The picture is taken instantaneously on a strip of sensitive film, which is moved into position by turning a key.

A DIVISION OF LABOR. After the one hundred pictures have been taken, the strip of film (which is wound on a spool) may be removed, and sent by mail to the factory to have the pictures finished. Any amateur can finish his own pictures, and any number of duplicates can be made of each picture. A spool of film to reload the camera for one hundred pictures costs only two dollars.

No tripod is required, no focusing, no adjustment whatever. Rapid rectilinear lens. The Kodak will photograph anything, still or moving, indoors or out.

A PICTURESQUE DIARY of your trip to Europe, to the mountains, or the sea-shore, may be obtained without trouble with a Kodak Camera, that will be worth a hundred times its cost in after years.

A BEAUTIFUL INSTRUMENT is the Kodak, covered with dark Turkey morocco, nickel and lacquered brass trimmings, enclosed in a neat sole leather carrying case with shoulder-strap—about the size of a large field-glass.

Send for a copy of the **KODAK PRIMER** with Kodak photograph.

THE EASTMAN DRY PLATE AND FILM CO.,

Branch: 115 Oxford St., London. **ROCHESTER, N. Y.**

SENSING MEMORIES: THE HAPTIC AND KINESTHETIC IN GEORGE EASTMAN'S CAMERA

Makeda Best

Makeda Best teaches at the California College of the Arts, where she is assistant professor in the history of photography in the Visual Studies Program. She is currently at work on a book manuscript on Civil War photography. Additional forthcoming publications address photography and Hiroshima, and contemporary war photography of the conflicts in Iraq and Afghanistan. Her research has been supported by fellowships from the Andrew W. Mellon Foundation and the Smithsonian Institution.

fig. 1
Eastman Dry Plate and Film Company advertisement, *Outing* (October 1888), xlvii. Wayne P. Ellis Collection of Kodakiana. John W. Hartman Center for Sales, Advertising, and Marketing History, Rubenstein Rare Book and Manuscript Library, Duke University.

In the late fall of 1888, readers of American magazines like *Scientific American*, *Scribner's*, *Century*, *Harper's Weekly*, and the sports magazine *Outing* began to see advertisements by the Eastman Dry Plate and Film Company for a new product, the Kodak camera (fig. 1).[1] Touting the new camera's innovative features and remarkable ease of use, these advertisements promised readers that the camera would serve the purposes of memory. The Kodak would help create a "picturesque diary of your trips to Europe, to the mountains, or the sea-shore," according to one advertisement from that year[2]; or "a complete illustrated record of interesting scenes and incidents," according to another.[3] My purpose in this essay is to examine how the design for the new camera by Rochester, New York–based inventor George Eastman (1854–1932)—and the marketing that accompanied it—engaged the user's nonvisual senses in this process of recording scenes for memory.

Scholars have increasingly turned to considering the multisensorial and intersensorial history of photography. Margaret Olin reminds us that touch has always been part of photography: the word *photograph*, literally meaning "light writing," suggests both vision and touch. Olin argues that, through the "slippage between the two parts of its name, photography gains power as a relational art, its meaning determined not only by what it looks like but also by the relationship we are invited to have with it."[4] In *Forget Me Not: Photography and Remembrance*, Geoffrey Batchen writes of a different kind of slippage. To Batchen, the feel of the daguerreotype case in the hand of the nineteenth-century viewer facilitated the "virtual" touch of loved ones and enhanced visual interaction with the mirrorlike image.[5] To Elizabeth Edwards, attention to the convergences of touch and photography serves to "extend our theory of photography beyond the dominant semiotic, linguistic, and instrumental models to a more strongly phenomenological approach, in which materiality and the sensual play a central role in how photographs are understood."[6] Contemporary writing on the senses and photography examines how photographs have been touched, worn, adorned, traded, and collected.[7]

This essay does not approach the analysis of photography and the senses in relation to the photograph, the photographed, or the photographic image, but rather in relation to the camera apparatus itself. In particular, it seeks to consider the contributions of touch (the haptic) and movement (the kinesthetic) to the experience of recording memories using Eastman's Kodak camera. By fostering interpretation through touch, haptic perception is called "proximal," in order to differentiate it from the visual sense, which perceives from a distance.[8] (In cognitive psychology, haptic is differentiated from tactile as a more active engagement by the subject with the object of perception.[9]) The definition of the kinesthetic sense also involves a binary opposition. As opposed to the aesthetic (concerned with still images and objects), the kinesthetic concerns the body's movement in space over time. The haptic and the kinesthetic are both linked to the visual, because the brain quickly translates information gathered from these senses into visual memories and associations.[10] If, as film critic and theorist Laura Marks writes, the proximal senses are senses of knowledge, what can we learn about memory and photography from these initial moments of sensory data gathering?[11] Can the camera itself function as an active sensory interface between the user and the world? Eastman's presentation of the camera during the few years following the Kodak's introduction demonstrates a consciousness of the materiality and sensuality of the apparatus as an integral part of the experience of recording memories. The Kodak camera design, and Eastman's marketing of it, facilitated haptic and kinesthetic experiences, which expanded the process and meaning of visual memory production via photography.

Out of the "Darkened Laboratory"

Eastman's innovation was to reduce camera operation to a few simple steps and to relieve the user of having to process the film and produce the prints. From the announcement of its invention in 1839 until the late 1870s, the technical complexities of photography were so great that only professionals and a few chemically and technically savvy amateurs (with the required facilities and disposable income) chose to pursue the practice. To make a photograph in the 1870s, the photographer had to, among other steps, prepare photosensitive materials; adjust camera settings; expose, develop,

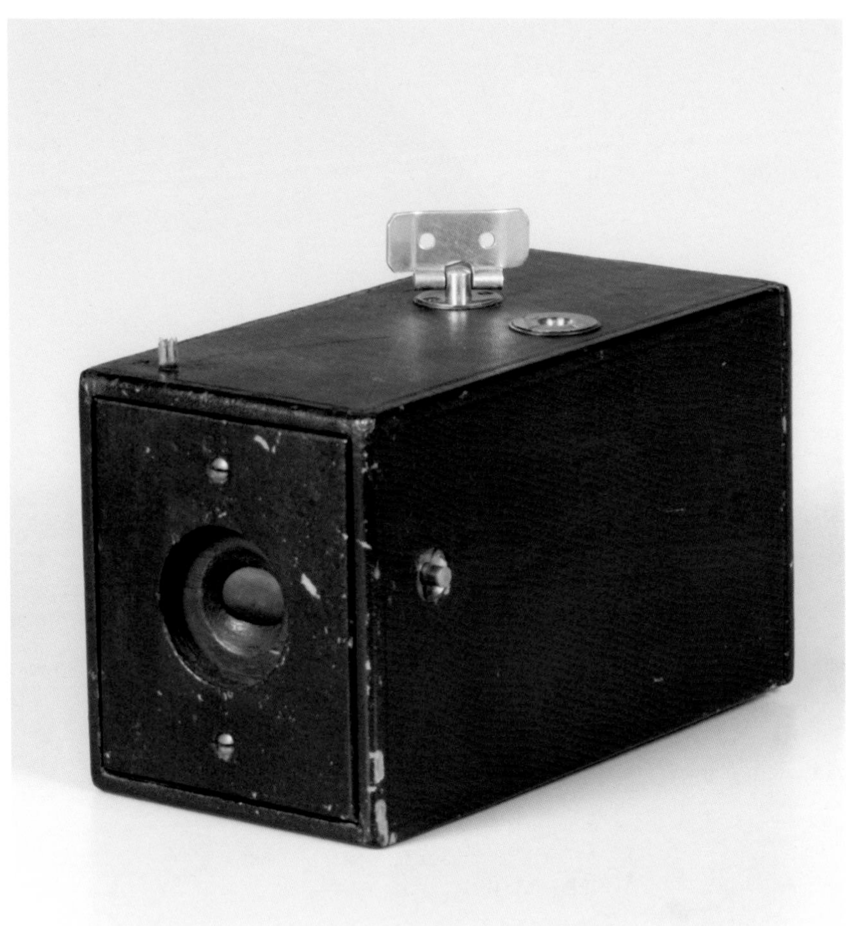

fig. 2
Kodak No. 1 camera, manufactured by Eastman Dry Plate and Film Company, 1888. George Eastman House, International Museum of Photography and Film.

and fix a fragile glass-plate negative; and print and fix the positive paper copy—all within a circumscribed amount of time. Photography was a familiar part of Victorian culture, but it was not an everyday activity for ordinary Americans.

Eastman's "self-contained" Kodak No. 1 camera (fig. 2), as texts described it, was an "oblong box covered with black Morocco" leather outfitted with a lens and a roll winder.[12] The Kodak system reduced the process of making a photograph to three steps: turn the key (to move the film into place), pull the cord (to cock the shutter), and press the button. An accompanying carrying case with a shoulder strap allowed for easy portability. The camera cost twenty-five dollars and came preloaded with a roll of sensitized film capable of making one hundred exposures. After exposing the film, the user returned the camera to Eastman's Rochester headquarters, and the Eastman Company factory processed the film and produced two-and-a-half-inch circular images from each exposure (figs. 3, 4).[13] In addition to the processing arrangement, several technical and practical novelties distinguished Eastman's camera from its predecessors, including its perfection of the roll film mechanism.[14]

fig. 3
Uriah Hunt Painter, "A small girl standing on sidewalk, three-quarters length, facing slightly right," 1889. Library of Congress Prints and Photographs Division.

fig. 4 (opposite)
Postcard, Eastman Dry Plate and Film Company headquarters, 1891. George Eastman House, International Museum of Photography and Film.

The concept of the Kodak was not entirely new. In fact, another Rochester-based inventor named William Walker anticipated Eastman's product by seven years with his camera system, Walker's Pocket Camera. Employing language that Eastman would later refine in such slogans as "Photography Made Easy for Everybody," Walker's promotional materials promised universal ease of use. The "carefully prepared" instructional booklet that accompanied Walker's camera was "free from technicalities and ambiguities [which] so simplifies the art of Photography that it is readily acquired by anyone *without previous experience*."[15] The relatively affordable ten-dollar price for the packaged kit (including camera and manual) also made Walker a forerunner of Eastman.[16] But his box camera was made of cherry wood, and it weighed about two pounds; like other cameras of its time, it was not meant to be handheld and required a tripod, table, or other surface for use.

The fact that within only a few years audiences came to connect the revolutionary amateur camera system exclusively with the Kodak is an indication of the impact of Eastman's design modifications and the effectiveness of his marketing. The Kodak was an international sensation (fig. 5). A writer for *British Architect* wrote: "With the ordinary camera, as our readers know, there is a good deal of skill and knowledge required in

"You press the button, we do the rest."
KODAK
THE EASTMAN COMPANY.
KODAK
PHOTOGRAPHIC MATERIALS.
OFFICE
CITY RAG STORE
CASH

the adjustment and manipulation of the apparatus, but with the 'Kodak' only ordinary intelligence and no preliminary study or long practice is necessary to its successful operation."[17] Advertising copy that ran in American magazines in 1891 proclaimed: "Photography is no longer the secret of the darkened laboratory. . . . The click of the Kodak button is now heard around the world."[18]

The immediate popularity of the Kodak owed much to the particular historical context into which the new camera was introduced in 1888. The fast pace of industrialization and urbanization; new relationships among consumers and producers, and workers and managers; labor unrest; and a welter of new consumer goods—all these factors contributed to a perception of rapid social change.[19] The Kodak was the perfect camera for this moment. Because it enabled its users to easily record the events, experiences, and people that mattered in their lives for the purposes of memory, it affirmed the value of the unique personal history during a time when impersonal forces seemed to be transforming the world. It was a thoroughly modern device that also offered an antidote to some of the anxieties of modern life.

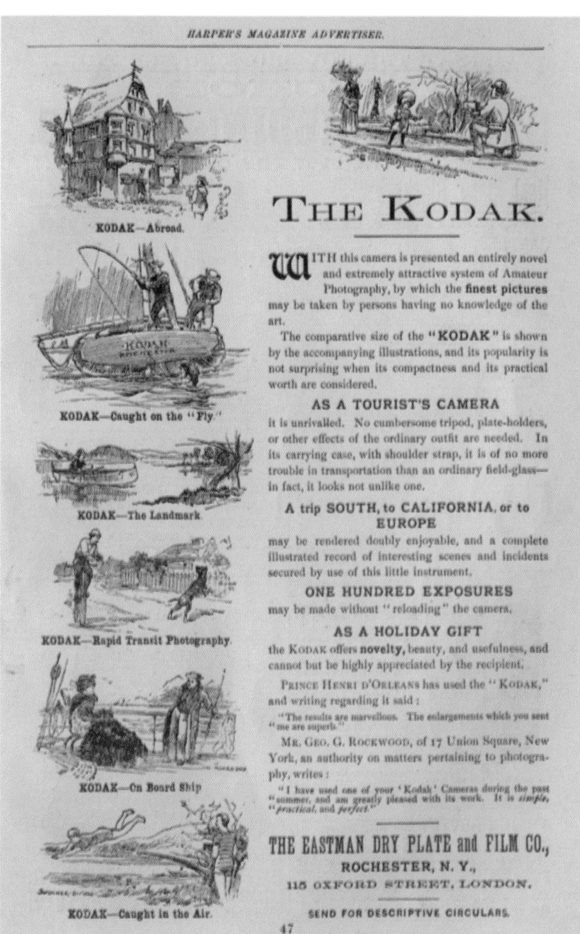

HARPER'S MAGAZINE ADVERTISER.
KODAK—Abroad.
KODAK—Caught on the "Fly."
KODAK—The Landmark.
KODAK—Rapid Transit Photography.
KODAK—On Board Ship
KODAK—Caught in the Air.
THE KODAK.
WITH this camera is presented an entirely novel and extremely attractive system of Amateur Photography, by which the **finest pictures** may be taken by persons having no knowledge of the art.
The comparative size of the "KODAK" is shown by the accompanying illustrations, and its popularity is not surprising when its compactness and its practical worth are considered.
AS A TOURIST'S CAMERA
it is unrivalled. No cumbersome tripod, plate-holders, or other effects of the ordinary outfit are needed. In its carrying case, with shoulder strap, it is of no more trouble in transportation than an ordinary field-glass—in fact, it looks not unlike one.
A trip SOUTH, to CALIFORNIA, or to EUROPE
may be rendered doubly enjoyable, and a complete illustrated record of interesting scenes and incidents secured by use of this little instrument.
ONE HUNDRED EXPOSURES
may be made without "reloading" the camera.
AS A HOLIDAY GIFT
the KODAK offers **novelty,** beauty, and usefulness, and cannot but be highly appreciated by the recipient.
PRINCE HENRI D'ORLEANS has used the "KODAK," and writing regarding it said:
"The results are marvellous. The enlargements which you sent "me are superb."
MR. GEO. G. ROCKWOOD, of 17 Union Square, New York, an authority on matters pertaining to photography, writes:
"I have used one of your 'Kodak' Cameras during the past "summer, and am greatly pleased with its work. It is *simple*, "*practical*, and *perfect*."
THE EASTMAN DRY PLATE and FILM CO.,
ROCHESTER, N. Y.,
115 OXFORD STREET, LONDON.
SEND FOR DESCRIPTIVE CIRCULARS.
47

W. S. Mullaly's and Webster Fulton's 1891 song inspired by the popularity of the Kodak acknowledged the camera's suitability for its moment: "We're living at a rapid pace I vow, / These times are filled with fancies strange and queer, / Electric snaps are now familiar things, / New wonders great are bobbing up each year."[20] Fulton's lyrics further align the Kodak with modernity by contrasting its ease of use and corresponding casualness of its aesthetic with older, outdated forms of photography: "In olden days for pictures they would sit, / In an attitude like this awful guy." Fulton celebrated the Kodak as a practice and personal aesthetic of the contemporary moment, which was not dictated by conventions but by individual desires: "But nowadays the Kodak changes that, / And photographs are captured on the fly! / Isn't it simple? Isn't it quick? / Such a small box, it must be a trick!"

Among the changes in American society that set the context for the immediate popularity of the Kodak, the growing role of travel was especially important. Travel was at the center of the modern middle-class lifestyle in the late nineteenth century, fostered by such developments as the opening of the nation's first continental rail lines in 1883 and the addition of short lines and branches in the 1890s.[21] The ability to afford travel affirmed one's middle-class status, while recording personal memories served the formation of this group identity.[22]

fig. 5 (opposite)
Frances Benjamin Johnston, "A Kodak creates a sensation," c. 1895. Library of Congress Prints and Photographs Division, Frances Benjamin Johnston Collection.

fig. 6
Eastman Dry Plate and Film Company advertisement, *Harper's Weekly* (1888), 44. Wayne P. Ellis Collection of Kodakiana. John W. Hartman Center for Sales, Advertising, and Marketing History, Rubenstein Rare Book and Manuscript Library, Duke University.

Kodak advertisements made readers aware of the necessity of memory, inspiring them to consider not only the activities of their trip, but also their return. One advertisement called the new device "a tourist's camera" and illustrated the kinds of leisure scenes that it could capture (fig. 6). Flipping through a guidebook in 1891, a reader might find under a Kodak advertisement for excursion trains these simple words, set off against a plain white background: "Take a KODAK with you."[23] Standing on the platforms of the New York Central Railroad, riders would have noticed yet another variation of the company slogan: "Take a Kodak with You—It will perpetuate the pleasure of your summer trip." The phrase "perpetuate the pleasure" invites multiple interpretations. The activity of photography itself is a pleasure to be enjoyed throughout the trip, while the snapshots are to be enjoyed long after.

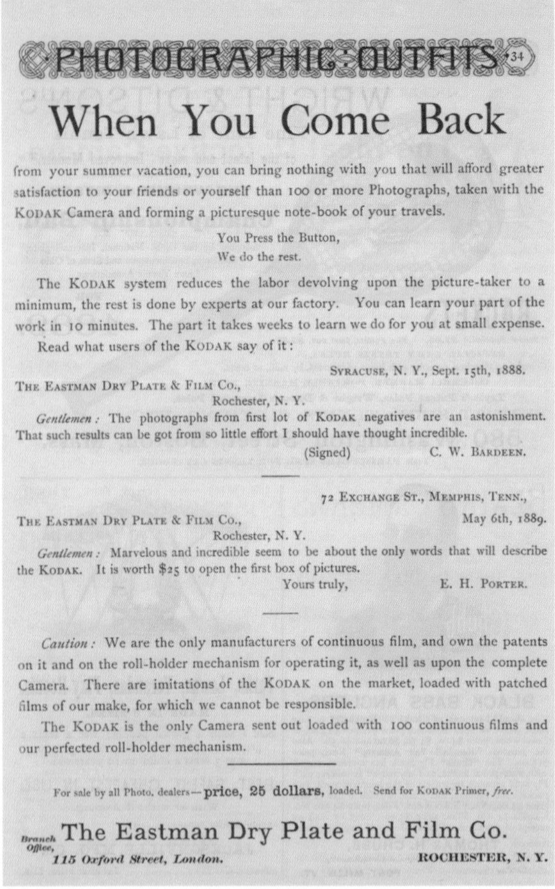

PHOTOGRAPHIC OUTFITS 34

When You Come Back

from your summer vacation, you can bring nothing with you that will afford greater satisfaction to your friends or yourself than 100 or more Photographs, taken with the KODAK Camera and forming a picturesque note-book of your travels.

You Press the Button,
We do the rest.

The KODAK system reduces the labor devolving upon the picture-taker to a minimum, the rest is done by experts at our factory. You can learn your part of the work in 10 minutes. The part it takes weeks to learn we do for you at small expense.

Read what users of the KODAK say of it:

SYRACUSE, N. Y., Sept. 15th, 1888.

THE EASTMAN DRY PLATE & FILM CO.,
Rochester, N. Y.

Gentlemen: The photographs from first lot of KODAK negatives are an astonishment. That such results can be got from so little effort I should have thought incredible.

(Signed) C. W. BARDEEN.

72 EXCHANGE ST., MEMPHIS, TENN.,
May 6th, 1889.

THE EASTMAN DRY PLATE & FILM CO.,
Rochester, N. Y.

Gentlemen: Marvelous and incredible seem to be about the only words that will describe the KODAK. It is worth $25 to open the first box of pictures.

Yours truly, E. H. PORTER.

Caution: We are the only manufacturers of continuous film, and own the patents on it and on the roll-holder mechanism for operating it, as well as upon the complete Camera. There are imitations of the KODAK on the market, loaded with patched films of our make, for which we cannot be responsible.

The KODAK is the only Camera sent out loaded with 100 continuous films and our perfected roll-holder mechanism.

For sale by all Photo. dealers—**price, 25 dollars,** loaded. Send for KODAK Primer, *free.*

The Eastman Dry Plate and Film Co.

Branch Office, 115 Oxford Street, London. **ROCHESTER, N. Y.**

THE KODAK CAMERA.

"You press the button, we do the rest."

Anybody can take good photographs with the Kodak. Send for the Primer, free.

The Kodak is for sale by all Photo stock dealers.

The Eastman Dry Plate and Film Co.

Price, $25.00. Loaded for 100 pictures. ROCHESTER, N. Y.

The words "when you come back" were introduced in an 1889 advertisement that ran in travel magazines.[24] Drawing readers in through the direct address implied in the word "you," the text that followed referred to mingled desires of the past and the present. The imagined reader was coming back from a summer trip with a "picturesque note-book," as the copy described it, courtesy of the Kodak camera. A Kodak slogan from the early 1890s reminded travelers that "what's worth seeing is worth remembering."

Middle-class Americans viewed travel from a moral and spiritual perspective. While vacations could be associated with idleness, another form of travel—touring, to see sites of historical significance or natural beauty—offered opportunities for self-improvement and spiritual awakening.[25] This kind of directed travel was made even more purposeful by the introduction of the "work" of memory making with a camera, which, like keeping a travel journal, served as a restorative outlet. The act of making photographs could be nearly spiritual. One writer speculated about what took place when making a picture: "The ray of light that penetrates this little box reaches something more than blank, empty space."[26] In addition, the production of personal photographic mementos offered an alternative to the heavily commercialized tourist experience.[27] Kodak owners did not need to purchase packaged, generic photographic views, and could instead preserve their personal vision of the sights they encountered.

Kodak's Promise

Between 1888 and 1893, Eastman conceived of and oversaw the creation of promotional materials that highlighted specific camera features, and in the process presented the camera as a magical vehicle to personal fulfillment and pleasure through the production of visual memories.[28] But while Eastman's advertisements touted the camera as a device for recording memories, the technical limitations of print advertising at this time meant that he was unable to attract buyers through high-quality reproductions of the kinds photographic memories users could potentially produce. Instead, appealing to the user's haptic and kinesthetic senses, these materials used text and line drawings—and sometimes text alone (fig. 7)—to present a new interpretation of photography and of the user's relationship with the camera. Eastman anchored the advertisements on the user's sensual experience with the camera and imaginatively suggested other experiences.

Eastman's camera-centered approach reflected a transactional relationship between the user and the Eastman Company that was based on the movement of the camera, since, in the beginning, users were required to return the camera (not just the exposed film) to the Rochester plant for processing. Eastman understood the power of voice in advertising to simulate personal relationships and interactions. He introduced audiences to the Kodak through a straightforward slogan that he coined: "You press the button, we do the rest" (fig. 8). The text made a promise to its users, employing a kind of voice that Eastman pioneered—a familiar, neighborly tone that implied social standing and sometimes even expressed concern.[29] In a pin produced by the company, the unpunctuated "you press the button" phrase drifts off, enticing the reader to imagine any number of scenes to record, but "we do the rest" is a definitive promise (fig. 9). Using "we" instead of "the Eastman Company" makes the transaction seem personal. "We" is a friend (the Eastman Company, of course, and maybe even George Eastman himself) who is there to help and to facilitate.[30] In an era of increasing social and economic stratification, "you" addressed everyone equally and singularly. The direct address by a voice that is both seen and "heard" prompts a personal response from its audience, proposing the need and encouraging the desire for visual records. Much of Eastman's potential customer base had never considered making a photograph, and the concept of processing film and printing the images was even more unfamiliar.[31] In reality, there was no physical contact, but there was a "contact" of sorts through the camera. The user had to trust the unseen "Kodak man" because he was responsible for the processing and return of the user's memories.

fig. 7 (opposite, top) Eastman Dry Plate and Film Company advertisement, *Century* (1889). Wayne P. Ellis Collection of Kodakiana. John W. Hartman Center for Sales, Advertising, and Marketing History, Rubenstein Rare Book and Manuscript Library, Duke University Library.

fig. 8 (opposite, bottom) Eastman Dry Plate and Film Company advertisement, 1888. George Eastman House, International Museum of Photography and Film.

fig. 9
Pin, c. 1888. George Eastman House, International Museum of Photography and Film.

The simulation of physical contact in these advertisements reinforces the arrangement stated in the slogan. In one version, the words surround an image of an unseen man's hand in profile, holding a camera (fig. 9). The hand is extended gently, as if in anticipation of a person ready to receive it and to respond to the offer. The hand and text function together to convey a

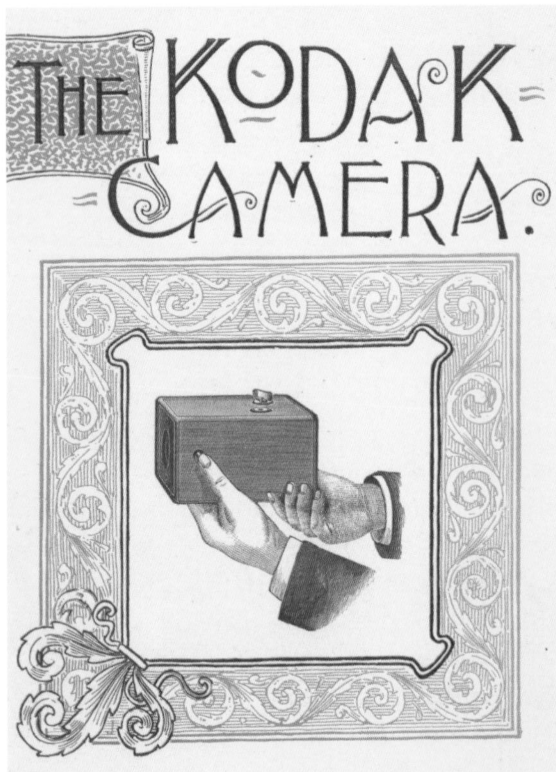

fig. 10
Eastman Dry Plate and Film Company promotional brochure. Emergence of Advertising in America Collection – K0013. Wayne P. Ellis Collection of Kodakiana. John W. Hartman Center for Sales, Advertising, and Marketing History, Rubenstein Rare Book and Manuscript Library, Duke University.

fig. 11 (opposite)
Eastman Dry Plate and Film Company advertisement, 1889. George Eastman House, International Museum of Photography and Film.

message to the potential user: "You press the button" is written along the top. The cuffed white shirt and black jacket from which the hand extends demonstrates credibility. The same hand appears regularly in advertisements, booklets, and instruction sheets, making it a familiar symbol for the company (fig. 10; see also fig. 1).

Once the user's hands received the camera, its feel conveyed an understanding of it as an object and tool for making memory. Earlier camera models (even Walker's inexpensive version) were often made, much like scientific instruments, from expensive fine woods like cherry or mahogany, referencing by visual and haptic association the technically complex process of using these devices. Eastman made a tellingly different design choice. He covered the Kodak camera box with a material known for its use in high-quality goods—stippled "Morocco" (sometimes called "Turkey") leather, the feel of which was occasionally likened to skin. Prized for being pliable and for its "glossy and otherwise attractive appearance," Morocco leather became especially popular during the late nineteenth century, when it was frequently used in children's and men's shoes, in bindings for large gift books (especially bibles), and in linings for baby carriages and purses.[32] Significantly for the purposes of evoking memory, Morocco leather was also used, along with silk and metal trimmings, for picture albums, such as the popular Longfellow photographic album.[33]

Morocco leather was a key feature through which Eastman cultivated the appreciation of the camera as a sensuous object rather than a technological instrument. In an advertisement from 1889, three women stand around a table looking at a Kodak, above a caption reading: "Isn't it lovely!" (fig. 11). Advertising copy called the camera "handsome" and described it as a "beautiful instrument." According to the Eastman Company, a "fact" about the Kodak was that it offers "beauty," among other things, that could not help but be "highly appreciated" by the recipient.

The Kodak featured a technical mechanism, referred to in advertising material as a "magazine," that allowed users to make continuous exposures, rather than having to cap the camera in order to prevent the film from being exposed as the next section of unexposed film moved into place. For this reason, Eastman labeled the camera "a magazine camera."[34]

A GIFT WORTH HAVING.
(Feminine Chorus): Oh! isn't it lovely! I must have a Kodak!

Novices likely would not have understood the technical innovation that supported continuous exposures, but they would respond to the word itself, during a period when magazines had become a significant aspect of American life, with the development of cheaper typesetting (after 1880) and halftone printing (after 1888).[35] To use the Kodak was to make a magazine of one's own life, to "turn the page" of the story. To explain the action of making a photograph as if it were like turning a page was important for an audience that did not understand how photography worked. What consumers would understand was the motion of turning a page and the sense of anticipation that accompanies that gesture. After Kodak advertisements introduced the phrase, other camera makers soon adopted it for their products.[36]

Advertisements likened the camera to a "picturesque diary," referring to the freedom and spontaneity in recording intimate memories that the continuous exposure mechanism allowed.[37] Like the term "magazine camera," the metaphor of the "picturesque diary" associated the Kodak with objects that users would interact with in personal and haptic ways. Like the camera, the diary "holds" only the personal and the meaningful. Because of its personal content, owners often perceive the diary as an extension of the body. Haptic touch is a central aspect of its material identity—the complex feelings evoked by the tactile perception of leather, linen, or silk bindings, and of fine writing paper, function as physical surrogates for the impalpable

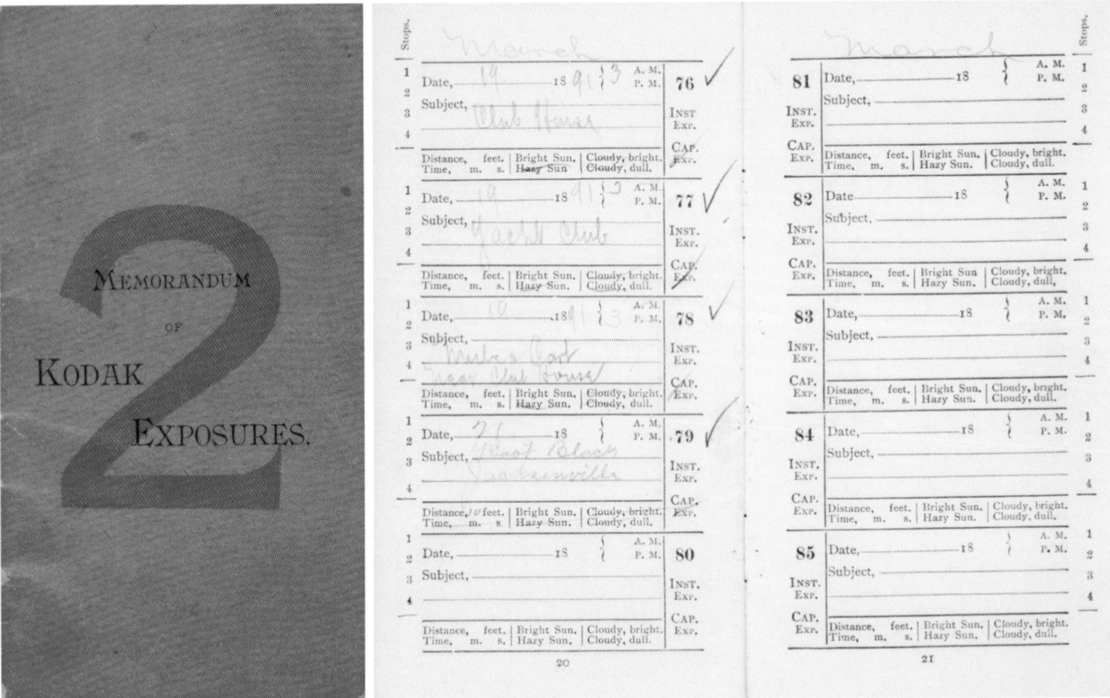

Stops. 1 2 3 4

March

Date, 19 18 91 A. M. P. M. | 76 | Subject, | INST. EXP. | CAP. EXP.
Distance, feet. | Bright Sun. | Cloudy, bright. / Time, m. s. | Hazy Sun. | Cloudy, dull.

Date, 19 18 91 A. M. P. M. | 77 | Subject, | INST. EXP. | CAP. EXP.
Distance, feet. | Bright Sun. | Cloudy, bright. / Time, m. s. | Hazy Sun. | Cloudy, dull.

Date, 19 18 91 A. M. P. M. | 78 | Subject, | INST. EXP. | CAP. EXP.
Distance, feet. | Bright Sun. | Cloudy, bright. / Time, m. s. | Hazy Sun. | Cloudy, dull.

Date, 21 18 A. M. P. M. | 79 | Subject, | INST. EXP. | CAP. EXP.
Distance, feet. | Bright Sun. | Cloudy, bright. / Time, m. s. | Hazy Sun. | Cloudy, dull.

Date, 18 A. M. P. M. | 80 | Subject, | INST. EXP. | CAP. EXP.
Distance, feet. | Bright Sun. | Cloudy, bright. / Time, m. s. | Hazy Sun. | Cloudy, dull.

20

March

81 | Date, 18 A. M. P. M. | Subject, | INST. EXP. | CAP. EXP.
Distance, feet. | Bright Sun. | Cloudy, bright. / Time, m. s. | Hazy Sun. | Cloudy, dull.

82 | Date 18 A. M. P. M. | Subject, | INST. EXP. | CAP. EXP.
Distance, feet. | Bright Sun | Cloudy, bright. / Time, m. s. | Hazy Sun. | Cloudy, dull.

83 | Date, 18 A. M. P. M. | Subject, | INST. EXP. | CAP. EXP.
Distance, feet. | Bright Sun. | Cloudy, bright. / Time, m. s. | Hazy Sun. | Cloudy, dull.

84 | Date, 18 A. M. P. M. | Subject, | INST. EXP. | CAP. EXP.
Distance, feet. | Bright Sun. | Cloudy, bright. / Time, m. s. | Hazy Sun. | Cloudy, dull.

85 | Date, 18 A. M. P. M. | Subject, | INST. EXP. | CAP. EXP.
Distance, feet. | Bright Sun. | Cloudy, bright. / Time, m. s. | Hazy Sun. | Cloudy, dull.

21

figs. 12, 13
Eastman Dry Plate and Film Company, "Memorandum of Kodak Exposures," c. 1888. George Eastman House, International Museum of Photography and Film.

words inside. Along with the camera, purchasers of Kodaks received a paper memorandum book (titled "Memorandum of Kodak Exposures") so that they could make notes on the photographs as they exposed them (figs. 12, 13).[38] The ostensible function of these entries was to indicate to users the number of exposures they had left on the roll, but the practice of jotting down notes following exposures strengthened the perception of the camera as a tool for preservation of memories.

Advertising texts further taught users to understand the camera as a tool to preserve time through allusions to haptic movements. The introductory text of an 1888 advertisement stated that "anybody who can wind a watch can use the Kodak Camera."[39] One winds a watch so that it can continue to keep time, and one makes photographs in order to sustain memories against erosion by the passage of time. By likening the daily winding of a watch to the practice of photography, the text normalizes the once formal act of photography as just another aspect of daily life—as regular an activity as winding a watch. Haptic touch unites the Kodak with objects as diverse as Longfellow albums, pocket watches, diaries, and popular magazines, devices sought after by consumers for whom recording memories was becoming a part of their middle-class identity.

If the body of the camera felt like skin, Eastman and his team further strengthened the Kodak's capacity to serve as an extension of the user's body by designing it to move with the user and to be operated through intuitive motions. The Kodak camera was unique because of the freedom of mobility it offered users, who did not require a table or a tripod upon which to rest it. Instead, Eastman's team designed the camera to be held by hand against the user's chest. The action of making a photograph was designed not to disrupt the flow of bodily movement, allowing the photographer a more dynamic interaction with the outside world. There were no bulky film plate holders that needed insertion or adjustment, as on previous camera models. The buttons had no confusing numbers or settings—the process of using the camera, as advertisements described it, consisted of "automatic arrangements." A device meant to be held in front of the body instead of the face instigated a different relationship between user and camera; corporeal orientation and kinesthetic sensations contributed to the act of recording, just as visual perception did.

Forgetting Touch

One of the reasons scholars overlook the role of the haptic and the kinesthetic in discussions of memory and amateur photography has to do with the technical evolution of the company's own promotional campaigns toward a strategy that favored vision above the other senses.[40] During the late 1890s, Kodak's most persuasive advertising coincided with expanding media markets and technical modernization in image reproduction and design. Authors in trade magazines began to speak frequently of "eye appeal."[41] Pursuing what William Leach describes as the "iconographic trend" of the visual culture of the era—full-page display advertising with bold headlines and distinct pictures of goods for sale—consumer goods manufacturers like the Eastman Company responded to the new capacity to produce visually stimulating material.[42] The Eastman Company's core graphic design strategy after the late 1890s featured single, large black-and-white (and eventually, color) photographs along with a few lines of simple text (fig. 14).

Because of how they explicitly taught Americans to value and conceive of photographic memories, these advertisements have received more attention than have the earlier Kodak advertisements discussed here.[43] Advertisements made before 1895 lacked the technical capacity for photographic reproduction and color. Kodak's earliest advertisements were black-and-white designs that relied heavily on text, typographical contrasts for emphasis, and line drawings for illustration. In other words, the role of memory in this earlier period is often unrecognized by historians of visual culture because it was presented in a different syntax that stressed the proximal senses instead of the visual.

As far back as Aristotle, philosophers argued that touch mediates every other type of sense perception, even vision.[44] Thomas Brown wrote in 1827: "If priority of sensation alone were to be regarded, the sense of *touch* might deserve to be considered in the first place; as it must have been exercised long before birth, and is probably the very feeling with which sentient life begins."[45] German philosopher David Katz, a pioneer in theories of tactical perception, wrote about the role of "active touch," and recognized that movements (especially those that are user-initiated) and vibrations enhanced the perception of objects and, thus, the experience of them.[46] British geographer and writer David Kay's *Memory: What It is and How to Improve It* was one of the most talked-about books of the era. He wrote: "the senses are not only necessary for the receiving of impressions, but also concerned in the recollection of them, and the muscles are not only requisite for the remembrance of them."[47]

The neglect of the earlier Kodak period is an example of what Mark Paterson calls the "visualistic bias" of Western culture and of the need to "reveal the underlying haptic (tactile, proprioceptive, kinesthetic) aspects of spatial experience and to re-inscribe them into that cultural history."[48] "Forgetting" to acknowledge the role of touch as an aspect of cultural experience diminishes our historical knowledge, Paterson writes.[49] The stakes for acknowledging sensual perception are real. Constance Classen points out that perception is a cultural act as well as a physical one.[50] We associate and invest acts of perception with cultural values.[51] Throughout history, the proximal senses have functioned as vehicles of politics and expressions of social status.[52]

Eastman's marketing may have promoted photography for "everyone," but the perceptual sensations of the Kodak experience of memory production were distinctly embedded within a specific modern, late nineteenth-century middle-class identity—an identity defined in large part by consumption and everyday practices relating to memory. From the beginning, Eastman linked the Kodak experience to this consumer identity, and relied on these other consumer experiences as means through which to both shape and distinguish the meaning of the user experience of his product. The Kodak experience demonstrates that the proximal senses are not "pre-modern": they are products of place and time, and their meanings change historically.[53] During these "times strange and queer," members of this emerging class sought (and had the means and the leisure time) to preserve moments in their personal experience against the rapid changes and social tumult that surrounded them in the broader society. Acknowledging the camera as an active sensory interface exposes the role of the haptic and the kinesthetic in photographic memory production, and expands our understanding of the relationship between class formation in late nineteenth-century America and amateur photography.

fig. 14
Kodak Company advertisement, 1915. Wayne P. Ellis Collection of Kodakiana. John W. Hartman Center for Sales, Advertising, and Marketing History. Rubenstein Rare Book and Manuscript Library, Duke University.

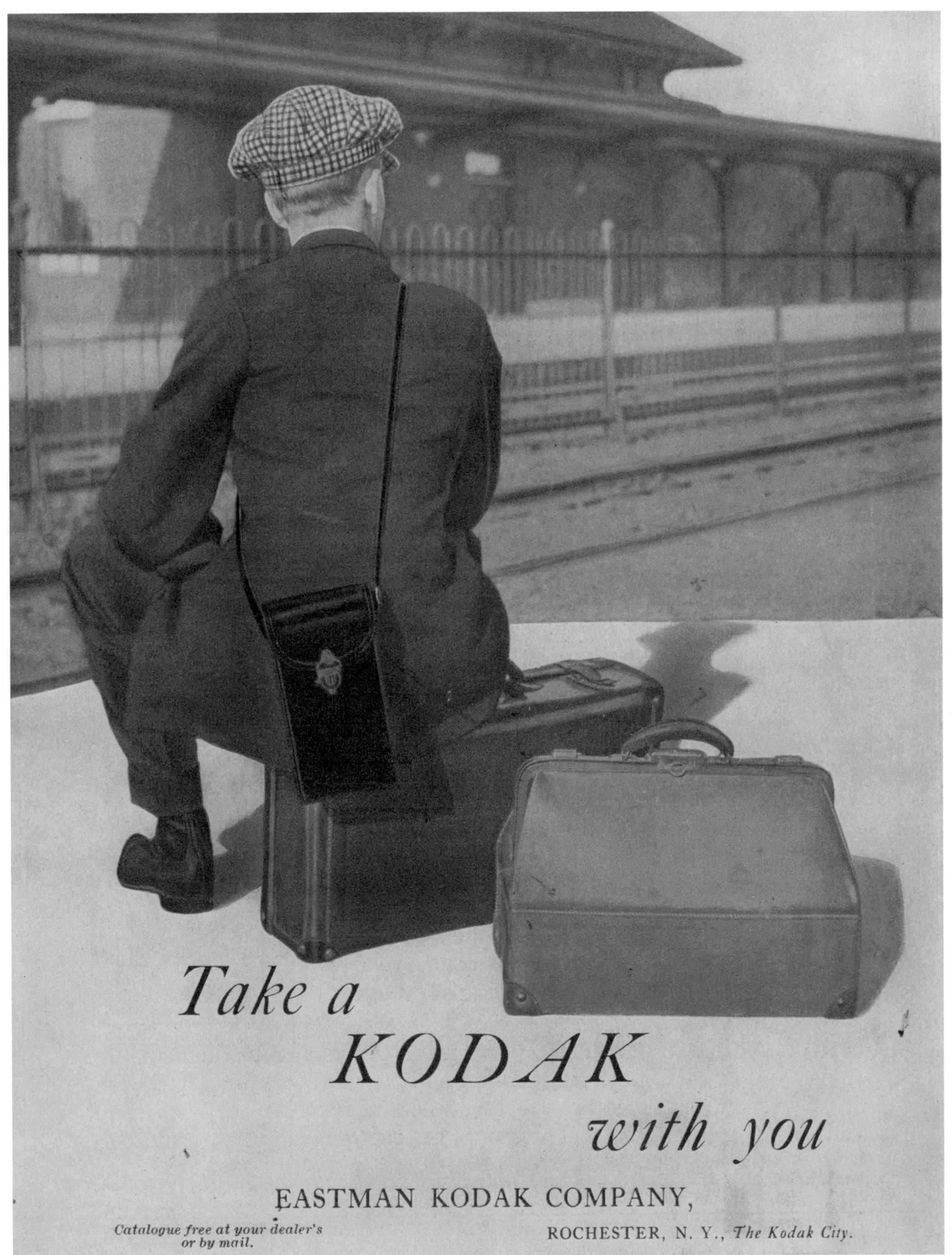
Take a
KODAK
with you
EASTMAN KODAK COMPANY,
Catalogue free at your dealer's
or by mail.
ROCHESTER, N. Y., The Kodak City.

NOTES

1. The Eastman Company did not become the Kodak Company until 1893.
2. Eastman Company advertisement, *Outing* (October 1888), xlvii.
3. Eastman Company advertisement that appeared in *Harper's Weekly* in 1888. The Eastman Company ran weekly advertisements (sometimes multiple advertisements per issue) in publications such as *Harper's Weekly* and *Century* magazine.
4. Margaret Olin, *Touching Photographs* (Chicago: University of Chicago Press, 2012), 3.
5. Geoffrey Batchen, *Forget Me Not: Photography and Remembrance* (New York: Princeton Architectural Press, 2004), 14.
6. Elizabeth Edwards, "Thinking Photography beyond the Visual," in *Photography: Theoretical Snapshots*, ed. J. J. Long, Andrea Noble, and Edward Welch (New York: Routledge, 2009), 33.
7. See, for example, Elizabeth Edwards, "Photographs as Objects of Memory," in *Material Memories: Design and Evocation*, ed. Jeremy Aynsley, Christopher Breward, and Marius Kwint (London: Oxford University Press, 1999), 221–36.
8. Nina Gaissert, *Perceiving Complex Objects: A Comparison of the Visual and the Haptic Modalities* (Berlin: Logos Verlag, 2011), 20–23
9. Yvette Hatwell, Arlette Streri, and Edouard Gentaz, eds., *Touching for Knowing: Cognitive Psychology of Haptic Manual Perception* (Amsterdam: John Benjamins Publishing Company, 2003), 2.
10. Gaissert, *Perceiving Complex Objects*, 20–23.
11. Laura U. Marks, "Thinking Multisensory Culture," *Paragraph* 31, no. 2 (2008): 125.
12. Eastman introduced nearly a dozen cameras in the next few years, with various modifications, but all retained the same shape and the use of the leather.
13. After 1891, users had the option of returning the camera or developing the film themselves.
14. For more on the technical aspects of the camera, see Reese Jenkins, *Images and Enterprise: Technology and the American Photographic Industry, 1839 to 1925* (Baltimore: Johns Hopkins University Press, 1987), 114.
15. "Pictures by the Roll," *Image* 4, no. 6 (September 1955): 43
16. Walker eventually joined Eastman's team. Ibid.: 42–43.
17. "What is the Kodak?" *British Architect* 31 (March 8, 1889): 187
18. "At the Home of the Kodak," *Scribner's* (June 1891), advertising supplement, 31.
19. See William Leach, *Land of Desire: Merchants, Power, and the Rise of a New American Culture* (New York: Vintage Books, 1993), 3; Arthur M. Schlesinger, *The Rise of the City, 1878–1898* (New York: Macmillan, 1956), 79; Walter Licht, *Industrializing America: The Nineteenth Century* (Baltimore: Johns Hopkins University Press, 1995), 161, 168; Susan Strasser, *Satisfaction Guaranteed: The Making of the American Mass Market* (Washington, DC: Smithsonian Books, 2004), 15; Alan Trachtenberg, *The Incorporation of America: Culture and Society in the Gilded Age* (New York: Hill and Wang, 1992), 80, 90–92; Roger H. Wiebe, *The Search For Order, 1877–1920* (New York: Hill and Wang, 1966) 12, 134–48.
20. "You Press the Button, We Do the Rest," lyrics by Webster C. Fulton, music by W. S. Mullaly (Willis Woodward & Co., 1891).
21. Marguerite Shaffer, *See America First: Tourism and National Identity, 1880–1910* (Washington, DC: Smithsonian Books, 2001), 21.
22. David Lowenthal, *The Past is a Foreign Country* (Cambridge: Cambridge University Press, 1985), 38. Lowenthal writes that one of the benefits of the past is its capacity to offer "reaffirmation and validation" as well as "individual and group identity."
23. S. W. Hoke, "Is Insertion Best?" *Printers' Ink* 4, no. 24 (June 17, 1891): 796
24. Eastman Company advertisement that appeared in *Century*, 1889.
25. Cindy S. Aron, *Working at Play: A History of Vacations in the United States* (New York: Oxford University Press, 2001), 9, 128.
26. "How to Prepare—A Suggestion for the World's Fair," *A Handbook of Agriculture, Wisconsin Farmer's Institute Bulletin*, no. 6 (1892): 80.
27. Shaffer, *See America First*, 267–68.
28. Eastman hired Lewis B. Jones to oversee advertising in 1892. Bruce Bliven, "Teaching the Nation to Want Kodak," *Printer's Ink* 102, no. 6 (February 7, 1918): 6.
29. Richard Malin Ohmann, *Selling Culture: Magazines, Markets, and Class at the Turn of the Century* (New York: Verso, 1996), 191.
30. Such friendly advertising belied the fact that Eastman was determined in his pursuit of his market. His advertising made him a pioneer of new techniques of persuasion, and his work soon became a case study in trade journals. See Henry Snowden Ward, *Process the Photomechanics of Printed Illustration* 5, no. 51 (March 1898): 399.

31. Jenkins, *Images and Enterprise*, 112.
32. *Stoddart's Encyclopedia Americana: A Dictionary of Arts, Sciences, and General Literature*, vol. 3 (1886), 582. Previously manufactured in Turkey and Morocco, this kind of leather had only recently begun to be produced in the United States.
33. "New Album Lines," *American Stationer* (June 30, 1889), 1363.
34. Eastman Company advertisement, *Outing* (October 1888), xlvii.
35. Frank Luther Mott, *A History of American Magazines. Volume IV, 1885–1905* (Cambridge: Harvard University Press, 1957).
36. The Boston Camera Company began marketing its Hawk-Eye Camera as an "automatic magazine camera" in 1889.
37. Eastman Company advertisement, *Outing* (October 1888), xlvii.
38. Brian Coe, *The Snapshot Photograph: The Rise of Popular Photography* (London: Ash and Grant, 1977), 17.
39. Eastman Company advertisement, *Outing* (October 1888), xlvii.
40. For example, since Brian Coe's *The Snapshot Photograph: The Rise of Popular Photography 1888–1939* (1977), numerous scholars and curators have addressed the cultural role and aesthetics of snapshots, including Marianne Hirsch, ed., *The Familial Gaze* (Hanover, N.H.: The University Press of New England, 1999); Douglas R. Nickel, *Snapshots: The Photography of Everyday Life, 1888 to the Present* (San Francisco: San Francisco Museum of Modern Art, 1998); Sarah Greenough et al., eds. *The Art of the American Snapshot, 1888–1978: From the Collection of Robert E. Jackson* (Washington, DC: National Gallery of Art, 2007).
41. Leach, "Color, Glass, and Light," in *Land of Desire.*
42. Leach, *Land of Desire*, 4.
43. Nancy Martha West, *Kodak and the Lens of Nostalgia* (Charlottesville, VA: University Press of Virginia, 2000), 1. West's central argument is that "Kodak taught amateur photographers to apprehend their experiences and memories as objects of nostalgia."
44. L. E. Krueger, "Historical Perspective," in *Tactual Perception: A Sourcebook*, ed. William Schiff and Emerson Foulke (Cambridge: Cambridge University Press, 1982), 5.
45. Thomas Brown, *Lectures on the Philosophy of the Human Mind* (Cambridge, MA: Hilliard and Brown, 1827), 143.
46. Krueger, "Historical Perspective," 8.
47. David Kay, *Memory: What It is and How to Improve It* (New York: Appleton, 1888), vii.
48. Mark Paterson, *The Senses of Touch: Haptics, Affects, and Technologies* (London: Bloomsbury Academic, 2007), 59.
49. Ibid.
50. Constance Classen, *Worlds of Sense: Exploring the Senses in History and Across Cultures* (New York: Routledge, 1993), 1.
51. Ibid.
52. See, for example, Constance Classen, David Howes, and Anthony Synnott, *Aroma: The Cultural History of Smell* (London: Routledge, 1994).
53. Mark Michael Smith, *Sensing the Past: Seeing, Hearing, Smelling, Tasting, and Touching in History* (Berkeley: University of California Press, 2007), 2–3.

CEYLON

Part of 1600 Columns. Ruins of the Brazen Temple.

INDIA

Banyan. (the Largest in the World) Tree.

CALCUTTA. Hindoo Temple.

Enroute to Darjeeling.

ALBUMS OF EMPIRE: PHOTOGRAPHY, COLLECTIVE MEMORY, AND THE BRITISH RAJ

Elizabeth Heath

Elizabeth Heath is a historian of modern France and the French empire. She received her Ph.D. from the University of Chicago in 2007 and is an assistant professor at Baruch College, City University of New York. She is the author of *Wine, Sugar, and the Making of Modern France: Global Crisis and the Racialization of French Citizenship* (2014), and is currently at work on a new project about the role that empire and colonial commerce played in shaping modern French economic, cultural, and social life.

In the late nineteenth and early twentieth centuries, British men and women traveled to South Asia carrying a new tool to record their experiences and adventures: the box camera. These travelers and colonial officers also collected professionally made stock photographs and postcards of colonial landscapes, peoples, and cultures, which they used to expand the breadth of their photograph collections. Both kinds of visual souvenirs eventually made their way into albums that provide an intimate perspective on British imperialism.

In working with these memory-objects, the historian encounters unexpected repetitions. Pages from albums like the Hobson family's 1901 *Le tour du monde I: 1899–1900–1901* transfix the viewer and draw her into a realm of individual memory and recollection glossed in black, white, and gray tones (figs. 1, 2). Yet, viewed alongside other British colonial photograph albums, it becomes clear that the albums bear remarkable similarities. Although produced by different travelers at different times, the albums contain photographs eerily reminiscent of one another. That the albums and images are so similar is both puzzling and unsettling, precisely because photograph albums are, by conventional wisdom, repositories of personal memory.

This essay seeks to unravel this paradox. Close scrutiny of several photograph albums—part of the Jean S. and Frederic A. Sharf Collection at The Wolfsonian–Florida International University—produced by British colonial travelers and agents reveals how these collections functioned simultaneously as personal memory-objects and collective souvenirs of empire. The albums are individual memoirs containing personal photographs and mementos. Like the *Le tour du monde* album, they are filled with photographs of temples and ruins, train and boat trips, and family, friends, and acquaintances preserved for future reminiscences. But closer inspection reveals that the albums are also repositories of a collective memory that justified British imperialism and the colonial state—the Raj. Pictures of ruined temples and modern railway systems did not simply bear witness to individual adventures, but also constituted pieces of a larger story that Britons told about British rule—and their own presence—in India. Likewise, images of state ceremonies, exploratory trips, and military missions reinforced notions of civility and barbarity that helped legitimize the colonial project. Read together, these albums present a complex understanding of the way that colonial agents and travelers constructed narratives of British rule in Asia.

Drawing on albums compiled by two military officers, a tourist family, and a group of missionaries, I explore how these personal photograph albums operated as "collective frameworks," a term that Maurice Halbwachs defined as "instruments used by the collective memory to reconstruct an image of the past which is in accord, in each epoch, with the predominant thoughts of the society."[1] Seen from this perspective, it is understandable why the albums contain key similarities. Though deeply personal, each album also reflected, and reinforced, a larger narrative about the British "civilizing mission" in India that drew on nostalgic longings for an aristocratic past and a self-proclaimed duty to restore social order and morally uplift India. Subtle differences among the four albums—two produced in the first decades of the Raj and two produced after 1910—likewise reveal the ways that collective understandings of British rule changed with the rise of Indian nationalism. In the early twentieth century, the albums gradually de-emphasized the idea that British India was a place where Britons could recover faded traditions of genteel privilege and instead focused more on Britain's duty to establish moral, political, and social order. Though images of temples and exotic traditions remained essentially the same, references to violence and trauma became more transparent. These changes were most obvious among those working on the ground as missionaries and military officers. Examining similarities and dissimilarities across the albums as reflections of a shifting collective ideal rather than simple personal idiosyncrasies, this essay explores the essential role that the camera, photograph, and photograph album played in advancing a broader colonial imaginary that sustained the British imperial project.

fig. 1 (previous spread, top) Cover and binding, *Le tour du monde I: 1899–1900–1901,* Hobson family photograph album, 10 1/4 x 15 3/4 in. (26 x 40 cm), 1901. The Wolfsonian–Florida International University, Jean S. and Frederic A. Sharf Collection, XC2011.08.2.150.

fig. 2 (previous spread, bottom) "Part of Iboa columns. Ruins of the Brazen Temple" – "Banyan tree" – "Hindoo temple" – Untitled – "En route to Darjeeling" – Untitled, from *Le tour du monde I: 1899–1900–1901.*

Photography and Imperialism

The modern British Empire developed contemporaneously with photography. When the first daguerreotypes appeared in the 1840s,

Photo: Bourne & Shepherd, Calcutta.
SNAKE-CHARMERS IN INDIA.
Few persons who have been in India have failed to witness the astonishing performances of the Snake-Charmers, who, as our illustration shows, handle with impunity the terrible cobra, the deadliest of Indian snakes. It has often been suggested that the snakes are rendered innocuous by the "Charmers," but there seems no sufficient evidence to prove that this is the case. Musical instruments are always an accompaniment of the performance, and it is clear that the snake is influenced by the sound—a circumstance which gives point to the Biblical description of the deaf adder which "will not hearken to the voice of charmers, charming never so wisely." The Snake-Charmers form a special caste, and their mystery is transmitted from father to son.
182

fig. 3
Bourne and Shepherd, "Snake charmers in India," from *The Queen's Empire: A Pictorial and Descriptive Record Illustrated from Photographs* (London: Cassell, 1897), 182. General Research Division, The New York Public Library, Astor, Lenox and Tilden Foundations.

the British Empire in Asia constituted a patchwork of territories and commercial interests largely controlled by the East India Company. After the Sepoy Mutiny in 1857, which revealed the military and administrative weaknesses of the East India Company, the British crown intervened, consolidated its holdings, and extended its territorial and administrative reach.[2] As British travelers, explorers, missionaries, and merchants laid the foundation for a more expansive empire, they used the new technology to document and record their missions. Queen Victoria's own fascination with photography encouraged this trend; by the time she was crowned Empress of India in 1876, the camera and photograph had become integral tools of colonial rule. Fittingly, Victoria commemorated her 1897 jubilee with the publication of several photograph books, including *The Queen's Empire: A Pictorial and Descriptive Record Illustrated from Photographs*, an album compiled from photographs taken by subjects of her vast colonial domain (fig. 3).

Early colonial photography was the reserve of trained photographers and officials dedicated to the idea that the camera captured reality in an unprecedented fashion. These cameramen persevered despite cumbersome equipment that required considerable training, patience, and manpower. Photographic missions like David Livingstone's 1858–64 Zambezi Expedition highlighted the exotic, and recorded the magnificent landscapes and resources of relatively unknown lands.[3] The camera soon became a standard piece of expedition equipment.[4] As imperial explorers captured the picturesque, military officials considered the camera's use for surveillance, reconnaissance, and defense. Photography provided officials a

fig. 4
J. Jackson, "Brinjaree dancing girl," from *Burma, 1870–1880*, compiled by Augustus John Lavie, 11 3/4 x 9 1/2 in. (30 x 24 cm), 1880. The Wolfsonian–Florida International University, Jean S. and Frederic A. Sharf Collection, XC2011.08.2.199.

new way of seeing and capturing information about the land, its people, and its resources. It became a critical tool for mapping out territories and demarcating boundaries as well as categorizing and cataloging the empire's populations (fig. 4). The eight-volume *The People of India* (1868–75), which claimed to provide a comprehensive guide to India's major tribes and ethnic groups through a series of 468 photographs, demonstrated one way that officials used photography to define the "essential" characteristics and cultural traits of a given people.[5] The camera thus operated as a critical knowledge-generating tool that influenced the Raj's administrative and political structures.[6]

Technological innovations expanded the popularity of photography. The development of the half-tone process facilitated photoreproduction, creating a new market for imperial images like those collected in *The People of India* and other publications. The invention of dry plates and then gelatin roll film in the late nineteenth century simplified the development process, encouraging more and more people to try their hand at photography. Smaller camera models made the technology more portable and, in the last years of the century, camera makers invented relatively affordable handheld cameras, like George Eastman's Kodak, that allowed people to take snapshots. With these innovations, photography became the domain of amateur and recreational photographers.[7] These technical changes followed shortly after the opening of the Suez Canal in 1869, which reduced travel time and encouraged Britons of all backgrounds to pursue careers, fortunes, and adventure in the colonies. Whether in India for official or unofficial purposes, they sought

fig. 5
Detail of fig. 2. "En route to Darjeeling," from *Le tour du monde I: 1899–1900–1901*.

opportunities that photography offered to record their travels for posterity. In so doing, they also created a set of collective frameworks and visual narratives with which to make sense of British imperialism in Asia.

Photographs as Objects of Memory

While crown photographers created an official narrative of British imperialism, soldiers, administrative agents, missionaries, and tourists employed cameras and albums to record and compile personal experiences and colonial lives. The resulting photographs and albums constituted an intimate memoir of an individual's imperial adventures that could also be shared with family and friends. Like diaries, photograph albums allowed people to recover a moment and experience from which they were separated temporally and to reclaim a "lost" fragment of themselves. Looking at their album *Le tour du monde*, for example, the Hobsons might relive something of the excitement they felt in exploring the temples and banyan trees in Calcutta and taking the train to Darjeeling (fig. 5).

The camera, though, not only recorded but also transformed the way that people lived their lives and experienced their travels. In a diary, people normally record memories and stories of life events some time after they have occurred. In contrast, the camera records these experiences at the very moment they happen. Though the photograph—like the diary—records a moment in anticipation of its future loss, photography is nevertheless a different kind of memory device insofar as it intervenes in the actual practice of everyday life.[8] This intervention is more acute in moments, like travel experiences, that are by definition extraordinary and therefore worthy of preservation.[9] Modern camera-bearing individuals view their experiences with a kind of double-consciousness; they simultaneously participate in the event and determine whether it is worth recording for the future.[10] Equipped with a camera, British travelers like the Hobsons no longer considered the train trip solely as the first step of a longer voyage, but also—evidently—as a significant moment to be recorded as part of a personal story preserved for future reflection. The camera thus engendered a new kind of subjectivity and sense of temporality.

The camera also provided a new avenue for self-representation. Writing of family photograph albums, Marianne Hirsch has argued that "photography quickly became the family's primary instrument of self-knowledge and representation—the means by which family memory would be continued and perpetuated, by which the family's story would henceforth be told."[11] This story, though, was highly mediated, revealing as much about what is longed for and desired as about what actually happened. Thus, while the camera ostensibly recorded life through an objective lens, it often captured something far more complex: insights into a collective ideal and an individual's (or family's) desire to achieve this ideal.[12] As a result, this visual record provides an unexpected insight into the collective narrative that a family—or any other group—tells about itself and the normative values that structure these relationships.[13]

Hirsch's observations about family albums might be extended to the albums of British colonial travelers and administrators. The British Empire was often envisioned as a family, and Britons routinely used familial metaphors to describe the relations between Britain and its colonies.[14] For British travelers and colonial agents, photographs and photograph albums were means to construct an imperial identity that resonated with Britain's colonial mission. From this perspective, we can dissect individual photographs, asking what any particular image—like the Hobsons embarking on the train for Darjeeling—reveals not just about the creators but also about broader British desires and ideals in India (fig. 5). In this photograph, for instance, the women's dress reveals not only their elevated social status, but also Victorian notions of decorum, propriety, and civility that guided the British mission in India. The way the four women are posed allows the photographer to capture the length of the train, a symbol of Britain's modernizing influence in India, and a contrast with the decidedly un-modern station and platform. The serious expressions on the women's faces suggest that the Hobsons' tour was at once a pleasure trip and a kind of imperial duty.

A single image, however, only provides a glimpse into the larger narrative, which unfolds in the way the photographs were organized into an album. Albums are edited to a lesser or greater extent through the processes of sorting, selecting, and arranging photographs into a coherent narrative. Collective ideas about which images and memories are remarkable and worthy of preservation influence seemingly personal decisions about which events and photographs to include and which to exclude. By convention, photograph albums are organized linearly; as viewers of *Le tour du monde*, for example, we assume that the Hobsons visited Calcutta first and then departed for Darjeeling. Gaps—like the entirety of the train ride—are expected, since snapshots only capture discrete moments; it is generally assumed that these exclusions are insignificant and can be glossed over when reconstructing the story. Textual annotations ("En route to Darjeeling") further code the images and tie together discrete episodes. Finally, visual juxtapositions—in this case the decision to frame the train image between untitled photographs of shoeless Indian porters and of a statue of Hindu gods or royalty riding an elephant (fig. 2)—provide another key narrative device. In the creator's absence, the album, its photographs, and its text assume an independent authority as a reliable record of a life or event. The album even supplants the authority of its creator at times, as the visual imprint left by photographs is often stronger and more compelling than those of fading memories. Albums, then, not only represent an ideal but also have the power to reshape the way individuals recollect and remember their own experiences and life, often aligning this personal narrative with the collective memory and ideal depicted in the album's pages.[15]

The photograph albums of Britons who traveled to the colonies thus offer an unusual vantage point into the workings of British colonial culture. An analysis of the four albums from the Sharf Collection illuminates how personal memory intertwined with and substantiated a collective narrative of the Raj that legitimated British rule in India. The first two albums—one by Lt. Colonel Henry W. Benson and one by the Hobsons, a family of tourists—document the British experience in India in the late nineteenth century. The second two—one by a visiting administrator from the Church Missionary Society and another by a member of the Royal Air Force—record the British colonial project in the early twentieth century.

Nostalgic Longings and Historicizing the Raj

Among the first to arrive in India with cameras were colonial officers like Lt. Colonel Henry W. Benson, a member of the First Battalion East Surrey Regiment, who mapped Kashmir for the colonial state. Benson photographed his battalion's surveying expeditions in 1886 and placed these photographs in a plain blue album with black corners and binding.

fig. 6
"Lake Pangong, 13900 ft. above the sea" – "Lake Pangong" – "Pass to northern end of Lake Pangong"– "My pony on the shores of Lake Pangong," from *Cashmere & Ladakh 1886*, Lt. Colonel Henry W. Benson photograph album, 10 1/8 x 13 3/8 in. (27 x 34 cm), 1886. The Wolfsonian–Florida International University, Jean S. and Frederic A. Sharf Collection, XC2011.08.2.24.

Opening the cover, the viewer is immediately struck by the topographic features and breathtaking landscapes he memorialized (fig. 6). It is, however, the way he interspersed these landscapes with portraits of individuals that best reveals the myths of British rule that motivated men like Benson to join the colonial force. A couple of pages from the album show how Benson and colonial officers drew on nostalgic memory for a disappearing aristocratic feudal order to justify the Raj's authority.

Benson's album reflects its particular historical moment in the 1880s, a period when the British were still consolidating rule in India. The Raj never possessed the manpower or weaponry to rule by force alone; it had to find a way to expand its administrative and military reach and inculcate popular support.[16] To do so, it drew on the past to create a multilayered political structure that mixed direct and indirect rule. The British crown directly administered nearly two-thirds of the country. In the remaining third, they relied on the "traditional" authority of regional rulers—rajahs, maharajahs, nawabs, and nizams—who pledged allegiance to the Raj.[17] This system of indirect rule extended British authority and secured critical allies; and, by co-opting traditional hierarchies, it enabled the British crown to bolster its claim as the legitimate successor to the Mughal emperor.[18]

fig. 7
"Lachman Dass. Governor of Cashmere and Officials," from *Cashmere & Ladakh 1886.*

Benson's album shows how the Raj incorporated elements of the local hierarchical and imperial order in an effort to stabilize its authority. A photograph in his album, which Benson likely purchased, depicts the Raj-appointed governor of Kashmir with his entourage in elaborate, official attire (fig. 7). At the center of the composition is an individual, presumably the governor, who is looking away from the camera at something outside the picture frame, projecting an aura of authority that will not bend to the commands of a simple cameraman. The group sits on a long, magnificent rug, itself a symbol of wealth and luxury and, to British eyes, the Orient. The way the subjects are posed, with two men forced to rest uncomfortably on their elbows at the feet of the group, makes the social hierarchy evident to the eye. Photographs like this played a role in popularizing British support for the Raj by showing Britons that India was a land with its own rich civilization and elaborate authority structures that could be easily assimilated into the British Empire.

Yet in Benson's album, as in British eyes in general, this was a civilization and social hierarchy that had become degraded. The rajah of Skardo, for example, appears in Benson's photograph with a motley crew of attendants (fig. 8). Benson placed the rajah's photograph alongside an image of a decrepit village and another one showing "coolies," suggesting that India had descended to a general state of social decay. He further illustrated India's decline in pictures of a Hindu temple near Naranag; the structures are physical remnants of an older order as well as testaments to

fig. 8
"Nungri. Village near Ganderbal. Sind Valley" – "Cashmere coolies with loads" – "The rajah of Skardo with attendants," from *Cashmere & Ladakh 1886.*

fig. 9 (opposite, top)
"Major & Mrs. Hillyard's Camp. Manasbal" – "Hindoo temple. Naranag." – "Hindoo temple. Naranag. Waugat," from *Cashmere & Ladakh 1886.*

fig. 10 (opposite, bottom)
"Self and shikaris. Ganderbal," from *Cashmere & Ladakh 1886.*

native indifference to indigenous culture and history (fig. 9). Interspersed between these images are two pages, each devoted to a single snapshot of Benson's own camp, which is clean and properly ordered (fig. 10). Through this juxtaposition, Benson justified for himself—and others—the idea that the Raj represented the Mughal Empire's legitimate successor and that the British alone could restore India to its former glory.

Benson's album reveals yet another aspect of British conceptions of India. According to David Cannadine, the British Raj seduced Britons with the idea that in India they could recuperate "an authentic world of ordered, harmonious, time-hallowed social relations of the kind that the Industrial Revolution was threatening (or destroying) in Britain."[19] To promote this longing, the British created elaborate political ceremonies based on imagined Mughal rituals and romanticized visions of Britain's feudal and aristocratic past.[20] This "time-hallowed" social order was also enacted before the camera by Britons like Benson and recorded in pictures pictures like "The resident's boat on the Dal Canal" and that of an elaborate and formal dinner (figs. 11, 12). Such scenes afforded Britons of all backgrounds a sense of place in the new collectivity they were helping to build and restore. They reinforced the idea that India was a place where Britons like Benson could potentially fill the role of the aristocrat.

Major & Mrs. Hillyard's Camp - Manasbal -

Hindoo temple - Naranag -

Hindoo temple - Naranag - Wangat -

Self and Shikaris - Ganderbal -

The Resident's Boat on the Dal Canal – Srinagar –

Benson's pictures further advanced this idealized vision of India as a land of aristocratic privilege by depicting Indians as a natural servant class. From the very beginning, Benson included images of the workers who made his expedition—and the British colonial state—possible. While he acknowledged their labor, he did not go so far as to acknowledge them as individuals with names, histories, and lives of their own. The individuals referred to as "coolies" are nameless, faceless servants; the men who stand behind the dinner guests or row the boats on the Resident's Lake are completely anonymous. The photographs contain few, if any, references to the structures of control that forced this social subordination. Benson's album reveals an emerging collective narrative about empire that assumed the labor of local populations, delegitimized the authority of indigenous leaders like the rajah, and reconfigured British rule into a nostalgia-laced mission to resurrect an aristocratic British past and reclaim India's former glory. This narrative would be reconfigured in subsequent albums as a mission that emphasized exoticism, civility, moral authority, and the legitimate exercise of violence in the name of social order.

Civility and the Colonial Gaze

The elaborate lacquered cover and professional binding of the Hobsons' *Le tour du monde* suggest something of the way that fin-de-siècle tourists intermingled older narratives of India as a land of aristocratic civility with a new fascination with the exotic (fig. 1). Imposing in size and weight, the album feels luxurious to the touch; these physical qualities inform the viewer that the photographs contained within, and the people they document, are important. It is clear from this album that the Hobsons were an affluent family, able to enjoy a leisurely trip to the colonies. After an extended voyage across the Pacific, the couple made their way to Ceylon and India, and sought out places, experiences, and images that typified the colonial experience for most Britons. Dressed in iconic colonial white, complete with hats and cane, the Hobsons pose for photographs to prove to family and friends that they had indeed experienced colonial life (figs. 2, 13). The family did not simply rely on their own photographic abilities, but also integrated stock photographs. Through these images, the Hobsons contributed to a collective narrative about the empire that linked exotic beauty, Orientalist fascinations, and British gentility.

The content of the Hobsons' album differs from Benson's in a number of ways that reflect the fact that one was the record of a military officer engaged in the work of establishing colonial rule and the other was created by tourists who enjoyed the opportunities that Benson's actions provided for travel and leisure. The Hobsons' album suggests that they had little sustained interaction with Indians or other native populations, and rarely ventured away from established routes and sites.

fig. 11
"The resident's boat on the Dal Canal. Srinagar," from *Cashmere & Ladakh 1886.*

fig. 12
Untitled, from *Cashmere & Ladakh 1886.*

fig. 13
"Vice governor's reception" – "Kandy" – "Prison methods" – "Xing Mahabella River" – Untitled – "Indian rubber tree," from *Le tour du monde I: 1899–1900–1901.*

Yet despite these differences, the *Le tour du monde* album, like the Benson album, projects a vision of the British Raj that valorized the colonies as a site where nostalgic longings for an aristocratic past could be embraced and lived. Neither engages with the violence and repression that colonial rule entailed. Whereas Benson portrayed colonial hierarchy as part of the natural order, the Hobson album represses the brutality of the colonial project, substituting what anthropologist Renato Rosaldo called the "elegance of manners governing relations of dominance and subordination between the races."[21] Photographs of the Raj's elaborate ceremonies of power, images of the Mughul Empire's fading glory, and snapshots of white-clothed gentility romanticized the colonial project and sanitized its violence. Only a few hints of the Raj's violence—like the photograph titled "Prison methods" (fig. 14) or an untitled image of an emaciated famine victim—appear in the album. The *Le tour du monde* album, in fact, shows little of the colonial state apart from its ceremonial aspects. The camera, which dissects the flow of life into discrete moments surrounded by gaps and absences, thus served a valuable function for a colonial state dependent on such silences to generate popular support.

The arrangements of pictures within the Hobson album show how the exotic and foreign helped justify the British civilizing mission. In planning their

fig. 14
Detail of fig. 13. "Prison methods," from *Le tour du monde I: 1899–1900–1901*.

itinerary, the Hobsons likely drew on a fairly well-established list of people, places, and events to see. In this way, they shared a certain commonality with tourists everywhere, for whom, John Frow has argued, "knowledge of a place precedes and informs experience."[22] The Hobsons gravitated toward well-known and imposing monuments like the Taj Mahal, which became an icon of the Mughul Empire and, after its restoration by Viceroy George Curzon, a symbol of the Raj's legitimate claim to authority. Its image, which was reproduced and sold abundantly, would have been immediately recognizable to almost any Briton. It is therefore not surprising that a professional photograph of the Taj Mahal occupies a whole page (fig. 15), followed by a number of smaller photographs, which offer the Hobsons' own perspective of the iconic building (fig. 16). The images of the Taj Mahal allowed the family to prove that they had in fact been there; the personal photographs also validated their identity as British colonial citizens who knew India and its treasures and understood the importance of British control, which valued, restored, and preserved these artifacts.

Tourists like the Hobsons did not simply adopt popular representations of India as a land of the exotic, but also used these images to advance a particular notion of British prestige that justified colonial rule. The Hobsons sought out and photographed exotic elements that would have captured any tourist's eye, but the *Le tour du monde* album arranges these titillating pieces into a narrative that juxtaposed images of aristocratic civility and British gentility with depictions of exoticism. The photographs of the rubber tree, the prison methods, the vice governor's reception, the elephant ride, the river crossing, and the visit to Kandy all demonstrate the Hobsons' privilege (fig. 13). The women, for instance, might try out native traditions, ride elephants, and pose with a prisoner's yoke, but they do so with the understanding that they will not be mistaken for colonial subjects and will never endure disciplinary measures that are tacitly marked for natives. The Hobsons enjoy the Raj's elaborate ceremonies, visit the empire's attractions, and seek out the unfamiliar, yet without risk. Little in the album suggests that they ever question the power structures that make their voyage and experiences enjoyable.

Their album records a world in which Britishness and whiteness united to define a new kind of aristocracy. Whereas England's real aristocratic past operated on hierarchy and difference *among* Britons, the aristocratic culture that the British hoped to create in the colonies relied on conceptions of race, nationality, and religion that united Britons in opposition to their colonial subjects. In this colonial ideal, actual lineage and social status mattered little; rather, all Britons could reimagine themselves as members of an aristocracy requiring a plenitude of servants to transport and serve.[23] The prospect of colonial aristocracy would likely have been appealing to wealthy individuals like the Hobsons who were not

fig. 15
"Taj Mahal," from *Le tour du monde I: 1899–1900–1901.*

fig. 16
Untitled – "Black throne" – "Balcony Jasmine Tower" – "Looking out of Jasmine Tower" – "Taj Mahal," from *Le tour du monde I: 1899–1900–1901.*

INDIA

Taj Mahal

INDIA

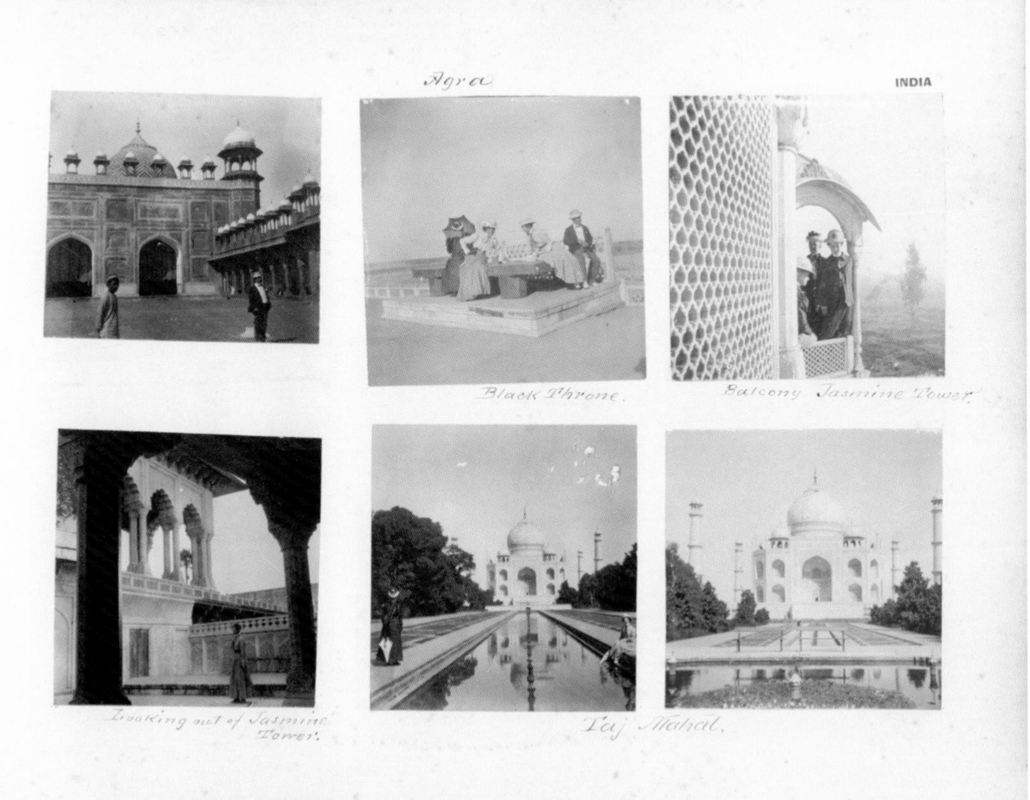
Agra
Black Throne.
Balcony Jasmine Tower.
Looking out of Jasmine Tower.
Taj Mahal.

Learning the Language

CMS Church, Amritsar & Rev Fazl-

fig. 17 (opposite)
"Learning the language" – "CMS Church, Amritsar & Rev. Farl.," from *Northwest frontier: 1910–1912*, Church Missionary Society photograph album, 7 7/8 x 10 5/8 in. (20 x 27 cm), 1912. The Wolfsonian–Florida International University, Jean S. and Frederic A. Sharf Collection, XC2011.08.2.21.

fig. 18
"En route," from *Northwest frontier: 1910–1912*.

aristocrats. In melding the promise of this reinvented aristocracy with collective images of the Raj and a wider visual culture that made the colonies "already" known, British tourists found a personal and emotional connection that made them feel at home in the empire. This connection, however, depended on their ability to omit the unseemly elements of colonial rule and erase its systematic violence or to gloss them as mere spectacle or necessary steps on the road to civilization.

Creating Moral Authority

The gaps in the accounts of tourists enamored with the exotic, however, occasionally came into focus in other albums, especially those of individuals who performed the concrete work of imperial rule. Missionaries, military officers, colonial administrators, and other agents had long confronted the daily difficulties of maintaining and legitimating British control in India. Colonial agents faced a new set of challenges in the early twentieth century with the rise of Indian nationalism, the Swadeshi (self-sufficiency) movement, and the growing radicalization of the Indian National Congress. The photograph albums from this period reflect the difficulties that many colonial agents faced as they tried to stabilize British rule and preserve the older ideals of British India as a genteel land of aristocratic privilege in the face of these anticolonial movements.

The plain leather cover of the 1912 Church Missionary Society (CMS) album already indicates the difference between this colonial tale and the one told by the Hobsons. The album's ordinary appearance serves as a reminder that for thousands of Britons the empire was not an exotic spectacle made familiar by popular images, but—quite literally—home. CMS missionaries working in the North-West Frontier were among those who settled in India for long periods, working to advance Britain's aim of creating a new moral order free of child-marriage, *sati* (self-immolation by widows), and the caste system. Living among the rural poor, CMS members sought to convert Hindus and Muslims and, in the process, create a new order based on Christianity and Victorian ideas of propriety, civility, and morality, to better assimilate natives to British norms and values.[24]

The album compiled by a London-based CMS executive reviewing the mission reflects the challenges faced by colonial agents who tried to balance the British Raj's official narrative with the social realities of the colonies. The executive occupied a peculiar position in the colonies. He was at once tourist and missionary, and his album reflects the complexities that these two perspectives entailed. Unlike the Hobsons' *Le tour du monde*, which wove a cohesive narrative that melded the ideal and real, the CMS album is fragmented. The album intersperses pictures of tourism, colonial life, and missionary calling with little apparent narrative order. Pictures of missionary work (fig. 17) are juxtaposed with images of picnics traveled to by palanquin, abandoned temples, and vice-regal processions (figs. 18, 19).

Two adjacent pages in particular reveal the fractured nature of this narrative and show how the ideal and real sometimes collided. The first of these pages in the album records Christmas 1910 (fig. 20). The top image is a kind of family portrait, though with the notable absence of men—a fragmented family. The missionary women stand with a group of girls, presumably orphans, and Indian women who perhaps helped with mission work. The girls generally look at the camera and smile, showing their willingness to engage the photographer and memorialize the day according to British conventions. This photograph suggests that the mission work has been, at least in some small part, successful in transforming the girls to meet British norms. The picture immediately below depicts a group of singers, an indication that the missionaries—and British Raj—have balanced their roles as civilizers and preservers of Indian traditions.

The page immediately following unsettles this narrative (fig. 21). While the photograph of missionary women and Indian girls suggests that conversion has been relatively easy, this picture suggests that the process is far from complete, causing strains on both sides. At the heart of this page is a picture titled "An Indian widow." A white missionary woman rests her hand on the shoulder of a young girl dressed completely in black. Two things about the picture stand out. First is the framing, which cuts off the head of the woman, robbing the viewer of her facial expression. The second is the young girl, whose gaze mixes incomprehension with defiance, challenging the photographer and the viewer to make sense of the scene. The child-bride, shown in this photograph as a child-widow, was a powerful symbol to most Britons of the allegedly corrupted morals of the East and a reminder of the civilizing work to be done in India. Yet the person who is there to carry out that work has been beheaded by the camera. Indeed the picture's various elements—the headless woman, the child's stare, and her widow's attire—thwart an uplifting reading. The picture's composition and the child's gaze compel the viewer to consider the tensions at the very heart of the British Raj and the fact that collective

fig. 19
"The tomb by his garden," from *Northwest frontier: 1910–1912.*

fig. 20 (following spread, left)
"CB bungalow, Ajnala. Miss Daliway & Miss Stiles, Xmas 1910" – "Bhajan singing, Xmas Day 1910, Anjala," from *Northwest frontier: 1910–1912.*

fig. 21 (following spread, right)
"An Indian widow" – "Edgehill Mussoorie," from *Northwest frontier: 1910–1912.*

The tomb by his garden -

C E Z
Bungalow
Ajnala
Miss Dalway
&
Miss Stiles
Xmas 1910

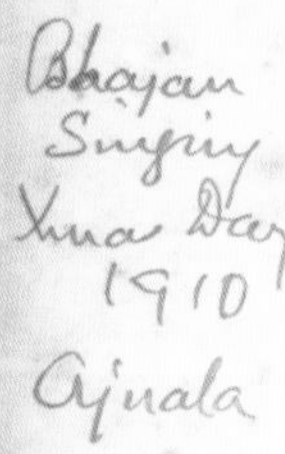

Bhajan
Singing
Xmas Day
1910
Ajnala

An Indian Widow

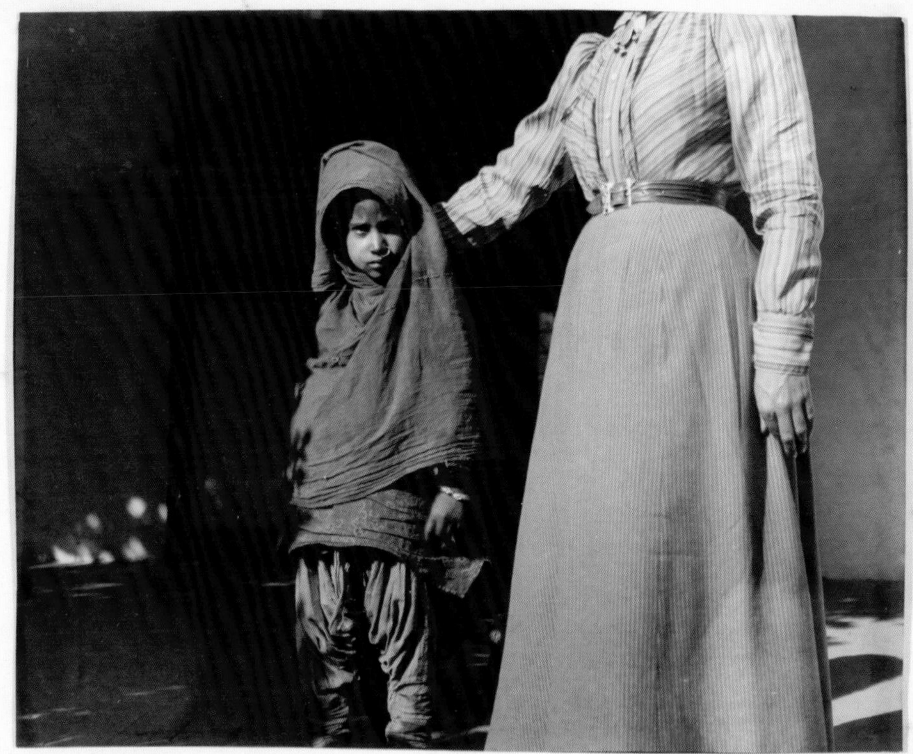

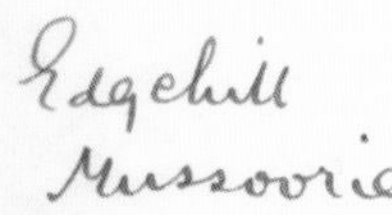

Edgehill Mussoorie

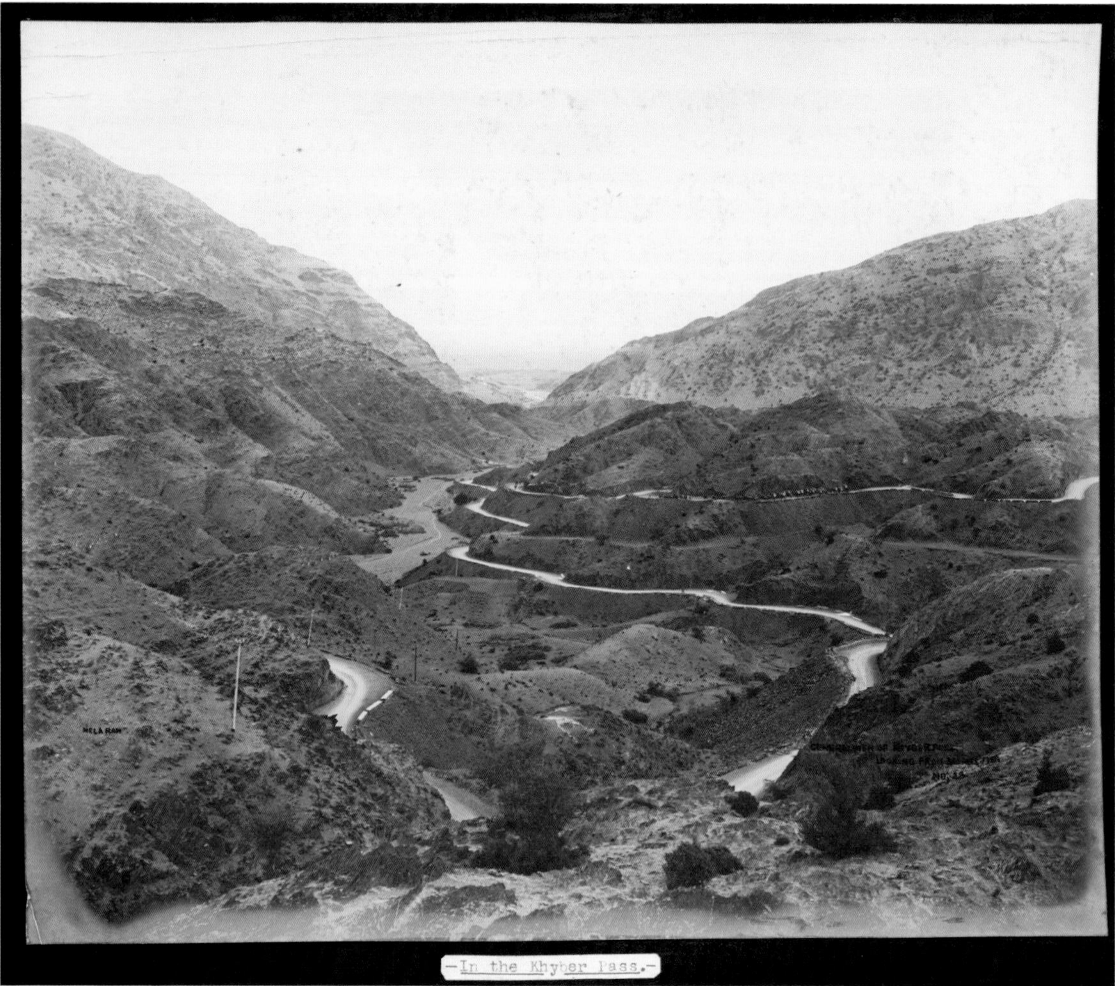

fig. 22
"In the Khyber Pass," from *R.A.F in Waziristan: 1922–23*, photograph album, 10 1/4 x 13 in. (26 x 33 cm), 1923. The Wolfsonian–Florida International University, Jean S. and Frederic A. Sharf Collection, XC2011.08.2.179.

fig. 23 (opposite)
"Inside the Jamid Masid, Mohammedan Temple, Delhi." – "The fort, Delhi," from *R.A.F in Waziristan: 1922–23*.

narratives about moral authority, social order, and white linen were increasingly challenged by Indians themselves.

Legitimizing Order, Legitimizing Violence

A final album shows how the collective narrative of the British Raj portrayed by Benson and the Hobsons began to disintegrate in the years before the Second World War. The 1923 photograph album was compiled by a young airman in the Royal Air Force 28th Squadron, likely part of the permanent garrison stationed in the region after the suppression of a rebellion in Waziristan during 1919–20. The album reveals little affection for a land and people who have challenged British control and stability. Rather, it exposes the daily strains of maintaining military control and discipline in a region where British authority was consistently under attack.

The album, with its simple, practical black cover, offers an initial sense of the photographs contained within. Inside, the viewer finds images of marches and convoys along the Kohat and Khyber Passes, fighter jets,

—Inside the Jamid Masid - Mohhammedan Temple- Delhi.-

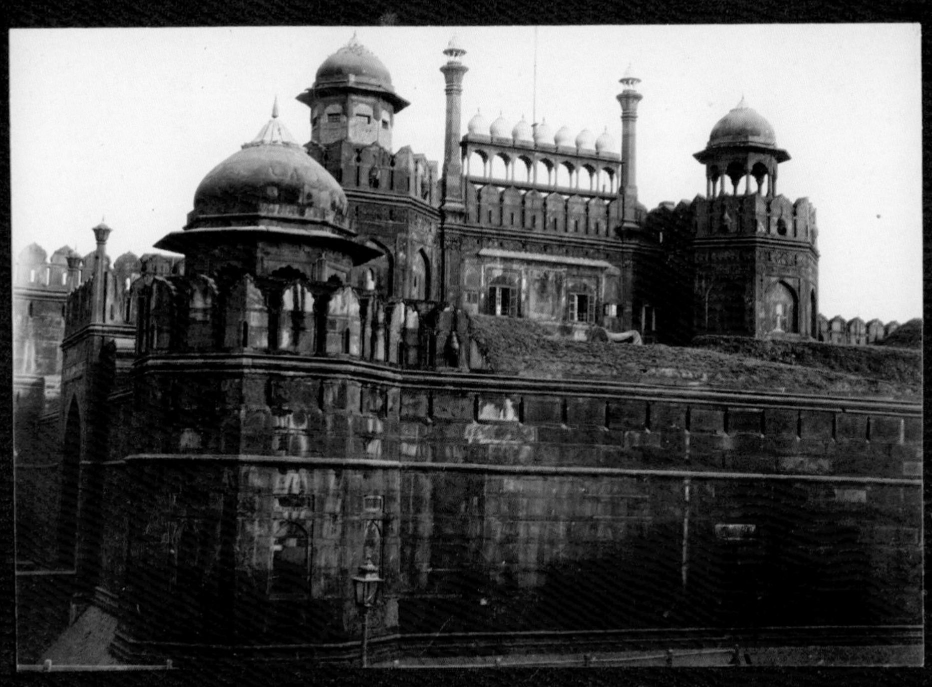

-The Fort - Delhi.-

PARACHINAR
ARRIVAL OF SIR JOHN SALMOND. K.C.B.
31 A 500 B.
1,500 FT 4-3-22
ARRIVAL OF H.R.H. THE PRINCE OF WALES AT PESHAWAR
TAKEN FROM LEADING MACHINE OF THE ROYAL ESCORT
31 A 512

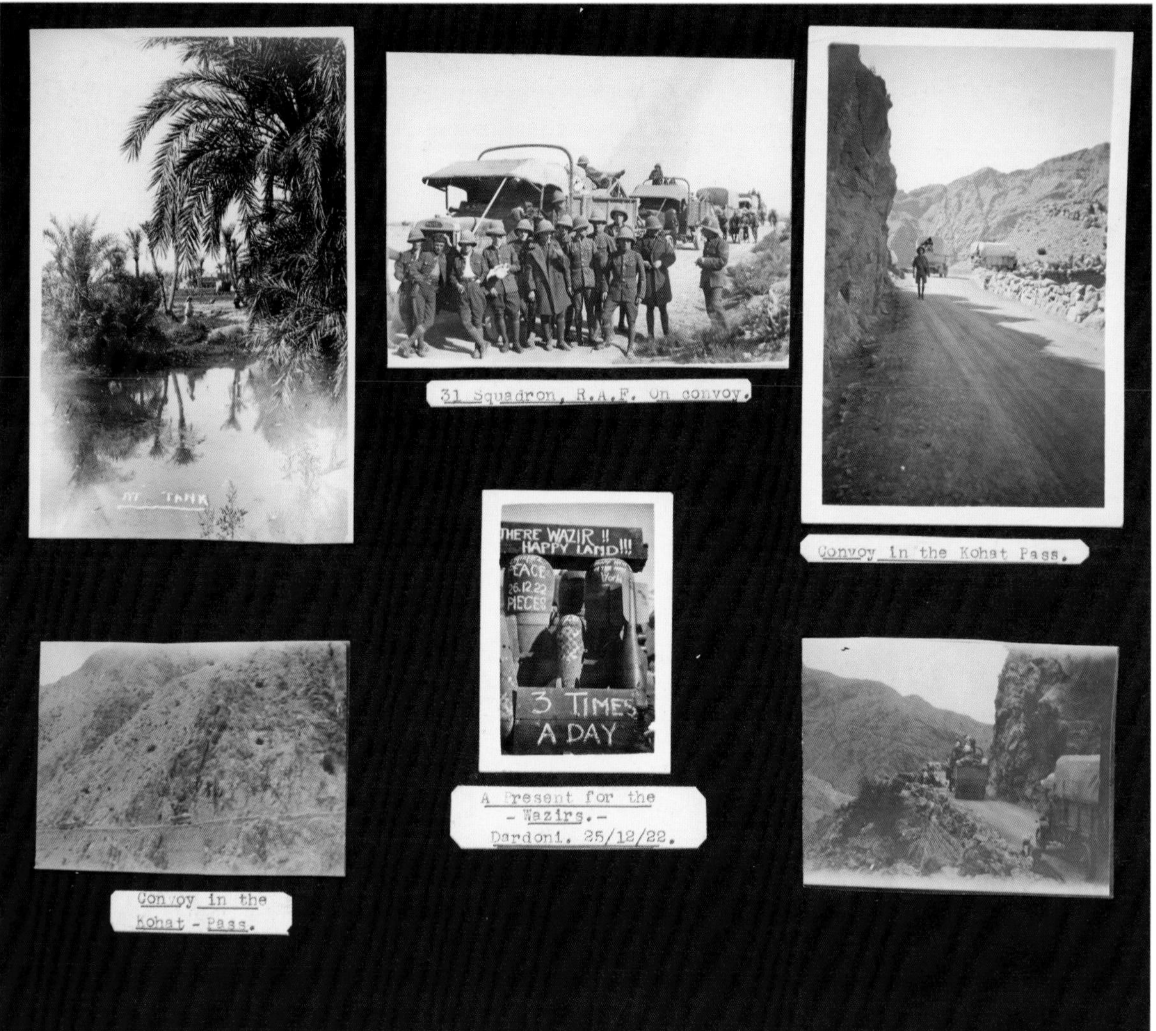

fig. 24 (opposite)
"Arrival of Sir John Salmond K.C.B., Parachinar" – "Arrival of HRH Prince of Wales at Peshawar" – "Taken from the leading machine of the Royal Escort," from *R.A.F in Waziristan: 1922–23.*

fig. 25
"At tank" – "31 Squadron, R.A.F. On Convoy" – "Convoy in the Kohat Pass" – "Convoy in the Kohat Pass" – "A present for the Wazirs. Dardoni. 25/12/22," from *R.A.F in Waziristan*: 1922–23.

and military camps, all of which present the daily experiences that preoccupied the album's creator (fig. 22). As with the earlier albums, the airman's collection includes pictures of decaying temples, beautiful landscapes, and regimental camaraderie interspersed with stock photographs of the Taj Mahal, Jama Masid, and other iconic images of British India (fig. 23). But the most striking images in this album are not those that depict the Taj Mahal found in countless other albums, but those that show what other albums neglected: the actual mechanics of British rule. The airman's album demonstrates that colonial governance required modern military technology and tactics (fig. 24). Aerial photographs taken during surveillance missions and images of troops marching through villages show the amount of force necessary to maintain colonial rule, especially in the interwar period. The album reveals that enforcing colonial rule among tribes that wished to free themselves of the British Raj was violent and dangerous, as well as monotonous and grueling.

The tension between British claims to rule and legitimacy and local anticolonialism comes to life on one particularly striking page of the album. Here the author combines an assortment of images, most fairly unremarkable: a picture of an oasis, a military convoy on the Kohat Pass, and a picture of the squadron (fig. 25). It is the bottom center photograph, though, that demands the viewer's attention. The photograph titled "A present for the Wazirs" lays bare the Raj's coercive tools. In its refusal to hide the violence needed to ensure the colonial regime, the album points to the erasures operating in the earlier albums as they promoted an image of civility unmarred by coercion.

Conclusion

Viewed together, these four albums (and others in the Sharf Collection) produce an uncanny sense of similarity and repetition. These repetitions reflect the fact that the albums worked as repositories of collective memory that intertwined personal experience with collective narratives. In the first two albums, colonial travelers not only legitimated but also extolled the virtues of the British Raj as a source of social and moral authority, and India as a place where Britons could regain a disappearing aristocratic gentility. The last two albums draw on these established narratives, but reveal the fact that conditions in India changed significantly between Benson's 1886 album and the 1920s, when the Royal Air Force was deployed to defeat the Wazirs in the North-West Frontier. In the missionary and R.A.F albums, the patina of white linen civility and Orientalist ceremonies performed on elephant backs was shown to be an ideal sustained by serious labor and military might. Yet even these albums justified British presence in Asia, ultimately showing how the forms of self-representation afforded by the camera, photograph, and the photograph album helped bolster collective narratives that legitimated the Raj even as the sun had begun to set on the British Empire.

Together these albums tell us something about how the British wished to see themselves in India. These mediated versions of British rule provide the historian with key insights into the collective narratives that British colonial military officers, tourists, and missionaries used to justify British rule and legitimate their own presence in the colony. In addition, the albums help later generations to understand what exactly was at stake for Britons who fought to preserve British rule in Asia even when it necessitated extreme violence that belied Britain's civilizing mission.

NOTES

1. Maurice Halbwachs, *On Collective Memory*, trans. Lewis Coser (Chicago: University of Chicago Press, 1992), 40.
2. On the British Empire and Sepoy Mutiny, see John Darwin, *The Empire Project: The Rise and Fall of the British World-System, 1830–1970* (Cambridge: Cambridge University Press, 2011); Thomas Metcalf, *The Aftermath of Revolt: India, 1857–70* (Princeton, NJ: Princeton University Press, 1964).
3. Livingstone's Zambezi Expedition was the first official expedition to include a camera. James Ryan, *Picturing Empire: Photography and the Visualization of the British Empire* (Chicago: University of Chicago Press, 1997), 30.
4. "Framing the View," chap. 2, and "The Art of Campaigning," chap. 3, in ibid.
5. See, among others, Thomas Metcalf, *Ideologies of the Raj* (Cambridge: Cambridge University Press, 1995); John Falconer, "'A pure labor of love': A publishing history of *The People of India*," in *Colonialist Photography: Imag(in)ing Race and Place*, eds. Eleanor M. Hight and Gary D. Sampson (London: Routledge, 2004), 51–83; Zahid Chaudhary, *Afterimage of Empire: Photography in Nineteenth-Century India* (Minneapolis: University of Minnesota Press, 2012).
6. Michel Foucault, *Discipline and Punish: The Birth of the Prison* (New York: Vintage, 1995).
7. Mary Marien, "Imagining the Social World," chap. 4 in *Photography: A Cultural History* (Upper Saddle River, NJ: Prentice Hall, 2002).
8. On the idea of the future anterior in photography, see Roland Barthes, *Camera Lucida: Reflections on Photography*, trans. Richard Howard (New York: Hill and Wang, 1980), 94–96.
9. Ryan, *Picturing Empire*, 17; Halbwachs, *On Collective Memory*.
10. I draw the term *double consciousness* from W. E. B. Dubois, who described this as the sensation of "always looking at one's self through the eyes of others." W. E. B. Dubois, *The Souls of Black Folks* (New York: Norton, 1999).
11. Marianne Hirsch, *Family Frames: Photography, Narrative, and Postmemory* (Cambridge: Harvard University Press, 1997), 6–7. See also Martha Langford, *Suspended Conversations: The Afterlife of Memory in Photographic Albums* (Montreal: McGill-Queen's University Press, 2001); Elizabeth Edwards and Janice Hart, eds., *Photographs, Objects, Histories: On the Materiality of Images* (London: Routledge, 2004).
12. Hirsch, *Family Frames*, 7.
13. Introduction to ibid.
14. Catherine Hall and Sonya Rose, introduction to *At Home with the Empire: Metropolitan Culture and the Imperial World* (Cambridge: Cambridge University Press, 2007).
15. Annette Kuhn, "Memory-texts and Memory Work: Performances of Media in and with Visual Media," *Memory Studies* 3, no. 4 (2010): 299, 303–4; "Resisting Images," chap. 6, in Hirsch, *Family Frames*.
16. Bernard S. Cohn, *Colonialism and Its Forms of Knowledge: The British in India* (Princeton, NJ: Princeton University Press, 1996); Metcalf, *Ideologies*.
17. Metcalf, *Ideologies*, 73.
18. David Cannadine, *Ornamentalism: How the British Saw Their Empire* (Oxford: Oxford University Press, 2001), 43–44.
19. Cannadine, *Ornamentalism*, 12–13.
20. Cohn, *Colonialism*, 3, 121.
21. Renato Rosaldo, "Imperialist Nostalgia," *Representations*, no. 26 (1989): 107–22. See also William Bissell, "Engaging Colonial Nostalgia," *Cultural Anthropology* 20, no. 2 (2005): 215–48; Ann Laura Stoler, *Carnal Knowledge and Imperial Power: Race and the Intimate in Colonial Rule* (Berkeley: University of California Press, 2010), especially "Memory Work in Java: A Cautionary Tale," chap. 7.
22. John Frow, "Tourism and the Semiotics of Nostalgia," *October*, no. 57 (1991): 125.
23. Cannadine, *Ornamentalism*. Cannadine, however, downplays the importance of race in the British colonial project, whereas I think albums like the Hobsons' make it clear that this was a central part of this aristocratic fantasy.
24. Hayden Bellenoit, "Missionary Education, Religion, and Knowledge in India, c. 1880–1915," *Modern Asian Studies* 41, no. 2 (2007): 369–94.

fig. 1
Real photographic postcard, August 1918. Author's collection.

MEMENTOS OF A DARK JOURNEY: GERMAN "REAL PHOTOGRAPHIC POSTCARDS" AND THE MAKING OF MEMORY

Mike Robinson

Mike Robinson holds the Chair of Cultural Heritage at the University of Birmingham, UK, and is director of the Ironbridge International Institute for Cultural Heritage. His research interests lie at the intersection of heritage, popular culture, and tourism. Recent books include *The Framed World: Tourism, Tourists and Photography* (2009) and *Emotion in Motion: Tourism, Affect and Transformation* (2012). He is currently working on German vernacular photography of the First World War as a form of travel narrative.

The centenary of the outbreak of the First World War has focused attention on how societies commemorate conflict in the form of highly visible public monuments and events. Much of what now informs and maintains collective interest and imagination about the First World War, however, began in the personal rather than the public sphere. Such objects, now stored and displayed in museums to assist in conveying insight and creating emotional connection, were once acquired and preserved for the purposes of personal and family remembrance. As souvenirs, they have particular resonance and prominence in family histories and inheritances. They also fit within the wider context of public interest in memory, referred to by Jay Winter as the "memory boom" that erupted in the second half of the twentieth century.[1] Present-day reflection on these souvenirs (many now disconnected from their original owners) by historians and collectors and their incorporation into the broadly defined heritage industry feed public remembrance, albeit sometimes without consideration for their production and the practices surrounding their original use.

In the absence of living survivors who can narrate their personal experiences, collective remembrance of the war draws heavily on a vast range of objects and texts produced during the conflict that now exist in various configurations as "heritage." The material culture of the war ranges from on-site built structures (graves, statues, monuments) to off-site personal collections (medals, letters, badges, trench art); from officially produced souvenirs, such as medallions, replete with their nationalist narratives, to artifacts of the battlefield (shell cases, pieces of shrapnel) spontaneously mobilized as mementos. As Nicholas Saunders and Paul Cornish indicate, the objects of the First World War are laden with emotional and symbolic meanings that are woven into the processes of remembrance.[2] These mementos, moreover, extend beyond objects of the battlefield to include objects reflecting concepts of home during wartime, and together they intertwine with mediated and received accounts of the war through poetry, literature, and film, to embed the Great War in the collective memory of both the victorious and defeated nations.[3]

This essay explores the role of one such object, the postcard, that was integral to the memory practices of German soldiers during the First World War. It focuses, in particular, on the "real photographic postcard" as a distinctive object and a particularly powerful agent of memory construction. As opposed to printed postcards, mechanically mass-produced from plates by large printing firms, real photographic postcards were genuine photographs, chemically produced from a negative directly onto photographic paper with a postcard back (fig. 1).

There were three types of real photographic postcards: those taken by professional photographers in studios that soldiers would visit while on leave and order a given number of prints; those taken by professional photographers in the field, often close to the front lines where, again, soldiers could order a number of prints; and those taken by the soldiers themselves using their own cameras. It was possible for photographs to be developed in the field, but the vast majority of negatives were mailed, directly or via a relative, to a local studio for developing, and the requested numbers of prints were then mailed back to the soldier. In contrast to commercially printed postcards, small numbers of prints were generally made from each negative. Well-composed photographs, particularly of large groups of soldiers, could result in many prints being produced, but there was a high frequency of single one-off prints. Names and studio locations on the reverse of the cards can refer to the photographer or the establishment that developed the soldiers' films, or both; many have no such markings at all.

I focus here on real photographic postcards of German soldiers from my own personal collection of over five thousand unpublished items. Some of these were inherited, but on the whole, the collection has been compiled over twenty years, sourced mainly from markets, shops, and other collectors inside and outside Germany. The postcards have long been disconnected from the families that once owned them and from the people they feature; they fall into the category of unclaimed objects. While part of the collection represents soldiers and their families and friends taken by professional studio photographers, the majority of the photographs were taken by soldiers and used as postcards in the field. A key feature of German real photographic postcards is that they were largely uncensored in terms of subject matter and were freely sent or taken home from the front, providing a wide horizon of material and situations that soldiers were able to capture as part of their experiences.

I place the practice of vernacular photography by German soldiers within the wider social context of what Susan Stewart terms "souveniring," a process closely linked to personal memory in which people use objects to create life histories and generate a sense of self.[4] Souveniring is a personal act of memory that, as Sarah Foot notes, involves the selection of people, places, and objects to be recorded so that future reminiscence can draw on one's own experience rather than on the collective remembrance of an event.[5]

I also link the role of real photographic postcards to the wider contexts of the emergence of a modern visual culture and the parallel development of mass travel. While the carnage of war disrupted (and often shattered) daily life, it also acted to overlay, magnify, and in part accelerate the cultural trends and social practices of the time. For the majority of the nations fighting the war, the battlefields functioned as destinations, places that were traveled to and from as part of an imposed, elongated journey. I use the idea of the soldier as a tourist to bring together the practices of collecting souvenirs, capturing experiences of both the unfamiliar and the familiar through photography, and of communicating encounters through postcards. While the experience of the war was far removed from anything that could be conceived of as pleasure, like tourism, it provided space and time for physical and metaphorical journeys, moments of leisure, and encounters with the foreign. As with tourism, it was framed by daily oscillations between ordinary and extraordinary life. German soldiers, like tourists, recorded, remembered, and communicated their meaningful experiences through the new technologies of the camera and the postcard. War photographs, like those from travel, intertwine to form not just a description of a journey and a destination but a meaningful narrative, selective, reflexively assembled, and capable of being reassembled in the future for the purposes of sharing knowledge and experience with others, or serving as a personal reminder of what was significant and formative. As souvenirs, the postcards of the soldiers and the relative moments of relief that they captured and embodied stand out sharply against the dark journeys the men were undertaking through battle. But through such journeys, the soldiers were nonetheless engaged in the daily construction of memory that related as much to ordinary life and personal connections as it did to the extraordinariness and historical significance of the war.

A Postcarded World

Soon after their introduction in Austria in the last quarter of the nineteenth century as "correspondence cards," postcards quickly established themselves as effective communication devices and, thanks to their combination of images on one side and personal messages on the other, versatile memory objects.[6] Illustrated souvenir cards can be traced to the Paris world's fair of 1889, at which tourists could purchase an image of the Eiffel Tower as a reminder of their visit,[7] and over the next twenty or so years the postcard established itself on a number of levels. As simple, cheap, and visually engaging objects, postcards opened up national and transnational communication networks that mapped onto movements of people relating to empire and trade, emigration and immigration, and the development of leisure tourism. The scale of production, sending, and collecting inspired terms such as the "postcard craze" or "postcard mania."[8] In the United States, postal service records suggest that nearly one billion cards were sent in 1913, with a similar figure estimated for Germany in 1903.[9]

The outbreak of war in 1914 led to shortages of paper and ink that, in turn, caused postcard production to decline. But in a context in which communicating with family and friends over distance became a necessity for millions of soldiers, postcards retained and arguably increased both their functional and symbolic importance. Soldiers on both sides of the conflict were already familiar with postcards, and they continued to buy, send, and collect them in considerable numbers. According to Andrés Mario Zervigón, each day of the First World War saw on average 9.9 million pieces of mail sent from Germans to the front and 6.8 million pieces posted from the front, with over half this total being postcards.[10] During the war there was considerable variety among the types of postcards available, from the basic British, non-pictorial "Field Service Post Card,"[11] to elaborately embroidered silk postcards produced by the millions by French and Belgian women and sold to soldiers as souvenirs.[12] The subject matter of picture postcards was shaped by blends of stylized patriotism, romanticism, and, as the war progressed, both comedic and increasingly explicit expressions of nationalist propaganda (fig. 2).[13]

Cards displaying artwork and selected professional photographs were produced en masse by large printing factories in Britain, France, and Germany. Real photographic postcards, on the other hand, were printed locally and derived in large measure from the amateur photography of the soldiers. Robert Bogdan and Todd Weseloh suggest that the "golden age" for the real photographic postcard in terms of quality and popularity was between 1906 and 1920.[14] This period coincided with a rise in the popularity of amateur photography led by technological advances, notably the introduction of affordable, easy-to-use cameras (pioneered by Kodak) and a system in which negatives could be sent by mail to be developed and

returned swiftly. Many German soldiers who served during the First World War had participated in the prewar trend of amateur photography and were familiar with the new technologies involved.[15] When it became evident that the war was not going to be over in a matter of months, soldiers sent letters home to request their cameras and also catalogues from which they could order photographic equipment.[16]

Most divisions in the German Army appear to have had a photographer working in a documentary role, but the use of personal cameras was common among the ranks of ordinary soldiers at the front. Soldiers would have used cameras such as the 1906 Ica Bebe strut-type folding plate camera with a good quality Tessar lens[17] or an Ernemann box camera that, like Kodak cameras from the United States, used flexible rolls of film that could be mailed to be developed and printed elsewhere. They were remarkably unrestricted in being able to send their negatives for printing and could also send their returned photographic postcards through the post without the significant degree of military censorship that French and British soldiers experienced. The German Army even supported amateur photographic competitions and published the entries, generally a mixture of classical landscape shots and scenes of the devastation soldiers encountered.

fig.2
Postcard, based on poster by Fritz Erler, *Vertraut Uns. Zeichnet Kriegsanleihe* (Trust Us. Subscribe to the War Loan), Dr. C. Wolf & Sohn (printer), Munich, c. 1917. The Wolfsonian–Florida International University, The Mitchell Wolfson, Jr. Collection, 87.19.119.

German soldiers produced millions of real photographic postcards over the course of the war. The experience of war consisted of long periods of calm, even boredom, and routine, noncombative work for the soldiers, so there was ample opportunity for taking photographs. The sheer number of cards, in a context of amateur photography and rapid processing, tempts us to think of both the objects and the practices surrounding them as somehow not serious. Rachel Snow, in reflecting on the mass availability of the Kodak Brownie in the years just before the First World War, draws a parallel to the banality and disposability of contemporary digital photography and identifies in this period the birth of the "snapshot aesthetic," an overproduction of photographs that arguably led to a decline in their value as both images and objects.[18] I would suggest, by contrast, that real photographic postcards from the First World War were infused with meaning and were deeply implicated in the memory practices of the soldiers and their loved ones as images and as souvenirs, purposely made to store or stimulate memories in relation to a particular experience, location, and time.[19] Soldiers purchased local souvenirs, but they also produced their own personalized, portable, transmittable souvenirs. The real photographic postcard performed the role of the souvenir, acting perfectly as an emblem of nostalgia and an object of validation of the "tour" or experience, in part as a literal *memento mori*—a symbol of inevitable death—and, in part, more speculatively, as an object for others to inherit and look to in grief or mourning.[20]

Travel Souvenirs in Wartime

Though the narratives generated by and through war are more profound and socially penetrating than those from the world of leisure, understanding the parallels between war and tourism helps us to understand the memory practices of soldiers and the role of the photographic postcard as an instrument of memory. Researchers, for example, have pointed to the ways that Australian soldiers in the First World War made sense of their experiences, not only as a military expedition but also as an emotional and cultural journey.[21] Ironically, while the outbreak of war in 1914 effectively brought a halt to middle-class leisure travel across Europe, it stimulated an unprecedented degree of travel among combatants, including long-haul travel from the territories of the British, French, and German empires, and from the United States in 1917. While German soldiers did not travel such great distances, they still made journeys into another landscape, another culture and language.

Like travel, war is both a literal and metaphorical journey, and as with other types of journeys, "souveniring" offered a way to make sense of the journey and secure memory through materiality.[22] The popular chronology of the First World War was punctuated by the places (destinations), battles, and tragedies now so familiar: the Somme, Passchendaele, Verdun, Argonne, and the like. But between these events, German soldiers engaged in daily routines in a foreign place, passing the time, making sense of their environments, and attempting to reconstitute feelings of home. Photography was part of this recreational time, and photographs acted to authenticate specific experiences and moments, serving as souvenirs for family, colleagues, and posterity, in much the same way as the holiday photograph performs its role as a prompt in the social processes of remembering. Just as the revelatory power, the playfulness of performance, and the pleasure of recall that have accompanied the photograph since its

fig. 3 (top left)
Real photographic postcard, Rob. Borowansky (studio), New Ulm, Germany, undated. Author's collection.

fig. 4 (top right)
Real photographic postcard, H. Cordes (studio), Hildesheim, Germany, undated. Author's collection.

fig. 5 (bottom)
Real photographic postcard, P. K. Bateriad (printer), Reichenbach im Vogtland, Germany, undated. Author's collection.

earliest days were all quickly employed in the practices of travel and tourism, so too did they lend themselves to the activities of war. Soldiers could produce their own postcard souvenirs swiftly and easily, to mark not only the novelty of their surroundings and the spectacle and drama of their journey, but also their daily realities and the more mundane aspects of life. Their "postcarding" of encounters and meaningful moments provided the visual narrative of the war as an event, acted as validation, and later provided an *aide memoire*, a trigger for memory.

Before departing for the front, soldiers would often visit a professional photography studio to record their embarkation, sometimes posing alone, sometimes with family members. A young recruit, for example, might pose in battledress against a painted Bavarian background (fig. 3). A studio portrait that survived in excellent condition would seem to indicate the postcard had resided with a soldier's family rather than in the field (fig. 4). At the front, soldiers arranged their own small displays of family photographs in barracks or dugouts as reminders of home. Figure 5 shows a postcard made from a photograph of such a shrine to home—most likely printed several times, so each soldier could have one to send to loved ones to illustrate how those at the front kept memories of family alive.

Drawing on a large corpus of German real photographic postcards from the First World War, it is possible to identify the sort of things that the soldiers thought were worth remembering as they journeyed through the conflict. Postcards sent home via the *feldpost* system often, but not always, contained messages and descriptions that can assist in explaining the images. A significant number of postcards bear no record of having been mailed (though they may have been included in parcels sent or taken home during leave). As creators of their own souvenirs, and faced with limited official censorship, soldiers had wide discretion in terms of what they recorded. However, it is likely that soldiers exercised some self-censorship, which limited what they were willing to share with their family and friends at home.

Broad subject categories can be detected among the postcards. By far the largest number of postcards record images of friends and comrades, often made by professional studio photographers either back in Germany or traveling closer to the front. These images convey a sense of relief and playfulness that was, in part, cleverly orchestrated by the studios through the use of painted backgrounds and elaborate three-dimensional sets in the form of airships and airplanes or other fanciful scenery (fig. 6).

German soldiers also documented friendships and camaraderie in the field with their own cameras. These friendships, which emerged from the shared experience of combat and living in close quarters, could be terminated in a

fig. 6 (bottom left)
Real photographic postcard, Schubert (studio), Berlin, 1916. Author's collection.

fig. 7 (top)
Real photographic postcard, undated. Author's collection.

fig. 8 (bottom right)
Real photographic postcard, undated. Author's collection.

moment through death or serious injury. As if in recognition of the precariousness of friendship under these conditions and readiness for future remembrance, soldiers made an ongoing record of friends at the battlefront, behind the lines, on leave, and even as prisoners of war, when allowed to retain their cameras. Many of these postcards do not appear to have been posted and were likely carried by soldiers as part of their own narratives of the war; but in the event of a comrade's death, they could be forwarded to his family.

At the outset of the war, groups of soldiers were photographed in line with regimental or divisional ordering in coordinated compositions that marked a ritualistic moment of passing into the military system. Formal photographs fed into narratives of the war that were destined for a home audience, as a ready memory marker—how soldiers would wish to be remembered and how families could mark and explain temporary or permanent absence. But they made informal records of friendship as well, such as one card showing a group of young friends, possibly brothers, holding flowers, which were often given as talismans of good luck (fig. 7). Even when temporarily or permanently out of the theater of war through injury, illness, and disability, soldiers would record the relationships they had built up through battle, relationships not only with one another but also with nurses and civilians (fig. 8).

Through photographic cards, soldiers were able to capture and preserve the intimacies among comrades that came about through living in close proximity over a prolonged period, sometimes choosing to record moments of normalcy that took place in a context of danger and deprivation, angst and uncertainty. There is a playful quality to postcards showing comrades and friends in the liminal spaces and moments that war creates, doing things they might normally do at home but under very different circumstances. The ordinary act of shaving (very important at the front in order to combat lice) becomes a public performance, something deemed memorable, particularly if it happens among friends (fig. 9). A scene of soldiers in a queue waiting to use a makeshift latrine is another example of humorous camera play with the aim of capturing the unusual that had become usual (fig. 10). Scenes of friends indulging in gambling, drinking, and smoking are also commonplace in the postcards (fig. 11).

fig. 9
Real photographic postcard, undated. Author's collection.

fig. 10
Real photographic postcard, 1915, inscribed: "Command in Champagne." Author's collection.

fig. 11
Real photographic postcard, 1917. Author's collection.

Like tourists, soldiers created a narrative of their journeys by recording images of their destinations. While some of the landscapes recorded consisted of images of forests and woodlands that could have been located anywhere, soldiers also took photographs of landscapes that showed the devastation wrought by war—a visual experience that was, arguably, difficult to express in any way other than through a photograph and probably recorded in part for the very sublime spectacle it conveyed.

Indeed, the extent of disturbance to the landscape—vast craters, caved-in trenches, fallen trees, and muddy expanses traversed by barbed wire—often made it difficult for recipients to interpret the scene, so senders scribbled short captions of location and date on the back of the postcard. "Between the first and second lines. Here I spent Christmas" is the inscription on the back of a card showing one such scene of a ruined landscape (fig. 12).

Such postcards sent home bearing these messages sought to commit to memory a landscape that others could not witness, nor would want to witness. Damage to the built environment, such as the destruction of towns and villages caused by shelling, was featured alongside scenes of the devastated natural environment in postcards made by German soldiers (fig. 13). The presence of fellow soldiers among the rubble and ruins of a conquered town could signal a moment of victory that might later spark remembrance of the war as a narrative of "progress" and advancement. But such images, particularly those showing the destruction of churches, cathedrals, and graveyards, were also records of scenes that might have provoked sadness and bewilderment.

As tourists seek out accommodation that temporarily anchors them in home comforts, so too did soldiers seek to build homes away from home. These accommodations ranged from small, cramped dugouts to highly elaborate wooden shelters built to withstand enemy bombardment. Postcards with photographs of such dwellings were commonly delivered back home to families as a kind of reassurance. These images documented the lengths soldiers would go to make their shelters homelike, such as a dugout complete with a decorative fence, a small garden, and outside table and benches (fig. 14). Similar images, showing elaborate planted areas,

fig. 12
Real photographic postcard, undated, inscribed: "Between the first and second lines. Here I spent Christmas." Author's collection.

fig. 13 (opposite, top)
Real photographic postcard, undated, inscribed: "Lille." Author's collection.

fig. 14 (opposite, bottom)
Real photographic postcard, undated. Author's collection.

fig. 15 Real photographic postcard, 1916. Author's collection.

fig. 16 (opposite) Real photographic postcard, 1917. Author's collection.

rock gardens, and identifying names of the "houses," are records of the soldiers' skill at woodcraft or gardening, and convey a genuine sense of achievement and pride in constructing a degree of permanence in an otherwise disturbed landscape.

Photographic postcards captured soldiers' encounters with the new military technologies and materials introduced during the war and recorded them for memory. Captured enemy tanks and field guns along with crashed airplanes provided backdrops and "props" for recording groups of comrades, marking small victories against the enemy. Postcards showing unexploded shells in the battlefield are common, such as one with a German private posing next to a large shell bearing the object's dimensions, but also the inscription "English dud-shot" (fig. 15); these images performed a morale-boosting function, drawing attention to the incompetence of the enemy, and were frequently posted home. But they also reflect the exoticism of the objects and the proximity of danger, acting as a surrogate trophy around which stories could be woven.

The war marked the first time most German soldiers would have traveled beyond the borders of their country. Outside of moments of combat and in spaces behind the battle lines, soldiers encountered foreign lands and civilian populations. While the invasions of Belgium and France brought soldiers into contact with cultures with which they would likely have been somewhat familiar, the Eastern front and East Africa were sites of more dramatic cultural difference. Postcards that record unfamiliar peoples and customs are prominent in the collections of soldiers and their families, markers of cultural encounters that would be largely unthinkable outside the context of war—for instance, a shot of German soldiers and officers posing with a peasant family somewhere on the Eastern front (fig. 16). Other postcards record soldiers handing over food to civilians, trying on foreign clothing, and playing with children. Such images speak of a

Hier
ruht
Adolf Wenzel
Ehre
dem
Helden

0
km

tourist-like fascination with otherness that would be carried in memory and feed storytelling, even as they also perhaps steered memories away from the fact that soldiers were in these lands on a mission of conquest.

For reasons of danger and the limits of technology (portable cameras did not allow for long-distance shots or long exposure times), few real photographic postcards from the First World War record battle in progress. German soldiers, however, did seek to record the tragedy of war, not as it unfolded in real time, but in terms of the legacies it left. Postcards that show the makeshift graves of comrades would be delivered back to the relatives of the fallen as a very practical way of recording the act of burial and as a way of displaying respect and duty done (fig. 17). Postcards that show the dead were almost never posted and seldom annotated, but they were made and kept. A postcard such as one showing corpses strewn on the ground—captioned in pencil, "Dead Romanian Company shot down early morning by machine guns"—marks out the extreme of personal memorabilia accumulated by soldiers (fig. 18). This postcard sits uneasily within the conventional notion of the term "souvenir." Yet as an object that could be displayed as a means of recollecting experiences and emotions from the past, it acts in the same way as a holiday souvenir to condense a moment and location for future reference. It appears that such material reminders of the ultimate consequences of war were more in evidence in the latter years of the conflict, as if self-censorship had waned in terms of what was deemed worthy of recording.

Working with real photographic postcards from this period, as vernacular objects that have been dislocated from their original cultural context, involves a fair degree of speculation. We do not know the life histories of the individuals who made them nor do we have access to their motivations. Many postcards bear messages on the reverse that are not related to the photographs, and a large number of the postcards do not carry any information at all. Accumulations of these postcards as souvenirs that have outlived the soldiers and their families now exist in archives and among collectors, as what Esther Leslie terms "particles of splintered memory in the modern era."[23] Nonetheless, examining them as souvenirs, as moments made material, and as objects that were distributed and collected during and after the war, sheds light on how and what soldiers chose to record for the purposes of memory. Within the context of a permissive attitude toward photography (compared, at least, with France and Britain), relatively easy access to cameras, and the effective *feldpost* system, the real photographic postcard may well have emerged as *the* primary device of recording for many German soldiers. As with postcards sent by holiday-makers and holiday snaps shared with family and friends, the postcards point to *what* was worth remembering as well as *how* memories were given substance to embody "personal event memory."[24]

fig. 17
Real photographic postcard, undated. Author's collection.

fig. 18
Real photographic postcard, undated, inscribed: "Dead Romanian Company shot down early morning by machine guns." Author's collection.

The last years of the twentieth century witnessed a sustained effort to record how the surviving Allied soldiers of the First World War remembered their participation. Oral recollections by these soldiers, as well as diary accounts, created not only narratives of violence, disruption, and pain, but also those of adventure, escape, encounter with the foreign and the exotic, boredom, the mundane, and camaraderie—all experiences closely associated with life, rather than death. For the vast majority of the First World War, ordinary Allied soldiers could not directly record and communicate such experiences through the medium of real photographic postcards. German soldiers, on the other hand, did not have such restrictions and, aided by the ready availability of quality cameras and a highly effective postal system, they produced postcard narratives of the war that closely paralleled vacation narratives. Though the horrors of the war were not excluded from these photo-narratives and were very much part of the soldier's memories, on the whole, the postcards consisted of images that would not be out of place in a holiday album. Indeed, postcard albums assembled by German families throughout the war that feature real photographic cards closely resemble records of a vacation; they were chronologically ordered, frequently annotated, and featured images of landscapes, places visited, and the subjects posing for the camera. The postcards captured the practices and performances of the German soldiers simultaneously engaged in both war and travel. Images of family and friendships, constructions of "home away from home," landscape views, scenes of play and enjoyment, experiences with food and drink, and glimpses of exotic cultures and encounters with locals, interspersed with snapshots of ordinary life in extraordinary circumstances, traveled on postcards between the shifting destinations of the battlefields of France, Belgium, Russia, Serbia, Bulgaria, Romania, and home, in Germany.

While there are parallels and intersections between war and tourism revealed in both the images and in the practices of recording, the tourist-like quality of these postcards masks the meta-narrative that, in the eyes of occupied local communities, the German soldiers were unwelcome invaders rather than welcome tourists. At the same time, many of the soldiers were likely not intruders by choice, and these souvenirs were, in general, not part of the German propaganda machine, but rather a genuine attempt on the part of the soldiers to make sense of the war and to preserve it for memory in a way that was tolerable and essentially human.

NOTES

1. Jay Winter, *Remembering War: The Great War between Memory and History in the Twentieth Century* (New Haven, CT: Yale University Press, 2006), 18.
2. Nicholas J. Saunders and Paul Cornish, introduction to *Contested Objects: Material Memories of the Great War* (London: Routledge, 2009), 1–10.
3. Paul Fussell, *The Great War and Modern Memory* (London: Oxford University Press, 1975).
4. Susan Stewart, *On Longing: Narratives of the Miniature, the Gigantic, the Souvenir, the Collection* (Durham, NC: Duke University Press, 1993).
5. Sarah Foot, "Remembering, Forgetting and Inventing Attitudes to the Past in England at the End of the First Viking Age," *Transactions of the Royal Historical Society* 6, no. 9 (1999): 187–88.
6. Bjarne Rogan, "An Entangled Object: The Picture Postcard as Souvenir and Collectible, Exchange and Ritual Communication," *Cultural Analysis* 4 (2005): 1–27.
7. Naomi Schor, "Collecting Paris," in *The Cultures of Collecting*, ed. John Elsner and Roger Cardinal (Cambridge, MA: Harvard University Press, 1994), 252–74.
8. Lynda Klich and Benjamin Weiss, *The Postcard Age: Selections from the Leonard A. Lauder Collection* (London: Thames and Hudson, 2012), 35.
9. George Miller and Dorothy Miller, *Picture Postcards in the United States, 1893–1918* (New York: Clarkson N. Potter/Crown, 1976).
10. Andrés Mario Zervigón, "Postcards to the Front: John Heartfield, George Grosz and the Birth of the Avant-Garde Photomontage," in *Postcards: Ephemeral Histories of Modernity*, ed. David Prochaska and Jordana Mendelson (University Park, PA: Pennsylvania State University Press, 2010), 54–69.
11. Allyson Booth, *Postcards from the Trenches: Negotiating the Space between Modernism and the First World War* (Oxford: Oxford University Press, 1996), 14.
12. Pat Tomczyszyn, "A Material Link Between War and Peace: First World War Silk Postcards," in *Matters of Conflict: Material Culture, Memory and the First World War*, ed. Nicholas J. Saunders (London: Routledge, 2004), 123–33.
13. Sophie Dehalle, "The Image of Belgium on German Post Cards in the First World War," *Guerres mondiales et conflits contemporains*, no. 241 (2011): 51–62.
14. Robert Bogdan and Todd Weseloh, *Real Photo Postcard Guide: The People's Photography* (Syracuse, NY: Syracuse University Press, 2006).
15. Jill Steward, "The Attractions of Place: The Making of Urban Tourism, 1860–1914," in *Creative Urban Milieus: Historical Perspectives on Culture, Economy, and the City*, ed. Martina Hessler and Clemens Zimmermann (Frankfurt: Campus Verlag, 2008), 255–84.
16. Sebastian Remus, *German Amateur Photographers in the First World War: A View from the Trenches on the Western Front* (Atglen, PA: Schiffer Military History, 2008).
17. Heinz K. Henisch and Bridget Ann Henisch, *The Photographic Experience, 1839–1914: Images and Attitudes* (University Park, PA: Pennsylvania State University Press, 1994).
18. Rachel Snow, "Correspondence Here: Real Photo Postcards and the Snapshot Aesthetic," in *Postcards: Ephemeral Histories of Modernity*, 42–53.
19. Nelson H. H. Graburn, foreword to *Souvenirs: The Material Culture of Tourism*, ed. Michael Hitchcock and Ken Teague (Aldershot: Ashgate, 2000), xii–xvii.
20. Stewart, *On Longing*, 140.
21. Bart Ziino, "A Kind of Round Trip: Australian Soldiers and the Tourist Analogy, 1914–1918," *War and Society* 25, no. 2 (2006): 39–52; Richard White, "The Soldier as Tourist: The Australian Experience of the Great War," *War and Society* 5, no. 1 (1987): 63–77.
22. Ian Baucom, *Out of Place: Englishness, Empire and the Locations of Identity* (Princeton, NJ: Princeton University Press, 1999), 119.
23. Esther Leslie, "Siegfried Kracauer and Walter Benjamin: Memory from Weimar to Hitler," in *Memory: Histories, Theories, Debates*, ed. Susannah Radstone and Bill Schwartz (New York: Fordham University Press, 2010), 123–35.
24. David B. Pillemer, *Momentous Events, Vivid Memories* (Cambridge, MA: Harvard University Press, 1998), 19.

満洲の回想
渕上白陽 編著

A LEGACY OF PERSUASION: JAPANESE PHOTOGRAPHY AND THE ARTFUL POLITICS OF REMEMBERING MANCHURIA

Kari Shepherdson-Scott

Kari Shepherdson-Scott is an assistant professor of Art History at Macalester College in St. Paul, Minnesota. She specializes in Japanese visual culture from the nineteenth and twentieth centuries, focusing on the visual expression of memory, national identity, and empire. A contributor to the anthology *Art and War in Japan and Its Empire, 1931–1960* (2012), her research examines how Japanese media and exhibitions produced idealized visions of Manchuria during the 1930s and early 1940s.

In 1958, noted art photographer Fuchikami Hakuyō (1889–1960) edited a publication titled *Manshū no Kaisō* (Reminiscences of Manchuria, 1958). A large, handsome volume measuring 10 x 14 inches, it consisted of a collection of photographs taken by Fuchikami and his colleagues in the Japanese puppet state of Manchukuo (1932–45) during the 1930s and early 1940s. A close-up of the Lama pagoda at Jinzhou (fig. 1) completely fills the front and back cover of the dust jacket, presenting the niche carvings of the Buddha and his attendants in fine detail.[1] The rough masonry edifice, each brick rendered with exquisite clarity, testifies to the long spiritual and cultural history of the region. *Manshū no Kaisō* takes the reader on a virtual, sentimental journey back to Japanese-occupied Manchuria, featuring images of smiling faces, sun-dappled beaches, expansive urban boulevards, plumes of smoke churning from factory stacks, picturesque rock walls, exotic portraits of native inhabitants, and bucolic Japanese settler farms. The photographs present an idealized vision of the past, while also showcasing the richness of Japanese artistic expression that developed in Manchuria during this period. Fuchikami and his cohort of photographers in the Manchuria Photographic Artists Association (Manshū shashin sakka kyōkai, or MPAA) experimented for more than a decade with various photographic and design trends, from the Japanese Besu-tan school and Pictorialism to Constructivism, straight photography, New Objectivity (Neue Sachlichkeit), and the dazzling light effects explored by László Moholy-Nagy in the 1930s. The diverse results ranged from the hazily atmospheric and sentimental *Kutsuya* (Shoemaker, fig. 2) by Yoneki

fig. 1
Photographer unknown, cover, *Manshū no Kaisō* (Tokyo: Keigadō, 1958). Author's collection.

fig. 2
Yoneki Zen'emon, *Kutsuya*, 1935. From *Manshū no Kaisō*, 21. Author's collection.

Zen'emon to Unoki Satoshi's dynamically vertiginous *Jōheki* (Castle Wall, fig. 3). The postwar publisher Keigadō acknowledged the incredible artistry of the works in *Manshū no Kaisō* by using a photogravure printing process to reproduce the images on an exceptionally heavy, finely grained paper stock, all of which enhanced the photographs' rich tones and remarkably subtle textures.

Manshū no Kaisō is a superb art object. It is also an object that exposes the fraught legacy of Japanese imperialism. Many of the photographs had been featured previously in media published by the South Manchuria Railway Company (Minami Manshū Tetsudō Kabushikikaisha, hereafter referred to as Mantetsu).[2] Fuchikami had worked for Mantetsu's public relations office from 1928 to 1941. Under the auspices of this Japanese company, he edited numerous illustrated publications, including the company's flagship promotional magazine *Manshū Graph* (Pictorial Manchuria) and the

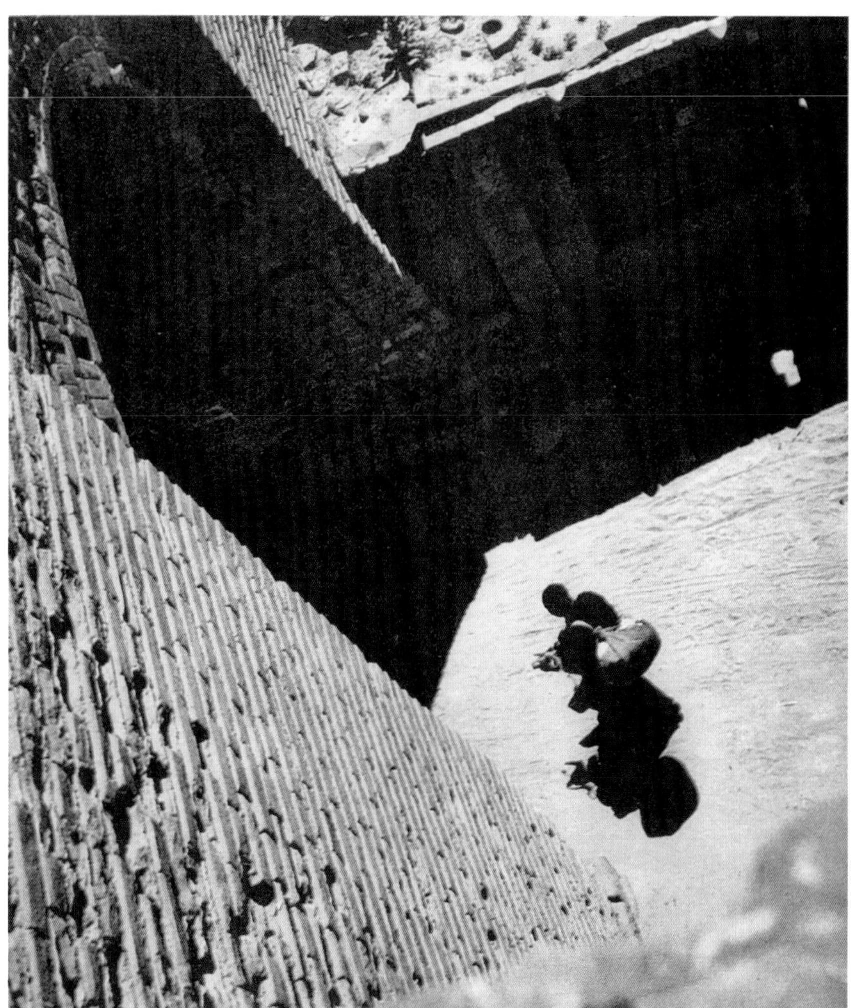

fig. 3
Unoki Satoshi, *Jōheki*, 1937. From *Manshū no Kaisō*, 26. Author's collection.

annual *Manshū Gaikan* (An Overview of Manchuria). These publications featured the highly evocative photography produced by Fuchikami and his colleagues in conjunction with short descriptive texts to advertise Mantetsu, the kinds of services the company provided on the continent, and reports on the latest events in Manchukuo. They were tools of persuasion, deployed to cultivate a desire to explore the continental frontier among a largely urban Japanese population. Additionally, they became an inextricable part of the visual lexicon that supported Japanese imperialism, as Mantetsu was one of the most important apparatuses of Japanese expansion on the continent. In short, the photography Fuchikami promoted in Manchuria and later revisited in the late 1950s exemplified the complex intersection between art and the contentious politics of empire.

Yet, the stakes of publishing these images had changed dramatically between the 1930s and 1950s. Initially they had functioned as tools inviting Japanese consumption of the new state of Manchukuo; republished in the postwar era, these works became poignant reminders of a bygone time and place. In order to examine the layers of meaning at work in *Manshū no Kaisō*, this essay first discusses the context of production in the 1930s and early 1940s, focusing on how the privileged position Fuchikami occupied as an esteemed Japanese culture producer contributed to a process of aesthetic colonization on the continent. I then discuss how the residue of the meaning accrued by the art photography that Fuchikami promoted during the Manchukuo era informed the works' visual and symbolic resonance in the 1950s. I argue that *Manshū no Kaisō* provokes a process of remembering—or, more specifically, nostalgically "reminiscing"—that maintains distance from inflammatory postwar narratives of violence, coercion, and displacement associated with the Japanese military occupation of Manchuria. This is not to suggest that the volume represents a conscious historical revisionism, but rather that it is indicative of the challenges individuals faced when seeking to reconcile memories of personal experience with the military atrocities publicized after the end of the war in 1945. In this way, *Manshū no Kaisō* can best be understood as what anthropologist Ann Laura Stoler calls "colonial aphasia," a kind of "dismembering, a difficulty speaking, a difficulty generating a vocabulary that associates appropriate words and concepts with appropriate things."[3] While Stoler applies this concept to the legacy of French imperialism, it is productive to consider how Fuchikami's volume visually manifests this process of remembering and forgetting the Japanese experience in northeast Asia. By interrogating the losses as well as the visual presences in *Manshū no Kaisō*, this essay will expose the tensions among aesthetics, privilege, nostalgia, and postwar discourses of Japanese empire that continue to resonate today.

Empire, Culture, and Privileged Vision

The postwar significance of *Manshū no Kaisō* derived partly from the fact that Manchuria was crucial to the expansion and maintenance of the Japanese empire in the first half of the twentieth century. Though the region first entered into the Japanese popular imagination during the Sino-Japanese War (1894–95), Japan did not secure a foothold there for another ten years. Following a Japanese victory over the Russians in the Russo-Japanese War (1904–05), the Treaty of Portsmouth awarded Japan continental concessions on the Liaodong Peninsula, which was then renamed the Kwantung Leased Territory.[4] This territory afforded the Japanese army a strategic position from which it could secure the Korean peninsula, often referred to as the "dagger pointed at the heart of Japan."[5] Eventually, Manchuria became an indispensable military bulwark between the Japanese homeland and Russian (eventually Soviet) interests in northeast Asia.

Japanese officials also regarded Manchuria, a vast space with abundant natural resources, as a panacea for the myriad problems that plagued Japan in the interwar period: a lack of rural opportunities, depressed export commodity markets, inflation, and urban overcrowding. They treated the region as a *hakushi* (blank page) where Japanese plans for industrial, urban, and agricultural expansion could unfold.[6] Mantetsu was critical to the development of Manchuria. It operated port facilities, offered freight and passenger transportation services, and established public institutions and infrastructure such as utilities, hospitals, and schools. It was also central to industrial development beyond providing transportation, founding subsidiary continental corporations such as the Anshan Iron and Steel Works. Enormous capital flowed into the region. By the end of 1931, the military and Mantetsu referred to Manchuria as the *seimeisen* (lifeline) of Japan; this term circulated so frequently that year that the Japan Broadcasting Corporation listed it as one the year's five "fashionable expressions."[7]

As a lifeline, Manchuria (or more specifically, Japanese interests there) had to be protected; yet, there was no clear consensus between the Japanese government and the army on the best way to do so. The army decided to proceed without government support. On September 18, 1931, the Japanese Kwantung Army detonated a section of railway outside the city of Mukden, blaming the act on Chinese dissidents. Referred to as the Mukden Incident or the Manchurian Incident, it marked the beginning of the Fifteen-Year War (1931–45), which encompassed the Second Sino-Japanese War (1937–45) and the Pacific War (1941–45). Moreover, this event gave the army a reason to invade the region. In 1932, it declared the founding of the nation-state of Manchukuo, claiming to liberate the region from the violence and political uncertainty of rule by regional Chinese warlords.

Manchukuo never became an official Japanese colony like Taiwan (Formosa) and Korea (Chōsen), but it nonetheless exemplified colonial systems of political and military subordination. Manchukuo was a paradox. It was born of war and sustained by military occupation, and yet Japanese media published on the Asian continent and in Japan presented it as a land of peace and order. In response to interwar global discourses of decolonization, Manchukuo was meant to exemplify the principles of self-determination and sovereignty.[8] It was purportedly a multiethnic utopia where the "five races"—Han-Chinese, Manchurians, Mongolians, Koreans, and the Japanese—could live in harmony (*gozoku kyōwa*). Manchukuo was as much a product of ideological optimism as of Japanese military aggression. Nonetheless, though peace, harmony, and equality made good media slogans, they were difficult to put into practice.[9] The sovereign identity of Manchukuo was caught in the power negotiation among numerous political agents, including the Japanese military, Japanese settlers, Chinese nationalists, warlords, Euro-American powers, even the League of Nations.[10] Struggles among these different groups resulted in an unequal sharing of power in Manchukuo. Japanese military and corporate interests played a dominant role there, overseeing extensive urban and industrial development as well as indigenous displacement, forced labor, and mass killings of political dissidents.[11] Yet, Japanese media published during the Manchukuo period did not address the troubling stakes of Japanese occupation, prefiguring the aphasia that would take place after the war.

Mantetsu's promotional campaigns demonstrate some of the ways that the dominant Japanese position on the continent became visually and culturally manifest. The company, like other Japanese agencies promoting tourism to the continent, invited numerous esteemed Japanese novelists, artists, and designers to visit. The work they produced placed Manchuria in the Japanese popular cultural imagination as an inspiring frontier, ripe for exploration. Their affective imagery, often focusing on bucolic rural scenes, young Manchurian women, exotic locals, and dynamic urban landscapes, connected with people on an emotional level.[12] These artistic narratives provided additional benefits for the company as well: they promoted the region as a cultural destination, balancing the image of Manchuria as the rugged hinterland with the idea of artistic refinement. As Louise Young notes, the "parade of literary luminaries" who went to Manchuria throughout the 1930s "turned the Manchuria tour into a badge of cultural distinction," making a trip to the continent a sign of cultural legitimacy for those in the fine arts.[13] In turn, the artists and authors who participated in Mantetsu-sponsored tours afforded the company cultural capital, a valuable component in its corporate image. The association with art and culture was but one tactic Japanese companies, drawing on the relatively new field of public relations, could employ to counter the perception they were "soulless" and thereby "avoid the stigma of mere profit seeking."[14] Yet, those same strategies that companies undertook to connect with the public were couched in elitist terms, predicated on a language of artistic connoisseurship.

Fuchikami Hakuyō was among the noted artists Mantetsu recruited to create images promoting the region and, after 1932, the new state of Manchukuo. Fuchikami had developed his artistic reputation in Kobe, Japan, where he had moved in 1918. The following year, he opened the Hakuyō Photography Studio.[15] While in Kobe, he actively promoted art photography by founding several photography associations in addition to publishing the monthly magazine *Hakuyō*, which featured high-quality collotype prints.[16] Through these endeavors, Fuchikami became renowned for a photographic vision that drew on multiple styles. For example, the

fig. 4
Fuchikami Hakuyō, *En to jintai no kōsei*, 1926. From *Fuchikami Hakuyō to Manshū Shashin Sakka Kyōkai* (Tokyo: Iwanami Shoten, 1998), unpaginated, from section titled "Fuchikami Hakuyō."

evocative play of light, shadow, shape, and texture in his work *En to jintai no kōsei* (Composition with Circle and Body, fig. 4) from 1926 exemplifies how he bridged the lyrical, atmospheric aesthetics of Pictorialism and the progressive geometry and abstraction of Constructivism.

Recognizing the artistic vision and the cultural cachet Fuchikami would bring to the corporate brand, Mantetsu invited him in 1928 to work in its public relations office, a well-paid and prestigious position associated with the office of the president of the company. As Fuchikami had fallen recently into financial straits in Japan, this job would provide him with the resources he needed to continue the promotion and development of photographic expression. The same year, Fuchikami emigrated from Kobe to the Manchurian city of Dalian, the site of Mantetsu's headquarters and

fig. 5
Chiba Yoshio, untitled photograph of Fuchikami Hakuyō (standing at center) and members of the Manchuria Photographic Artists Association on the Sungari River, 1940. From *Ikyō no modanizumu* (Nagoya: Nagoya City Art Museum, 1994), unpaginated, from chapter 6, "'Yu-topia' no puropaganda."

the urban center of the Liaodong Peninsula. With his Flex camera in hand, he became a continental flâneur, an artistic explorer of the Manchurian frontier (fig. 5).

Fuchikami's elite position on the continent complemented the kind of privileged gaze Mantetsu had already established in its promotional media, targeting primarily urban readers in Japan. Publications from the mid-1920s, such as the 1926 *Mantetsu Shashinchō* (The Mantetsu Photography Book), demonstrate how Mantetsu sold Manchuria as a tantalizing destination, a site of ethnic difference and bourgeois indulgence. For example, the photograph, captioned simply as "Shina fūzoku: buyō" (Chinese Scenery no. 1: Dancing), presents four figures—one man playing a *dizi* (Chinese flute), another playing a four-string *pipa*, and two dancers in elaborate costumes from the local opera—as bearers of an authentic Chinese culture (fig. 6).[17] They perform as if on a shallow stage, acting as a kind of ethnic scenery for Japanese readers to enjoy. A photograph of the beach near the northern city of Harbin focuses on foreign bodies in the Manchurian landscape; here most noticeably are two Caucasian women and a small child (likely Russian emigrés) (fig. 7). The photograph, which is captioned "Harbin: Sungari suieijō" (Harbin: Sungari River Swimming

figs. 6, 7
Photographers unknown, "Shina fūzoku: buyō" and "Harbin: Sungari suieijō." From *Mantetsu Shashinchō* (Minami Manshū Tetsudō Kabushikigaisha, 1926), 53, 48. The Wolfsonian–Florida International University, The Mitchell Wolfson, Jr. Collection, XC1992.51.

(53)

支那風俗(其一)……舞踊

(48)

哈爾賓(其四)……松花江水泳場

fig. 8
Photographer unknown, cover, *Manshū Graph* 10, no. 1 (January 1942). Yumani shobō, 2008, reprint. University of Minnesota Library.

Area), compels a general appreciation of the beaches stretching along the Sungari River, populated by a cosmopolitan mix of women in arm-baring sundresses and men in straw hats, indicative of the latest mid-1920s fashion. Mantetsu presented this space as an idyllic destination, perfect for indulging in sunbathing and other kinds of leisure.[18]

Following the establishment of the new nation-state of Manchukuo in 1932, Fuchikami worked with Mantetsu to develop new media like

Manshū Graph (1933–44) and the illustrated annual *Manshū Gaikan* (1934–41) to communicate current events in the new state. These publications were more than newsletters filled with photo-reportage. Created by the company's public relations division, they were also tools of persuasion, distributed in major urban centers like Tokyo, Osaka, and Nagoya. Fuchikami continued to use evocative imagery of exotic peoples and middle-class leisure pursuits to connect the Japanese metropole emotionally to the new state. There was a noticeable shift, however, in the social and political stakes of this connection during the Manchukuo period as compared to the 1920s. For example, the figure of a female ice-skater, deftly posing on her toes and fashionably attired in a matching hat, vest, and skirt, suggests Manchukuo is a land where middle-class fantasies of material consumption and the luxury of leisure could be realized (fig. 8). Interestingly, Mantetsu published this photo on the cover of *Manshū Graph* in 1942, when Japanese at home were exhorted to spurn such (Western) sartorial extravagances as they mobilized for total war. This image demonstrates how Mantetsu presented Manchukuo as a space of middle-class indulgence and, in the first years of the Second Sino-Japanese War, escape from realities of wartime sacrifice.[19]

Undoubtedly, the most significant contribution Fuchikami made to the development of Mantetsu's public relations programs was his promotion of art photography. In addition to transforming the design and quality of images featured routinely in Mantetsu promotional materials, Fuchikami spearheaded the publication of specific projects dedicated to art photography, including postcard sets featuring works like *Bafun wo hirō jiji* (Old man Gathering Horse Manure, fig. 9) and his own *Banshū* (Late Autumn, fig. 10), as well as three full issues of *Manshū Graph*.[20] These collections functioned as virtual gallery spaces and, particularly in the case of the postcard set, souvenirs of cultural production on the continent. They made the work of Fuchikami and his colleagues accessible to a broader audience than those who attended MPAA exhibitions in Manchuria, Japan, or overseas in Chicago (1933–34) and Paris (1937). Moreover, they underscored Fuchikami's status as a member of the cultural elite and, by extension, enhanced Mantetsu's cultural cachet.

The aestheticization of the continent in these kinds of works decontextualized subjects from the specificity of time and place to present them as evocative artistic objects. For example, both *Bafun wo hirō jiji* and *Banshū* deny any documentary function. The hazy, atmospheric effects of both images exemplify the continuing influence of Pictorialism; they also obscure the individual identities of the figures. The subjects become evocative symbols of local culture in Manchuria, occupying a timeless rural landscape. The captions that accompany the images on the postcards further enhance their aesthetic and poetic function, describing the general

馬糞を拾ふ爺

平和な朝に生れて、天の支配のまゝを
従順に平和な夕べを迎へたお爺さん。
赭色の皺の顔面は幸福に輝きわたつて
ゐる。

晩秋

農を本とする満州の秋
とりいれが済めば冬の
仕度だ。満州の稲とも
云ふべき高粱、その殼
を刈ることは、一面秋
のしめくゝりでもある
が、それよりも冬の仕
度と云つた方が好い。
それ程高粱は重要な燃
料である。

fig. 9
Photographer unknown, *Bafun wo hirō jiji*. From *Manshū bijutsu shashin ehagaki (dai isshū)* (Minami Manshū Tetsudō Kabushikigaisha, undated). Author's collection.

fig. 10
Fuchikami Hakuyō, *Banshū*. From *Manshū bijutsu shashin ehagaki (dai isshū)*. Author's collection.

ethos of the "old man's docile greeting of the peaceful evening" and the "preparation for winter at the end of the Manchurian autumn." While a seemingly innocuous act, this transformation of Manchurian people and spaces into art objects effected a kind visual and systemic violence, stripping the subjects of agency as the photographers privileged the poetic play of light and texture in their compositions. As David Spurr points out (using the example of American travel writer Stephen Crane in Mexico), this cultivation of a "purely aesthetic view" is a means to "escape the obligations of power."[21] In other words, a focus on formal, artistic expression can be a means for artists (and viewers) to distance themselves from the fraught imperial discourses of colonial subjugation. Fuchikami's writings from his time in Manchuria were almost wholly focused on aesthetics and artistic production: the development of art photography on the continent, the poetic transformation of subjects through artistic intervention, and even his optical response to the sun.[22] He did not address the social or political issues at stake in Manchukuo. Yet, as Spurr argues with regard to Crane, he is unable to sidestep fully those power relationships as this artistic identity was inextricably bound to the colonial interests with which he identified. Spurr makes it clear that the aesthetic transformation of the subject is far from a neutral act. Indeed, one must acknowledge how this process of objectification is made possible by a position of power and privilege, in the uneven relations between photographer and photographed, occupier and occupied.

Using his expensive Flex camera, Fuchikami transformed the Manchurian landscape and its people into exquisite art objects for consumption by middle-class urban Japanese readers.[23] In the process, the violence and displacement suffered by the native subjects in Manchuria disappear, replaced by richly tonal vignettes of Manchurian life and landscapes. His works and those of other MPAA photographers were lovely tools of persuasion that were also manifestations of visual domination. It is important to consider, then, how these photographs continued to articulate these aesthetic but violent erasures after the war as *Manshū no Kaisō* inherited their complex artistic and political legacy.

Remembering Manchuria in Postwar Japan

While Manchukuo had functioned as a space for the projection of middle-class Japanese fantasies from 1932 to 1945, it quickly fell into memory with the surrender of the Japanese on August 15, 1945. The region, once posited as a "blank page" of idealistic industrial, urban, and artistic pursuits, became entangled in much different, darker narratives in the first years of the postwar era. Hundreds of thousands Japanese settlers, abandoned by the decimated Kwantung Army in August 1945, attempted to evacuate the region, fleeing the Soviet Red Army and angry Chinese, many of whom had been physically displaced from their farms or forced

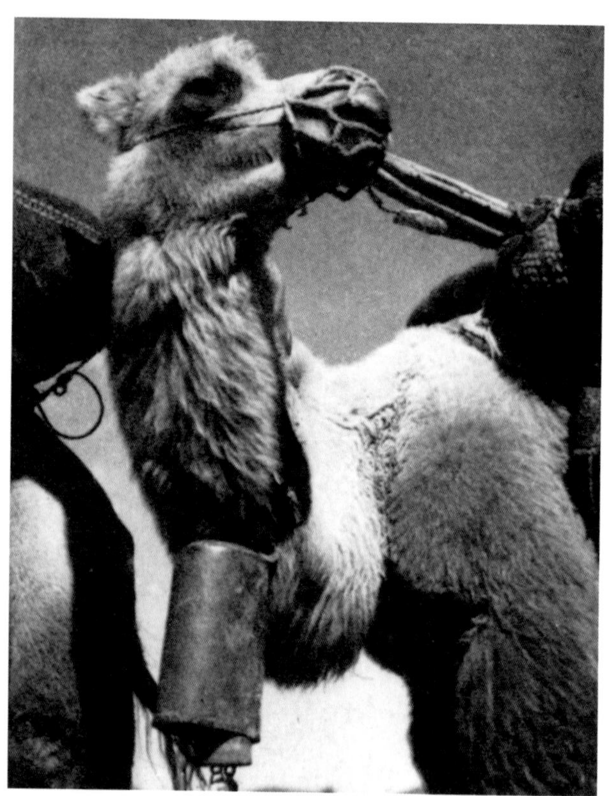

fig. 11
Photographer unknown, untitled photograph, c. 1937. From *Manshū no Kaisō*, title page. Author's collection.

into labor by the Japanese.[24] As many as sixty-seven thousand Japanese colonists died due to starvation and disease alone, while many Japanese children were abandoned on the continent by their parents.[25] In addition to the frightening narratives of Japanese flight from the continent at the end of the war, reports of atrocities committed by the Japanese Army began emerging through the Tokyo War Tribunal, which convened from May 1946 to November 1948. For more than two and a half years, the Japanese public learned of stories of forced labor, imprisonment, and massacres of civilian populations such as that in Nanking in 1937. These revelations fell on a weary public, coping with heavy feelings of betrayal, defeat, and personal culpability.

The end of the American occupation in 1952 opened a new era of reflection on the war and victimization. By the time Fuchikami spearheaded the production of *Manshū no Kaisō* in the late 1950s, it may be that sufficient time had passed to afford a nostalgic return to Manchuria. The conditions of the return in this large, visually rich volume, however, were quite specific, manifesting the ongoing relationship among privileged agency, aesthetics, and the production of continental memory. In a brief editorial statement for the volume, Fuchikami stated that he wanted the photographs featured in *Manshū no Kaisō* to communicate to readers "the aura of Manchuria and recollections of that time."[26] He meant the photographs to function as documents that could foster an understanding of the idealistic ethos and mystique of that period. In addition to their descriptive function, however, the photographs were also exquisite artistic artifacts. The quality of the volume beautifully presented the artistry of each work in the collection. The use of heavy, finely grained paper and the photogravure process, a printing method usually reserved for only high quality fine-art publications, underscores the value he placed on the photographs as artworks.[27] It is a fitting homage to the art photography produced on the continent during the Manchukuo era.

Of course, as many of the featured photographs were also included in *Manshū Graph* and *Manshū no Gaikan*, the "aura of Manchuria" Fuchikami referenced in his editorial statement was synonymous with Mantetsu's promotional lexicon and, by extension, the language of the

fig. 12
Baba Yashio, Bashafu, c. 1937. From *Manshū no Kaisō*, 3. Author's collection.

Japanese empire. The first page of *Manshū no Kaisō* features a photograph of a camel (fig. 11), one of the recurrent subjects that marked the exotic difference of the Manchurian frontier. On turning the page, the image *Bashafu* (Cart Man, fig. 12) by Baba Yashio presents a man wearing a fur-lined hat and heavy, padded coat, holding a rope whip. Both the portrait and image of the camel draw the reader in close to the subjects. This proximity and the quality of the printing allow for an appreciation of textures: the thick, soft hair of the camel, the bristles of the man's hat, and the wind-chafed texture of the cart-driver's cheeks. Neither subject directly engages the reader. The man and the animal are objects to be consumed, each looking to the right of the camera. These continental subjects compel us to look, yet do not look back. They become exotic icons of a distant land, once more offered up for Japanese consumption. Moreover, the minimal text opposite *Bashafu* demonstrates the abstract philosophical and aesthetic roles these figures play for Fuchikami:

"Manchurian nature conveys a deep philosophical impression; one can see that the Manchurian 'person' is a genuine 'person.' To the Manchurian land and people, be eternally beautiful."[28] Such images of continental people and animals became tropes during the Manchukuo era and operated without context; in *Manshū no Kaisō* they continued to float in a sea of signifiers unmoored from time and place, providing Fuchikami and his colleagues aesthetic inspiration.

Many of the later layouts are much more specific geographically and temporally, firmly locating Japanese readers in images of a past now long gone. These images are more poignant, as many portray Japanese settlers and tourists in Manchukuo, harkening back to a more idealistic time. For example, in the photographic layouts captioned "Dairen meisho tokoro dokoro" (Famous Places in Dalian: Here and There, fig. 13) and "Kantōshū" (Kwantung, fig. 14), smiling subjects relax on the beach, stroll in lush parks, or go ice-skating. The people inhabiting these sunny spaces are well-dressed in crisp white shirts and ties, fashionable swimwear, and beautifully patterned kimonos. The reader then embarks on a wider regional tour, taking in sights that include evocative factory landscapes, the crumbling rock walls of Fushun (fig. 15), and bucolic scenes of

fig. 13
"Dairen meisho tokoro dokoro," c. 1935. From *Manshū no Kaisō*, 16–17. Author's collection.

fig. 14 (opposite)
"Kantōshū," c. 1935. From *Manshū no Kaisō*, 18. Author's collection.

春の大正公園・旅順

秋のピクニック・大和尚山麓・響水寺

遠浅にめぐまれた夏家河子海岸

関　東　州

長い海岸線、恵まれた気候風土。ことに州内産のリンゴや新鮮な魚介は格別だった。それに金州と旅順は勝れた風致や戦蹟でくっきょうの行楽地。金州の古城。大和尚山、響水寺の紅葉と溪流。旅大バスの車窓にうつる星ケ浦、黒石礁、小平島、錦ケ浦の景勝。旅順の博物館、大正公園、戦蹟の巡遊。夏家河子、柳樹屯の臨海聚落など。それらは皆、ここに住む者の間に深く根ざしていた生活の落着きとよろこびを物語る州内ならではの感興をかもし出していた。

18

Japanese settler life on the vast frontier (fig. 16). These landscapes are among many that came directly from the pages of *Manshū Graph* and *Manshū Gaikan*.[29] The inclusion of these photographs from the Manchukuo period—originally intended to stimulate Japanese desire to visit the continent—in the postwar album is bittersweet. They no longer advertise a tantalizing destination. Rather, they revisit a now impossible place that exists only in memory. *Manshū no Kaisō* functions as a precious repository for this memory, a collection of artistic artifacts frozen in time. Moreover, as the original photographs had preceded widespread, popular knowledge of wartime atrocities, they scrub memory clean of militarism. They become critical tools for postwar aphasia.

To better understand the process of sanitizing and aestheticizing texts in the process of aphasia, it is useful to interrogate the function of nostalgia. Nostalgia, an affective relationship to the past, can be torturous in its contradictory production of both desire and denial. Svetlana Boym defines the complexities at work in the term's definition:

> Nostalgia (from *nostos*—return home, and *algia*—longing) is a longing for home that no longer exists or has never existed. Nostalgia is a sentiment of loss and displacement, but it is also a romance with one's

fig. 15
"Fushun no fūkei," c. 1937. From *Manshū no Kaisō*, 40–41. Author's collection.

> own fantasy. . . . Nostalgia inevitably reappears as a defense mechanism in a time of accelerated rhythms of life and historical upheavals.[30]

As this definition indicates, "place" may be an abstraction, some place that in fact never existed; rather, the paramount preoccupation of nostalgia is with time. This helps to clarify what Fuchikami may have longed for in the 1950s. It was not the physical land of Manchuria or Manchukuo, per se. Rather, it was what Manchukuo had come to signify: a *time* of unfettered Japanese artistic exploration and bourgeois indulgence. It was also a time when Fuchikami and his cohort were not burdened with the postwar knowledge of coercion, violence, and abandonment. In fact, a nostalgic return to the continent and recuperation of the art photographs produced during the Manchukuo period *requires* erasure, even if temporarily. It is productive to evaluate *Manshū no Kaisō* in terms of what Boym later describes as "restorative nostalgia," a "perfect snapshot" signifying a "return to the original stasis, the prelapsarian moment."[31] According to Boym's paradigm, the past does not show "decay"; rather, it remains "eternally young," posited as a "value for the present."[32] Fuchikami stakes the value of *Manshū no Kaisō* in retrieving art objects—reproduced with incredible artistic sensitivity in this collection—from the oblivion of a dark, imperial history. The volume is an artistic fantasy, an aphasia made possible through nostalgia for a simpler, more idealistic time.

The relationship among the photographs, nostalgia, and empire emerges textually in the first pages of the collection. Here, contributor Aikawa Yoshisuke,[33] the former head of Manchurian Heavy Industries (Mangyō), states "[h]olding this photo collection in one's hand is not only to experience things that have passed; it is also something to delight in savoring as if playing in one's old home town."[34] The sentimentality of Aikawa's recommendation of this book is unmistakable, particularly as he likens the feeling one has in consuming it to being in one's home village (*kokyō*). That this sentimental description comes from the former director of a major continental office (a position that eventually resulted in his designation as a Class A war criminal) speaks to how positions of power and favorable conditions of return influenced these recollections of Manchuria: Aikawa returned to Japan when he left his position in 1942, while Fuchikami himself moved to Tokyo from Dalian in 1941.[35] Each returned to Japan of his own volition and with assets intact, unlike Japanese repatriates, or *hikiagesha*, whose abominable experiences at the end of the war resulted in a shared lexicon that included phrases like "with only the clothes on my back" (*ki no mi ki no mama*) and "without a red cent" (*hadaka ikkan*).[36] Moreover, Aikawa and Fuchikami did not suffer the social stigmatization of Japanese returnees from the continent. This is not to say that *hikiagesha* never felt nostalgic for time spent in Manchuria.

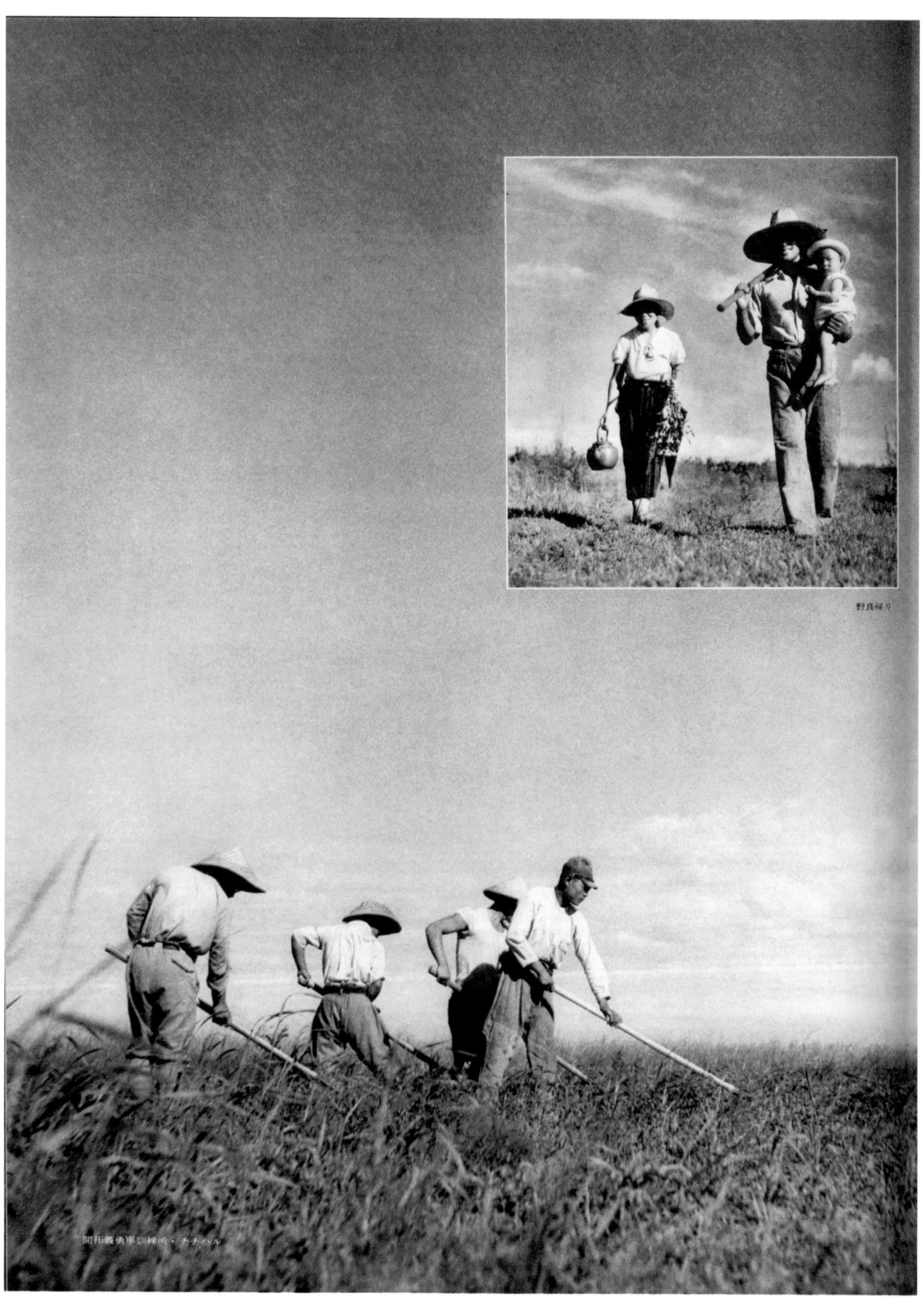

野良帰り

開拓義勇軍訓練所・チチハル

However, as Boym notes, nostalgia for a place is taboo among those who leave it "under difficult personal and political circumstances."[37] Public nostalgia for Manchuria was for the privileged, and an aesthetic return was only for the most elite sensibility.

While it may seem as though the union of nostalgia and aesthetics in *Manshū no Kaisō* completely occluded critical postwar narratives, the essay titled "Memories of Manchuria" (Manshū no omoide) reveals a more self-reflective perspective from art photographer Unoki Satoshi. Unoki expressed his personal struggle with the disjuncture between the "beauty and enjoyment" of his memories and "the gruesome reality (*seisan na genjitsu*) at the end of the war, that goes beyond the imagination to repatriation."[38] Here, he exposes the rupture between the fantasy of Manchukuo as a site for aesthetic exploration and the violence of postwar stories narrating the return of Japanese settlers from the continent. His photograph, *Jōheki* (Castle Wall, 1937) (fig. 3), also featured in the volume, does not reveal this inner turmoil during the Manchukuo period. Yet, it is clear that his relationship to Manchuria has become more complex and conflicted. For Unoki, there is no aphasia, no warm retreat into a timeless past. He states: "If remembering, I intend to compare the afterglow of the beauty of the continent, which has warmed my heart for years, and the reality of suffering."[39] This statement articulates the emotional complexity of remembering Manchukuo in 1958. How does one reconcile a deep connection to Manchuria and warm memories of artistic discovery and beauty with the horrors of repatriation? Moreover, his statement indicates a questioning of what was "real" on the continent. By associating "reality" with returning Japanese colonists, Unoki suggests that his joyful memories of the continent were then somehow false, revealing feelings of ideological betrayal and complicity felt by many Japanese in the years following defeat. For Unoki, ultimately, remembering Manchuria was not a means of nostalgic escape, but rather an opportunity to reconcile the past with the present.

Conclusion

Despite the inclusion of Unoki's self-reflective admission, *Manshū no Kaisō* is far from a cultural confessional. It is a rich repository of past artistic practices, its visually stunning presentation functioning as a physical reminder of the privileged legacy that such images and memories bear. Indeed, aesthetics act as a screen that mediates postwar memory of Japanese Manchuria. Two decades earlier, these photographs functioned as evocative instruments of persuasion. Atmospheric, dynamic, illuminated, and textural, the photographs produced by Fuchikami and his colleagues of the MPAA tantalized the eye while selling an image of Manchukuo as a space for consumption. They transformed landscapes and people into pleasurable aesthetic objects, ripe for scopic exploration by Japanese

fig. 16
"Hoku-Man kaitakumura," c. 1937. From *Manshū no Kaisō*, 78. Author's collection.

bourgeois readers. During the Manchukuo era, these images were sublime commodities that sold empire in cultural terms. In 1958, they became conduits for a nostalgic return to the continent.

It would seem that the desire to embark on a virtual, aesthetic return to Manchuria was shared by many Japanese. Keigadō published new editions of *Manshū no Kaisō* in 1966, 1968, and 1971. Given the importance of Manchukuo in the Japanese empire, its memory carried strong political and social stakes in postwar Japan and the rest of Asia. This photographic collection only enhanced the postwar affective potency of Manchukuo. As Susan Sontag has noted, "photographs actively promote nostalgia. Photography is an elegiac art, a twilight art. Most subjects are, just by virtue of being photographed, touched with pathos."[40] Indeed, this collection is at once replete with idealism and poignancy, evident in its erasures as much as its aesthetic inclusions. Contradictory and complex, it elegantly testifies to the fraught stakes of remembering Manchuria in postwar Japan. More broadly speaking, it points to the fragmentation of (post)colonial discourse, the aphasia, which occurs as individuals attempt to express their experiences in the context of a dark, imperial past.

NOTES

1. Prior to 1942, Jinzhou was called Chin Hsien. Fuchikami uses this earlier designation in *Manshū no Kaisō*. See *Manshū no Kaisō*, ed. Fuchikami Hakuyō (Tokyo: Keigadō, 1958), 51.
2. The South Manchuria Railway Company was founded in 1906, when the southernmost section of the Chinese Eastern Railway was transferred to Japanese control.
3. Ann Laura Stoler, "Colonial Aphasia: Race and Disabled Histories in France," *Public Culture* 23, no. 1 (2011): 125.
4. The Japanese army had initially won this territory ten years earlier after defeating the Chinese army in the first Sino-Japanese War (1894–95); however, the Tripartite Intervention of France, Russia, and Germany stripped Japan of its territorial prize.
5. Louise Young, *Japan's Total Empire: Manchuria and the Culture of Wartime Imperialism* (Berkeley: University of California Press, 1998), 23–24.
6. David Tucker, "City Planning without Cities: Order and Chaos in Utopian Manchukuo," in *Crossed Histories: Manchuria in the Age of Empire*, ed. Mariko Asano Tamanoi (Honolulu: Association for Asian Studies and University of Hawai'i Press, 2005), 55.
7. Sandra Wilson, *Manchurian Crisis and Japanese Society, 1931–33* (London: Routledge, 2002), 56.
8. Prasenjit Duara, *Sovereignty and Authenticity: Manchukuo and the East Asian Modern* (Lanham, MD: Rowman & Littlefield, 2003).
9. It is important to acknowledge the myriad relationships Japanese people had with these slogans. Indeed, some Japanese officials merely paid lip service to the concepts of "peace, harmony, and equality" and relished Japanese positions of dominance in Manchuria. However, others (primarily from the political left) were genuinely optimistic about the social and political ideals the state represented.
10. Duara, *Sovereignty and Authenticity*, 5.
11. Yamamuro Shin'ichi, *Manchuria under Japanese Dominion*, trans. Joshua A. Fogel (Philadelphia: University of Pennsylvania Press, 2006), 3–4. Yamamuro's study was originally published in Japan as *Kimera: Manshūkoku no shōzō* (Tokyo: Chūō Kōronsha, 1993).
12. Annika A. Culver, *Glorify the Empire: Japanese Avant-Garde Propaganda in Manchukuo* (Vancouver: University of British Columbia Press, 2013), 76–82.

13. Young, *Japan's Total Empire*, 267.
14. Roland Marchand, *Creating the Corporate Soul: The Rise of Public Relations and Corporate Imagery in American Big Business* (Berkeley: University of California Press, 1998), 9, 167.
15. Iizawa Kōtarō, *Fuchikami Hakuyō to Manshū Shashin Sakka Kyōkai* (Tokyo: Iwanami Shoten, 1998), 4. See also Kaneko Ryūichi, *Nihon no Pikutoriarizumu: fūkei he no manazashi* (Tokyo: Tokyo Metropolitan Museum of Photography, 1992), 130.
16. See Iizawa, *Fuchikami Hakuyō*, 4; Kaneko, *Nihon no Pikutoriarizumu*, 130.
17. While I use italics to denote proper names of photographs presented as titled artworks, I use quotation marks to refer to captions.
18. Little text accompanies the photographs in this collection. The examples discussed here feature only the basic descriptive captions "Shina fuzoku: buyō" and "Harbin: Sungari suieijō."
19. This virtual escape in the pages of *Manshū Graph* would be fleeting, as the magazine increasingly featured wartime themes from 1942 to 1944. This change occurred after Fuchikami had left Manchukuo at the beginning of 1941 and signaled increasing pressure by the Kwantung Army on Mantetsu's promotional content.
20. Mantetsu published these issues in June 1936, June 1937, and January 1940.
21. David Spurr, *The Rhetoric of Empire: Colonial Discourse in Journalism, Travel Writing, and Imperial Administration* (Durham, NC: Duke University Press, 1993), 57.
22. Fuchikami Hakuyō, *Manshū shashin dokuhon* (Dalian: Minami Manshū Katsudō Kabushiki Kaisha, 1938); Fuchikami Hakuyō, "Taiyō," *Hikaru Oka* 2, no. 1 (Jan. 30, 1938): unpaginated; Fuchikami Hakuyō, caption for *The Setting Sun* (Rakujitsu), *Manshū shashin nenkan* (Dalian: Minami Manshū Tetsudō Kabushiki Kaisha, 1930), 77.
23. The Flex camera (the apparatus of choice for American art photographer Alfred Stieglitz) cost several hundred yen, a considerable sum at a time when a Japanese textile worker earned on average 1.16 yen per day. *Japan-Manchoukuo Year Book* (Tokyo: Japan-Manchoukuo Year Book Co, 1934), 248.
24. Young, *Japan's Total Empire*, 409. See also Mariko Asano Tamanoi, "Between Colonial Racism and Global Capitalism: Japanese Repatriates from Northeast China since 1946," *American Ethnologist* 30, no. 4 (November 2003): 528.
25. Young, *Japan's Total Empire*, 410. See also Mariko Asano Tamanoi, "A Road to 'A Redeemed Mankind': The Politics of Memory among the Former Japanese Peasant Settlers in Manchuria," *The South Atlantic Quarterly* 99, no. 1 (Winter 2000): 165
26. Fuchikami, "Atogaki," *Manshū no Kaisō*, 96.
27. *Manshū no Kaisō* cost two thousand yen. This was a formidable sum at a time when the average monthly wage of an employee working in a textile mill was 11,546 yen. See *Nihon tōkei nenkan*, vol. 11 (Tokyo: Nihon Tōkei Kyōkai: Mainichi Shinbunsha, 1960), 334. Nonetheless, the amount was fairly consistent with prices for other photography compilations.
28. Front matter, *Manshū no Kaisō*, 2.
29. The factory scene on the center left of left-hand page of fig. 15 was featured in the January 1939 art photography issue of *Manshū Graph*; the mining scene on the bottom right of the left-hand page was featured in the June 1937 art photography issue. The Fushun rock wall was repeated in both the 1935 and 1936 *Manshū Gaikan*. The photograph of the farmer holding the child came from a series of images taken in the late 1930s; similar photographs of him with his idealized continental family appeared in both the 1939 *Manshū Gaikan* and the 1939 art photography issue of *Manshū Graph*.
30. Sventlana Boym, *The Future of Nostalgia* (New York: Basic Books, 2001), xiii–xiv.
31. Ibid., 49.
32. Ibid.
33. Aikawa Yoshisuke is also known as Ayukawa Yoshisuke.
34. Aikawa Yoshisuke, "Suisen no kotoba," *Manshū no Kaisō*, 7.
35. Young, *Japan's Total Empire*, 217.
36. Lori Watt, *When Empire Comes Home: Repatriation and Reintegration in Postwar Japan* (Cambridge, MA: Harvard University Asia Center, 2009), 9. Watt notes that the literal translation of *hadaka ikkan* is "completely naked."
37. Boym, *The Future of Nostalgia*, xv.
38. Unoki Satoshi, "Manshū no omoide," *Manshū no kaisō*, 20–21.
39. Ibid.
40. Susan Sontag, *On Photography* (New York: Picador, 1973 [1977]), 15.

fig. 1
Werkstätte Emmy Zweybrück-Prochaska, chicken farm and nursery, turned and painted wooden toys, ca. 1926. Photo: *Deutsche Kunst und Dekoration* 59 (1926–27): 201.

CHILD'S PLAY? MEMORY AND NOSTALGIA IN THE TOYS OF THE WIENER WERKSTÄTTE

Megan Brandow-Faller

Megan Brandow-Faller, assistant professor of history at Kingsborough Community College, City University of New York, completed her doctorate in cultural history at Georgetown University. Her current book manuscript examines Vienna's "Female Secession," a movement provocatively reclaiming the stereotypes surrounding "women's art" and carrying the Klimt Group's artistic legacy into the interwar years. Her most recent publications deal with the interwar expressionist ceramics of the Wiener Werkstätte and "Art for the Child" at the 1908 Vienna Kunstschau exhibition.

An exhibition for what one critic called "an entirely new public... children small and large" opened at Vienna's Neue Galerie in December 1924.[1] The Austrian Artists' Christmas Bazaar featured handcrafted artistic toys, books, and games designed by artists associated with the Wiener Werkstätte (Vienna Workshops) and the Werkstätte Emmy Zweybrück-Prochaska (Emmy Zweybrück-Prochaska Workshops). The toys on view offered an alternative to mass-market technological miniatures—derided by one reviewer as "fashionable rubbish" purchased by parents ignorant of their children's preferences for simple playthings—that replicated the adult world in painstaking detail.[2] The toys at the exhibition, instead, seemed inspired by formal abstraction, stylization, and naïveté, evidenced in pieces produced by students at the Werkstätte Emmy Zweybrück-Prochaska just two years after the exhibition (fig. 1).

While a few critics joked that the proliferation of child's play at the Neue Galerie—widely regarded as the major advocate of German and Austrian Expressionism—might detract from its reputation as a forum for the "weighty seriousness of modern art," most reviewers grasped that important issues were at stake in this toy exhibition.[3] Favorable reviews framed the exhibition in terms of the meaning the toys held for adults, rather than for children, as expressions of nostalgia for handcrafted eighteenth- and nineteenth-century German wooden playthings and the timeless, supposedly purer and less-commercialized childhood they embodied.[4] This nostalgia for childhood fused with the desire—central to the aesthetic vision of the Wiener Werkstätte and the broader Viennese Secession movement from which it sprang—for a return to a childlike state of naïveté that transcended received ways of seeing; the idea, as Charles Baudelaire famously explicated in his *Painter of Modern Life* (1863), that "genius is nothing more or less than childhood regained at will."[5]

Tracing the overlapping discourses on memory, nostalgia, and modernist aesthetics that surfaced in the 1924 Neue Galerie exhibition back to the turn of the century, this essay analyzes toys created by artists associated with the Vienna Secession and the closely connected Wiener Werkstätte (1903–32), as well as the ideas that surrounded these objects. The Secession was launched in 1897 when Gustav Klimt (1862–1918), in response to the conservative artistic and commercial policies of the Genoßenschaft der bildender Künstler Wiens (Viennese Artists' Guild), founded a new league dedicated to creative freedom, originality, and artistic timeliness; the Viennese Secessionist motto ("To the Age Its Art/To Art Its Freedom") expressed this spirit. Given that the Secession's founding was framed as a generational struggle of *die Jungen* (the young) versus *die Alten* (the old), the idea of childhood as a time of artistic and material innovation was an apt trope for the Secessionists' broader goals of creative liberation from staid academicism. Yet, despite the fact that adult designers appropriated the stylistic vocabulary of children's drawings, Secessionist toys were designed at least as much with an eye to the desires—and memories—of adults as those of children. Whether or not the toys were ultimately intended to be played with by children or simply collected by adults, such playthings had to be marketed to the latter and appeal to their sensibilities if they were to find purchasers. Indeed, the aesthetic qualities of child art famously "discovered" by the Vienna Secessionists (for instance, a privileging of expressivity over verisimilitude, a penchant for stylized abstraction, and integration of pictorial information from dream and fantasy realms) were as much a discursive construct reflecting adult aesthetic sensibilities as characteristics universally inherent in children's drawings. What the toys ultimately reveal is adults' nostalgic preoccupation with childhood—both their personal childhoods and the idea of childhood as a metaphor for artistic newness.

Sacred Spring: Youth and Nostalgia in Secessionist Vienna

As suggested by critical reactions to the Neue Galerie's Christmas Bazaar, Secessionist toys expressed a longing on the part of their adult makers, purchasers, and critics to return to a similarly naive state of artistic development as the child. For the Viennese avant-garde, as well as counterparts elsewhere in Europe, children's art stood for such qualities as objectivity of vision, creative spontaneity, and expressive immediacy. The fascination with the childlike should be seen as part of the broader cult of primitivism that attracted European avant-gardes as a means of subverting academic formulas stifling creative authenticity: the untutored child, uncorrupted by socialization, was thought to be a sort of domestic "noble savage," at a similar stage of evolutionary development as prehistoric people or those living in folk cultures removed from urban civilization.[6]

Just as artists like Pablo Picasso, André Derain, and Maurice de Vlaminck famously "discovered" the formal qualities of African tribal objects around 1906–07, modernists also began to appreciate children's drawings as artworks rather than as socio-psychological artifacts. To avant-gardes across Europe, children's art seemed to possess modernist tendencies in its formal simplification and apparent eschewal of realism. This tendency was particularly pronounced in Vienna, where Secessionist Franz Cižek's progressive *Jugendkunstkursen* (youth art classes) were the first to offer children the chance to draw from their imagination; Cižek is routinely credited as being "largely responsible for bringing child art into the gallery."[7] But the Secessionist appreciation of child art was far more sophisticated than straightforward visual appropriation. Addressing the primitivist "double-exposure" in the catalogue to the controversial 1984 exhibition *"Primitivism" in 20th Century Art: Affinity of the Tribal and the Modern* at the Museum of Modern Art, New York, curator William Rubin pointed to the ways in which primitivizing artists inflected tribal objects with their own values, arguing that the Parisian avant-garde "became interested and began to collect primitive objects only because their own explorations had suddenly made such objects relevant to their work. . . . The 'discovery' of African art. . .took place when it was needed."[8] Primitivism was, thus, an aesthetic filter through which the art of peripheral, supposedly less rational cultures was absorbed as a means of subverting post-Renaissance aesthetic value systems. In an analogous way, child art was for the Vienna Secessionists not an accidental discovery, but a discursive construction that reinforced their own aesthetic rebellion.

The Vienna Secessionists' valorization of the childlike was rooted in their reverence for youth as a sacred spring of artistic renewal, or, as Max Burckhardt argued in the inaugural issue of the Secessionist journal *Ver Sacrum*, "the spirit of youth wafting through the spring…[as] a driving force for artistic creation."[9] The Secessionists' identification with the springtime of humanity as preserved in the *Urkunst* (primeval art) of the child reflected the spirit of rebellious protest central to Secessionist philosophies. The movement had its genesis in spring 1897, when a group of young artists led by Klimt marched out of a meeting of the conservative artists' guild, or Künstlergenoßenschaft, in protest of its supposed disdain for innovative styles that lacked an assured commercial value (what pro-Secessionist critic Hermann Bahr referred to as the guild's "market hall" policies).[10] While the split between the *Alten* and *Jungen* was not purely along stylistic lines, the early Secessionist movement was

fig. 2
Moritz Nähr, group portrait of Vienna Secession, from the Fourteenth Secession Exhibition, 1902. © Austrian Bildarchiv.

preoccupied with stylistic and metaphorical rebirth. Best reflecting these early "proclamations of youthful vitality" were Alfred Roller's woodcut for the cover of the inaugural issue of *Ver Sacrum* featuring a tree sapling whose roots break free from a restrictive barrel, and Klimt's 1898 drawing of a youthful *Nuda Veritas,* which expressed in visual terms the idea of contemporary art as a mirror of truth.[11] The Secessionists' self-identification with youth is also suggested by the informal group photograph taken before the opening of its well-known spring 1902 exhibition, themed around Klimt's *Beethoven Frieze* and Max Klinger's polychrome statue of the composer (fig. 2). The Secessionists' casual poses, dress, and comportment in the photograph suggest a disdain for bourgeois conventions, much like a rebellious child's defiance of adult rules.

It was after the group's so-called heroic years (1897–1905) that artists associated with the Secession—especially those connected to the Wiener Werkstätte and to the Klimt Group, which by then had seceded from the Secession—began to engage constructions of the childlike on a more immediate visual level. Reflecting its intellectual origins in the philosophies of the English Arts and Crafts movement and the model of C. R. Ashbee's Guild of Handcraft, the Wiener Werkstätte (established

fig. 3
Folk-art toys from the collection of Emmy Zweybrück-Prochaska. Photo: *Der Wiener Kunstwanderer* 2, no. 3 (March 1934): 7.

in May 1903) began with metalwork, but after several months expanded to encompass leatherwork, bookbinding, and cabinetmaking, and also began undertaking architectural projects. Werkstätte founders Josef Hoffmann (1870–1956) and Kolomon Moser (1868–1918) believed that the finely crafted furniture and decorative objects produced by the Werkstätte could not only beautify everyday life, but also usher in closer contact among artists, craftsmen, and society at large—an approach reflecting the philosophies of members of the Klimt Group more broadly.[12] Toy making was one of the fields of work that resulted from the cross-pollination of art, architecture, and design that thrived in this milieu.

The valorization of the "childlike" and its conflation with the "primitive" provided the foundations for the Viennese avant-garde's rediscovery of handmade *Bauernspielzeuge* (peasant toys). Informed by the desire to integrate art and artifact, Secessionist toymakers looked to a preindustrial era when toys were products of guild workshops—before, as art historian Karl Gröber put it in his landmark cultural history of toys, the factory robbed "the toy of the individual face that made old toys so charming."[13] Such carved and turned wooden toys, produced by cottage-industry networks in the Erzgebirge, Grödnertal, Oberammergau, and Berchtesgaden regions, were collected by Viennese artists including Hoffmann, Dagobert Peche, and Egon Schiele. Hoffmann assembled an impressive collection through regular trips to Viennese flea markets and the Erzgebirge region bordering his hometown. His students recalled how their professor's afternoons were spent "poking around all the places where he found old toys for his toy collection" and how he presented them with "pictures of primitive toys" from his personal reference library as a creative stimulus to their own work.[14]

In addition to this longing for the preindustrial golden age of German toys, cultural nostalgia for handmade playthings tended to overlap with Secessionists' personal nostalgia for toys from their own childhoods. For instance, objects from the childhood toy box of the teacher, children's book illustrator, and toy maker Emmy Zweybrück-Prochaska (1890–1956) formed the basis of the extensive collection of *Volkstümliche Spielzeuge* (folk-art toys) she amassed as an adult, supplemented by further acquisitions from East Asia, the Americas, and Oceania (fig. 3). That the

fig. 4
Emmy Zweybrück-Prochaska, hand-painted and stenciled cabinet from the artist's apartment. Universität für angewandte Kunst Wien, Kunstsammlung und Archiv.

collection was prominently displayed in Zweybrück-Prochaska's hand-painted and stenciled cabinet—whose design grafts the childlike onto the tradition of brightly painted Central European *Bauernschränke* (peasant cupboards)—illustrates how the artist's signature style tapped distinct, yet intellectually linked sources of artistic naïveté (fig. 4). Recalling her collection's genesis, Zweybrück-Prochaska suggested that it provided her with an avenue to reconnect not only with her own childhood, but also with her toys' intended users:

> When a little girl of eight, I was very fond of those carved wooden toys that are exhibited for sale in the stalls of our fairs. I used to buy some of them for the coppers from my saving-box. These primitive, queer looking things form the origin of a now very rich collection of toys. And whenever I look at all those tiny, colorful objects, I feel that the best of them are those which were the playmates of my early childhood. The toys we used to play with have kept the faint perfume of remembrance.[15]

Recalling a crudely carved wooden horse as her very first purchase at a Christmas market, Zweybrück-Prochaska posited linkages between adulthood and a "childlike" state of creativity:

> This primitive little horse gave me the first motivation to collect toys. . . . Soon a longing developed in me to make similar things, equally abstract, symbolic, full of color and luster as those that I discovered on my wanderings, [yet] simultaneously bearing the stamp of our own times.[16]

Zweybrück-Prochaska, who was widely recognized as an embroiderer and children's book illustrator, also ran a progressive craft school for girls founded in 1915, which was based on pedagogical principles similar to those of Franz Cižek, with whom she studied at the Austrian Kunstgewerbeschule (School of Applied Arts). Connected to the school was an applied arts workshop—the Werkstätte Emmy Zweybrück-Prochaska, mentioned earlier—teaching pupils aged fourteen to eighteen proficiency in crafts, such as production of toys, lace, embroidery, textiles, ceramics, clothing, children's books, and graphic art, as well as undertaking interior design projects. There, she cultivated in her students a design language characterized by stylized naïveté and deliberate awkwardness (see fig. 1) that drew inspiration from the colors and patterns of the vernacular toys of the kind she collected.[17]

Not all commentators shared Zweybrück-Prochaska's belief that the "childlike" could be excavated and reanimated from adult memory. While displaying a similar nostalgia for eighteenth- and nineteenth-century German toys, Karl Gröber believed that the child's ability to transcend everyday reality and enter a parallel world of illusion was something that could never be regained later in life:

> The fantasy of a grown-up, however animated it may be, cannot recover the wealth of visions which roll past the heart of every child when it is absorbed in its toys, quiet and oblivious of its surroundings. The world of reality melts away and the young soul is wrapped up in another dream-like existence.... Once in a while, when he takes in his hand a poor little toy from his youth, a flash of memory, phantomlike and vague, gleams in the grown-up. A little gap opens into the thick curtains of the past, through which he catches a glimpse of the long-gone magical land of childhood.[18]

But, Gröber maintained, this fantasy world of memory "dissolves into gray mist and the adult is overcome by a bittersweet nostalgic feeling."[19] It was on this very point—the ability of adult artists to return to a childlike state of vision, as opposed to merely longing for childhood—where Zweybrück-Prochaska parted ways with Gröber. The best toys, she argued, are "made by children or people who work like children—half playing, half-dreaming. . .artists and peasants. . . hit the true child-like note."[20] For Zweybrück-Prochaska, Hoffmann, and other Secessionists, vernacular folk toys unearthed vanished memories of "the magical land of childhood" while simultaneously serving as positive examples of naïveté and simplicity in design. Complex layers of memory and nostalgia informed the design of the toys of the Wiener Werkstätte.

Wiener Werkstätte Toys for Children and Adults

Around 1905–06, the Wiener Werkstätte began producing artistic objects for children to complement its aim of an all-encompassing aestheticization of everyday life. The Werkstätte's commencement of toy production coincided with a shift away from the geometrical style that defined its early "purist" phase (1904–06), toward work reflecting the interest in folk art and children's art that exploded around 1906–07. Women artists, such as Fanny Harlfinger-Zakucka (1873–1953) and Minka Podhájská (1881–1963), were particularly celebrated as toy designers and children's book illustrators, which is not surprising given contemporary perceptions of women's supposedly intuitive understanding of children's minds.[21] Female designers negotiated such essentialist stereotypes of women's natural connection to children by harnessing a childlike formal vocabulary that played on their own status as naive outsiders to Viennese institutions.

As early as 1903, even before Wiener Werkstätte toy production began, Podhájská demonstrated her fascination with vernacular toys in a boldly stenciled image that appeared in the book *Schablonen Drucke* (Stencil Prints) that she and Harlfinger-Zakucka illustrated (fig. 5). Her illustration shows wood-turned *Bauernspielzeuge* of the kind praised in Gröber's book and eagerly collected by Hoffmann and Zweybrück-Prochaska, while simultaneously drawing on the flattened rhythmic vocabulary that Secessionist artists associated with both folk art and child art. A wooden chess set from 1906 designed by Harlfinger-Zakucka and Podhájská together echoes the forms captured by Podhájská's earlier illustration (figs. 6, 7). The simply formed and painted figures evoke the bold colors of vernacular folk toys and traditional peasant household artifacts, such as textiles, ceramics, and painted furniture, with which the creativity of the untutored child was conflated in Secessionist discourse. Clearly, however, the work refers as much to sophisticated Secessionist design language, particularly in the nod to the characteristic Werkstätte checkerboard pattern bordering the queen figures' clothing, which simultaneously reflects the artist's interest in historical costume as filtered through a sense of folk naïveté. That the set was bought by Otto and Eugenia Primavesi—important Klimt collectors and the Werkstätte's main financial backers in the postwar period—for their daughter Mäda (who would go on to become a devoted student of the art pedagogue Franz Cižek) attests to the appeal of the nostalgic impulses expressed by these objects.

fig. 5 (opposite, top) Minka Podhájská, *Schablonen Drucke*, c. 1903. Princeton University Library, Cotsen Children's Library, Department of Rare Books and Special Collections.

figs. 6, 7 (opposite, bottom; following spread) Fanny Harlfinger-Zakucka and Minka Podhájská, chess set, turned and painted wood, made by the Wiener Werkstätte, heights: 2–3 1/2 in. (5–8.7 cm), 1906. Wolfgang Bauer/Bel Etage Kunsthandel, Vienna.

Following the Werkstätte's 1905 exhibition at the Galerie Miethke, Werkstätte toys and other objects for children debuted to a broader public in the January 1906 issue of *Kind und Kunst* (Child and Art), a lavish art periodical dedicated to "awakening a love of art in children through play."[22] The journal was published by progressive Darmstadt entrepreneur Alexander Koch, whose publishing house owned exclusive rights to reproductions of Werkstätte products; its page layout and border monograms were presented in typical Werkstätte *Gesamtkunstwerk* (total work of art) fashion. The jocular text accompanying the twenty-eight-page spread suggests that the

toys were animated by a particularly Viennese penchant for musicality, sensuality, and the diverse folk arts of its imperial hinterlands. Viennese modernist interpretations of traditional *Bauernspielzeuge*, despite the stiff bowling pin-like shapes resulting from construction at the turning lathe, were found to be enlivened by a dynamic energy and *Lebensfreude* (love of life) rooted in their evocation both of the bourgeois and/or aristocratic lifestyles associated with (ostensibly) happier eras from the Habsburg past, and of the wooden toys remembered by the magazine's upper-class readers from their own childhoods.

Rather like Podhájská's stenciled image, which acquired its aesthetic appeal through its reductionist forms, the stiff-yet-lively turned forms designed by her and Harlfinger-Zakucka seemed, as the accompanying text put it, to invite the journal's readers to play with them "right now. . .even though they are just in the picture and not real."[23] Harlfinger's trademark "Viennese Types" borrowed freely from the costumes of golden ages in the city's past, yet her interpretations are offered up in a simplified manner drawing on the stylized anonymity typical of vernacular toys. The idea of the Biedermeier era as representing a time "when the 'golden heart' of Vienna had beaten proudest, when the Congress had waltzed and Austria had been the paternal protector of order in Europe"[24] is subtly

fig. 8
Fanny Harlfinger-Zakucka and Minka Podhájská, Biedermeier pair with poodles, turned and painted wooden figurines, c. 1906. Photo: *Kind und Kunst* 3, no. 4 (January 1906): 134.

fig. 9
Fanny Harlfinger-Zakucka, Rococo pair, turned and painted wooden figurines, c. 1906. Photo: *Kind und Kunst* 3, no. 4 (January 1906): 130.

fig. 10
Studio of Madame d'Ora, with staged toys designed by Fanny Harlfinger-Zakucka, c. 1920. Private collection, Vienna.

conveyed by Harlfinger-Zakucka's Biedermeier couple, seemingly attired for a winter stroll through a park (fig. 8). Similarly reflecting the artist's modernist filtering of historical costume with a simplified design language were her Rococo figurines, illustrated in the same spread, endowed with references to the golden age of the Empress Maria Theresa, who reigned from 1740 to 1780 (fig. 9).

In other images from the periodical, one sees such Rococo figures posed with Biedermeier types next to Spanish courtiers and Turkish figures. Evidently Harlfinger-Zakucka was less concerned with historical accuracy than with awakening latent fantasies of children and adults who could create their own narratives about the figures. The likelihood that Harlfinger's nostalgic toys served as a source of amusement to adults—potentially awakening the "magical land of childhood" Gröber believed was hermetically sealed from adulthood—is suggested by a mysterious 1920 photograph (fig. 10) from the studio of Viennese portrait photographer Dora Kallmus, or Madame d'Ora, in which the figurines have been posed in a theatrical setting redolent of Diego Velázquez's *Las Meninas* (1656). The "sort of animated [quality]" that reviewers frequently found present in the figures is apparent in the elaborately staged image, in which a crinolined infanta figurine, flanked by a retinue of courtiers and what appear to be dwarfs, proceeds into a stately hall.[25] So strong are the connotative resonances to the Spanish Habsburg

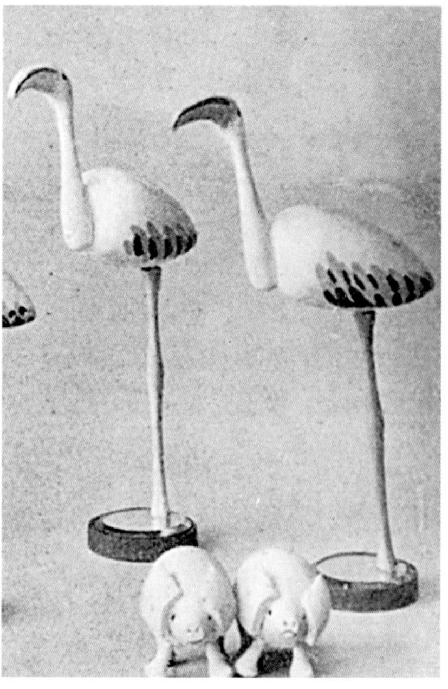

fig. 11
Minka Podhájská, flamingos and pigs, turned and painted wood, c. 1906. Photo: *The Studio* 38, no. 159 (June 1906): 217.

fig. 12
Minka Podhájská, quail, turned and painted wood, c. 1906. Photo: *Kind und Kunst* 3, no. 4 (January 1906): 133.

golden age immortalized by Velázquez, particularly the ways in which both artists play with various levels of reality, image, and reflection, that it is easy to forget that the mise-en-scene is one of miniature playthings.

The toys of Podhájská, Harlfinger-Zakucka's frequent collaborator, were likewise featured in the journal, illustrating the designer's trademark interpretations of exotic animals and fantasy creatures. While grounded in the wood turning methods predominant in traditional toy making, Podhájská used the turning lathe to produce highly original, idiosyncratic, and delicate forms, often referencing their manner of construction in a humorous fashion. These wooden animals—poodles, flamingos, pigs, quail—were enlivened by a sense of dynamic, explosive energy (figs. 11, 12). The text accompanying the images was written in a seemingly naive style targeted to *Kind und Kunst*'s adult subscribers that, through its childlike visual description, implied that readers might transcend adult ways of seeing and relive childhood memories by purchasing such objects for their offspring. The childlike voice observed that the carefully groomed poodles, standing behind the Biedermeier couple on turned legs not unlike those of a chair (fig. 8), "seemed proud of their coiffure, and rightly so."[26] Another anonymous reviewer employed a similarly humorous voice, comparing the poodles' smooth, cylindrical bodies to "a cannon connected to a gun-carriage: naturally, four-footed which is much more practical than the actual cannon's wheels."[27]

Although Viennese critics found toy making essentially suited to women, male Wiener Werkstätte artists like Hoffmann, Moser, Peche, and Carl Otto Czeschka were equally interested in bringing art into children's

figs. 13, 14
Koloman Moser, wooden building sets, 1905/06. Photo: *Kind und Kunst* 3, no. 4 (January 1906): 129, 130.

everyday lives while appealing to their parents' aesthetic and nostalgic impulses.[28] For these artists embodying the multitalented *Tausendsassa* (artistic jack-of-all-trades) type, central to the Werkstätte ideal, toy making complemented their broader artistic output in furniture and graphic design and harkened back to the preindustrial era of German handicraft when toys, as Walter Benjamin put it in his favorable review of Gröber's book, were the "side-products of guild-regulated handcraft-workshops."[29] That his illustrated children's books and wooden playthings represent a lesser-known aspect of Moser's artistic oeuvre exemplifies how design history has treated toy making as a distraction from more "serious" pursuits.[30] Illustrated close to Podhájská's toys in the special issue of *Kind und Kunst* were Moser's wooden building sets, including two variations of *Die Stadt* (the town) from 1905 or 1906 (figs. 13, 14). It was particularly the second version, capturing the timelessness of an idyllic village, with its spires,

fig. 15
Koloman Moser, Easter egg, painted wood, length: 3 ½ in. (9 cm), c. 1906. © Bonham's Images.

fig. 16
Josef Hoffmann, Easter egg, silver inlaid with semiprecious stones, c. 1906. Photo: *Kind und Kunst* 3, no. 4 (1906): 140.

half-timbered buildings, and trees rendered in a stylized geometric fashion, that might have resonated with adult purchasers. Other Moser toys featured in the journal, such as his exquisitely designed wooden Easter eggs, suggested that even though children were the end-users, buying such toys allowed adults to indulge their own artistic sensibilities.

Demonstrating his genius for the optical effects of positive and negative space, Moser's Secessionist egg (fig. 15), as well as a model by Hoffmann made of silver featuring inlaid ovoid semiprecious stones resting on cylindrical bases (fig. 16), begged the childish question of whether "the content is perhaps sweeter?"[31] The text accompanying the illustrations seemed fully complicit in the adult humor: the fine workmanship, and, in the case of the Hoffmann egg, sumptuous material, likely suited the aesthetic proclivities of adult collectors more than children, who, as the text suggested, were presumably more interested in the confectionaries housed inside the decorative shell.

fig. 17
Magda Mautner von Markhof, dollhouse, painted wood, Friedrich Zeymer (woodworker), 59 5/8 x 35 3/8 x 50 3/8 in. (151.5 x 90 x 128 cm), 1908. © Badisches Landesmuseum Karlsruhe. Photograph by Thomas Goldschmidt.

While, despite their appeal to adult consumers, Moser's play sets and Easter eggs were presumably destined for the nursery, other Werkstätte products were intended as playthings for adults alone. An apt example of the adult nostalgia for an idealized landscape of child's play—and the raw "childlike" aesthetic of early Viennese Expressionist graphics—is found in the so-called *Sezessionstarock* (Secession tarok) cards that Moser's wife Ditha (née Mautner von Markhof) created for the Werkstätte.[32] Much like the elaborate Secessionist dollhouse designed by her older sister Magda Mautner von Markhof, a miniaturized *Gesamtkunstwerk* quoting Hoffmann's garden villas on Vienna's Hohe Warte (fig. 17), Ditha Moser filtered Secessionist *Flächenkunst* (planar or surface art) through a deliberately simplified eye (fig. 18). Produced in limited editions for the Mosers' friends, the cards were dotted with vernacular toys, as well as with human figures whose formal qualities echo the stiff rigidity of the *Bauernspielzeuge* that Secessionists remembered. Critic Ludwig Hevesi was so taken by the color-lithographic set's "primitive, healthy little vignettes, in their childish palpability, pieced together of naive primary colors in a mosaic-like fashion," that he proceeded to immediately play with his.[33] The wall clock in the background of the III card's afternoon *Jause* (coffee/tea time) scene cleverly references the fact, as Hevesi observed, "that it was the three card," a move typical of the way "the modernists thought about the details of the details" (fig. 19).[34] The cards were profuse with idealized images of the artist's own childhood, for instance the garden facade of the country estate where she was born (XVI), and the yellow facade and rolling beer kegs of the Mautner-Markhof family brewery (XX). A stylized Noah's ark (XV, fig. 20), a popular subject in traditional toy making regions, and a childlike rendering of the Prater's giant Ferris wheel (XVII) are also recognizable. So stylized were the trump cards' Roman numerals that Hevesi admitted that they were "really not intended as proper playing cards for tarok-players."[35] Like her sister's Secessionist dollhouse—so

fig. 18
Edith Moser, *Tarockspiele*, set of fifty-four playing cards, printed by Alfred Berger, color lithography, card size: 4 9/16 x 2 3/16 in. (11.6 x 5.5 cm), 1906.
© Christie's Images.

perfect and complete in every detail that critics jested that "any modernist doll would be ready to move in immediately"—Moser's Secessionist tarok set ultimately seemed more appropriate for aesthetic contemplation than for ease of use.[36] Once again, modernist interpretations of the childlike were interwoven with adult fascination with the vernacular.

Gustav Klimt's *Mäda Primavesi*

One of the most profound collisions between toys and adult memories of childhood is found in Gustav Klimt's 1912 portrait of Mäda Primavesi (1903–2000), the strong-willed daughter of Wiener Werkstätte patrons Otto and Eugenia Primavesi (fig. 21).[37] The Primavesis were devoted to the progressive cult of the child that was fashionable in Secessionist circles and

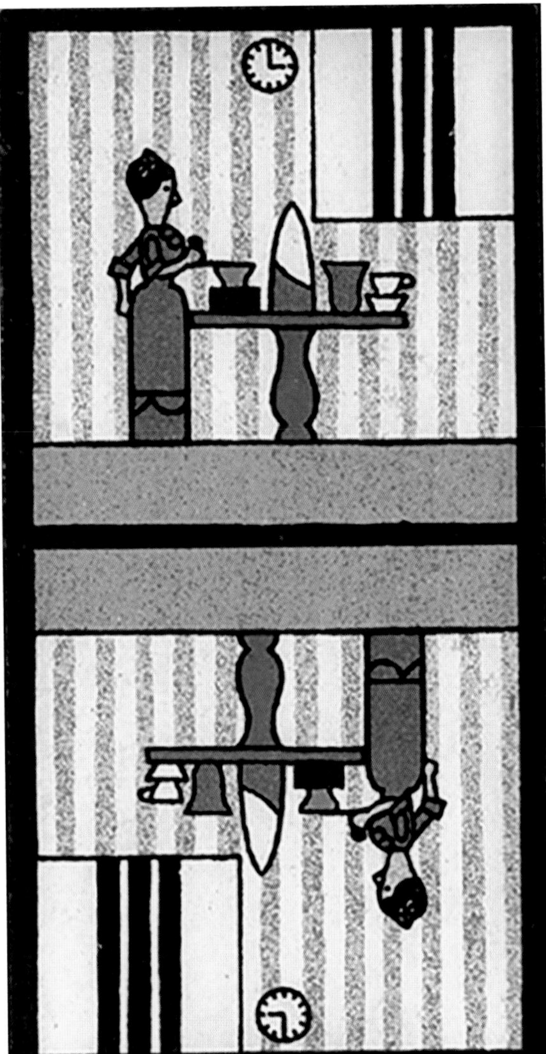

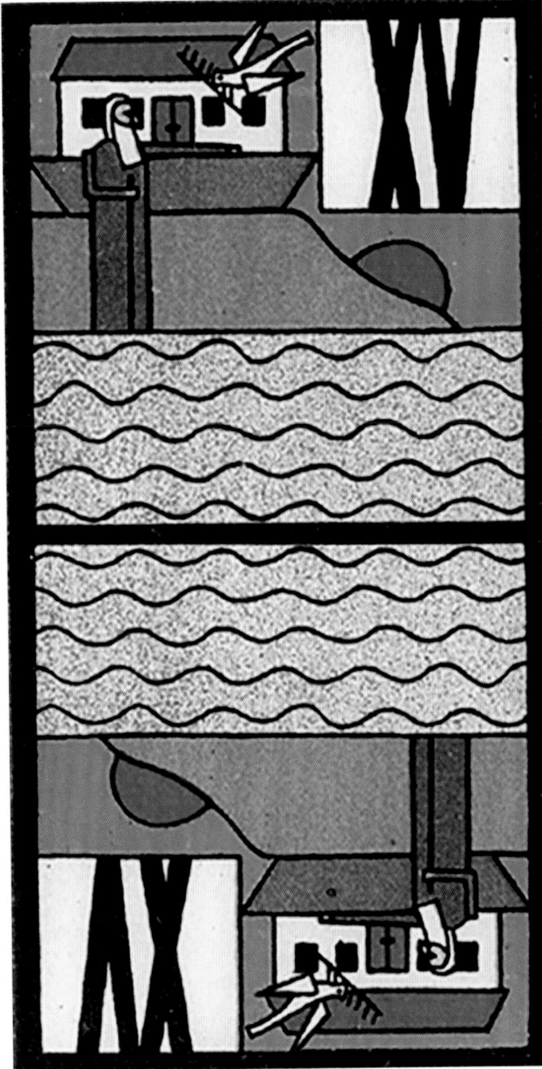

figs. 19, 20
Edith Moser, III and XV cards from *Tarockspiele* set, 1906. © Christie's Images.

showered their four children with artistic toys, such as the Harlfinger-Zakucka/Podhájská chess set they purchased for Mäda (figs. 6, 7) several years before the portrait commission.[38] Completed in time for the girl's tenth birthday on December 22, 1913, the canvas ranks as the artist's only commissioned child portrait.

What is striking about the work is the contrast between the unusual precocity of the willful child-subject and the playful ornamentalism of the childlike dreamscape surrounding her. Mäda straddles, with weight evenly distributed, a triangular white carpet populated with childish objects: fish, birds, and other whimsical animals. These toys strongly recall Podhájská's stylized animals, which Klimt undoubtedly remembered from the 1908

GUSTAV
KLIMT

Kunstschau exhibition—the important exhibition of the Klimt Group that is typically regarded as the high point of the Wiener Werkstätte *Gesamtkunstwerk* unifying art, architecture, and design—where her toys were featured in the "Art for the Child" section. Compare, for instance, the flamingos below the left edge of Mäda's skirt and the pug/piglike figures directly above (fig. 22) with the Podhájská figurines in figure 11; similar formal affinities are apparent between Podhájská's quail (fig. 12) and the fantastical winged animals below the right side of the skirt (fig. 23).

fig. 21
Gustav Klimt, *Mäda Primavesi*, oil on canvas, 59 x 43 1/2 in. (149.9 x 110.5 cm), 1912. The Metropolitan Museum of Art. Gift of André and Clara Mertens, in memory of her mother, Jenny Pulitzer Steiner, 1964 (64.148). © The Metropolitan Museum of Art. Photograph by Schecter Lee. Image source: Art Resource, NY.

According to interviews with the sitter, these playthings were the product of the artist's, not the child's, imagination. There is no evidence that actual toys were used as models during the sitting, and it was Klimt rather than Mäda who decided to include them in the scene.[39] The depiction of Mäda, indeed, separates her from the environment in which the artist placed her. As art historian Tobias Natter observed, "the representation is neither an adult nor child-portrait."[40] At Klimt's instigation, Mäda was portrayed in an iridescent white lawn dress accented with wired flowers and colored beads commissioned from his companion Emilie Flöge, a reform-dress couturier hardly known for making children's clothes. The viewer is immediately struck by the self-assured precosity of the child, her gaze unswervingly meeting the viewer as she assumes what was reportedly a characteristic pose of shoving her left arm behind her back, with her right elbow jutting out.[41] Her dress, her pose, her expression, and her position at the very edge of the picture plane together signal Mäda's psychological distance from the adult fantasy of childhood opening up behind her.

figs. 22, 23
Details of fig. 21. Gustav Klimt, *Mäda Primavesi*, 1912. The Metropolitan Museum of Art. Gift of André and Clara Mertens, in memory of her mother, Jenny Pulitzer Steiner, 1964 (64.148). © The Metropolitan Museum of Art. Photograph by Schecter Lee. Image source: Art Resource, NY.

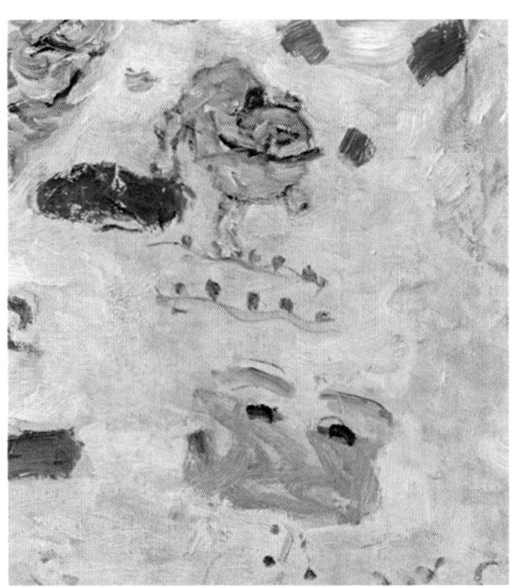

Klimt's painting brings together key themes addressed in this essay. Childhood had powerful and multivalent meanings for Secession-era Viennese, meanings that informed the design of handcrafted artistic toys. Secessionists believed that children were blessed with uncorrupted aesthetic vision, a characteristic they apparently shared with the vernacular culture of "primitive" peoples. Both offered sources for "unlearning" the stale conventions of academic art in the service of the Secessionist artistic rebellion. Toys were significant within this cultural milieu because, as the key artifacts of childhood *and* a traditional product of peasant production, they existed at the nexus of these various concerns. Traditional wooden toys, *Bauernspielzeuge*, offered examples of the vernacular aesthetics so valued by the Secessionists, while also awakening the memories of their own childhood playthings. And such toys provided the inspiration for new products, appealing to the tastes of cultivated and wealthy Viennese, designed by artists associated with the Wiener Werkstätte. It was natural, then, that such wooden toys would form part of the background of the childhood that Klimt imagined for Mäda Primavesi. His painting, though—like the arguments presented here—suggests that the toys may have meant at least as much to the adult as to the child.

NOTES

All translations are by the author.

1. "Spielzeug und Kunst," *Die Bühne* (December 1924): 32. Consulted in newspaper clippings scrapbook Wiener Werkstätte Annalen [WWAN] 84/777, Wiener Werkstätte Archives, Museum of Applied Arts, Vienna.
2. V. Tr., "Künstlerisches Spielzeug" *Reichspost*, no. 338 (December 10, 1924): 9. WWAN 84/773.
3. Max Eisler, "Neues Kinderspielzeug," *Der Tag* (December 14, 1924). WWAN 84/778.
4. For the harsh reality of German toy making, see David D. Hamlin, *Work and Play: The Production and Consumption of Toys in Germany, 1870–1914* (Ann Arbor: University of Michigan Press, 2007), 189–93.
5. Quoted in Jonathan Fineberg, *The Innocent Eye: Children's Art and the Modern Artist* (Princeton, NJ: Princeton University Press, 1997), 5.
6. Jonathan Fineberg, "Child's Play and the Origins of Art," in *When We Were Young: New Perspectives on the Art of the Child*, ed. Jonathan Fineberg (Berkeley: University of California Press, 2006), 87–96.
7. Colin Rhodes, *Primitivism and Modern Art* (New York: Thames and Hudson, 1994), 55.
8. William Rubin, "Modernist Primitivism: An Introduction," in *"Primitivism" in 20th Century Art: The Affinity of the Tribal and the Modern*, ed. William Rubin (New York: Museum of Modern Art, 1984), I: 11.
9. Max Burckhardt, "Ver Sacrum," *Ver Sacrum* 1, no. 1 (January 1898): 3.
10. Hermann Bahr, *Secession* (Vienna: Wiener Verlag, 1900), 2.
11. Christian Weikop, "Ver Sacrum (1898–1903): The Printed Face of the Vienna Secession," in *Birth of the Modern: Style and Identity in Vienna 1900*, ed. Jill Lloyd and Christian Witt-Dörring (New York: Neue Galerie/Hirmer Verlag, 2011), 221.
12. Josef Hoffmann and Koloman Moser, "Arbeitsprogramm der Wiener Werkstätte," *Hohe Warte* 1 (1904): 268.

13. Karl Gröber, *Kinder-Spielzeug aus alter Zeit: Eine Geschichte des Spielzeugs* (Berlin: Deutscher Kunstverlag, 1928), 62.
14. Lillian Langseth-Christensen, *A Design for Living: Vienna in the Twenties* (New York: Viking, 1987), 112, 141.
15. Emmy Zweybrück, "Toys—A Modern Art Problem," *Design* 34, no. 8 (January 1933): 184.
16. Emmy Zweybrück-Prochaska, "Wie mein Spielzeug entstand," *Der Wiener Kunstwanderer* 2, no. 3 (March 1934): 6.
17. Beginning in the 1920s, and more regularly throughout the 1930s, Zweybrück-Prochaska taught summer courses for drawing instructors in the United States, and served as a guest lecturer at various American universities, including Columbia University, the University of Southern California, and the University of California, Los Angeles. Through publications such as *The Stencil Book* (1935), she became internationally known for her theories on introducing art and design to children at an early age, as well as for her English-language children's books, *Come and Play* (1934) and *Children and Animals* (1935), similar in approach to her illustrations for Erwin Redslob's *Das Spielzeugschrank* (1934). Upon emigrating to the United States in 1939, she became director of the educational division of the American Crayon Company in New York and Los Angeles, editing its periodical *Everyday Art*. For her role in promoting Austrian applied arts abroad, she was honored with the title of professor in 1935; in 1955, largely due to the efforts of Josef Hoffmann, a retrospective of her work took place at the Vienna Secession.
18. Gröber, *Kinder-Spielzeug*, 1.
19. Ibid.
20. Zweybrück, "Toys—A Modern Art Problem," 184.
21. A. S. Levetus, "Studio Talk—Vienna," *The Studio* 38, no. 159 (June 1906): 219; Juliet Kinchin, "Hide and Seek: Remapping Modern Design and Childhood," in *Century of the Child: Growing by Design, 1900–2000*, ed. Juliet Kinchin and Aiden O'Connor, et al. (New York: Museum of Modern Art, 2012), 17–18.
22. Alexander Koch, "Die Kunst im Leben des Kindes," *Kind und Kunst* 1, no. 1 (September 1904): 3.
23. "Wiener Werkstätte," *Kind und Kunst* 3, no. 4 (January 1906): 125.
24. Steven Beller, "The World of Yesterday Revisited: Nostalgia, Memory and the Jews of *fin-de-siècle* Vienna," *Jewish Social Studies* 2, no. 2 (1996): 41.
25. "Das Kind," *Kunst und Kunsthandwerk* 10 (1907): 400.
26. "Wiener Werkstätte," 125.
27. "Das Kind," 400.
28. A. S. Levetus, "Modern Viennese Toys," *The Studio* 38, no. 159 (June 1906): 214.
29. Walter Benjamin, "Kulturgeschichte des Spielzeugs," *Gesammelte Schriften*, Band III (Frankfurt: Suhrkamp, 1972), 117.
30. See Kinchin, "Hide and Seek: Remapping Modern Design and Childhood," 16–17.
31. "Wiener Werskstätte," 125.
32. *Koloman Moser 1868–1918* (Munich: Prestel, 2007), 414–15.
33. Ludwig Hevesi, "Sezessions-Tarock," *Fremden-Blatt* 1, no. 1 (January 1, 1907): 21.
34. Ibid.
35. Ibid.
36. Ludwig Hevesi, "Kunstschau 1908," in *Altkunst-Neukunst: Wien 1894–1908* (Vienna: Carl Konegen, 1909), 315.
37. On the Primavesis, see Tobias Natter, "Otto and Eugenia Primavesi," in *Gustav Klimt: Painting, Design and Modern Life* (London: Tate, 2008), 182–83.
38. Ibid.
39. Katharine Baetjer, "About Mäda," *Metropolitan Museum Journal* 40 (2005): 131–50.
40. Tobias Natter, *Die Welt von Klimt, Schiele und Kokoschka* (Cologne: Dumont, 2003), 77.
41. Many of the numerous studies preceding the finished canvas recall, as Alice Strobl has suggested in *Gustav Klimt: Die Zeichnungen 1904–1912*, vol. 2 (Salzburg: Galerie Welz, 1992), 273–74, Velázquez's portrait-series of the Infanta Margarita Theresa depicting the youngest daughter (also the central figure in the take on *Las Meninas* photographed by Madame d'Ora) of Philip IV in various stages of childhood. The bold frontal composition of Klimt's final result, with the child-subject centered symmetrically on a dreamlike ornamental backdrop, evokes the Velázquez canvases from 1656 and 1659, particularly in terms of their symmetrical formal arrangements and commanding bearings of the child-subjects. The Velázquez portraits (housed in Vienna's Kunsthistorisches Museum) were sent to Vienna to anchor the diplomatic marriage alliance between the Infanta and her maternal uncle/cousin, Emperor Leopold I.

fig. 1
Paul Dubois, *Le Souvenir d'Alsace-Lorraine*, bronze, Place Maginot, Nancy, 1899–1902, installed 1910. Author's photograph.

MEMORY AND MASS MOBILIZATION: THE MATERIAL CULTURE OF THE ALSACE-LORRAINE QUESTION, 1885–1919

Peter Clericuzio

Peter Clericuzio teaches the history of architecture, urbanism, and material culture at Florida International University in Miami. His work focuses on architecture, design, and the graphic arts in francophone countries and the United States, and international expositions, with an emphasis on regionalism, identity, and collective memory. He is currently preparing a book manuscript on the Art Nouveau architecture of the city of Nancy, France, between 1889 and 1914.

The loss of the territories of Alsace-Lorraine in 1871 to the newly formed German Empire in the aftermath of the Franco-Prussian War was a national embarrassment for France. As the Third Republic emerged uneasily from this defeat over the following three decades, most French citizens steadfastly attempted to forget the military disaster and its consequences. And yet, the so-called Alsace-Lorraine question once again rose to national and international prominence after 1900, and the return of these regions became a rallying point for the French cause during the First World War. This essay examines a key aspect of the process of forgetting and resurrecting the Alsace-Lorraine question by suggesting that it was the efforts of residents of the region of Lorraine that kept alive the memory of the conflict and stoked French hopes of recapturing the "lost provinces" from the 1880s through the early 1900s.

Although the Germans incorporated nearly all of Alsace into the Kaiserreich in 1871, they left the southern two-thirds of Lorraine, including the city of Nancy, to France. Lorrainers merged an intense desire to restore the entire region to French control with a formidable sense of regional identity to shape the province's fin-de-siècle cultural production. Their work in the fine and decorative arts and architecture created, in Pierre Nora's words, *lieux de mémoire,* or objects and sites serving as touchstones for collective remembrance (fig. 1)—in this case, the memory of the catastrophic events of 1870–71, the dismembering of Lorraine, and the loss of Alsace. The relentless efforts of Lorraine's citizens to reawaken the issue

fig. 2
Emmanuel Héré de Corny and Jean Lamour, Place Stanislas, Nancy, 1753–55. Photo: courtesy Aurélien Schvartz, via Flickr Creative Commons Attribution-NonCommercial-Sharealike 2.0 license.

in the national consciousness were aided by the techniques of industrial production of such mass-circulation items as postcards, posters, board games, and children's books, whose explicit references to the Alsace-Lorraine question allowed it to resurface among all French citizens. This combination of art and architecture with a flood of modern popular media saturated the French cultural landscape with emblems of the cultural identity of the "lost provinces" and helped mobilize the nation behind the aim of regaining Alsace-Lorraine during the First World War.

Remembering and Forgetting the "Lost Provinces"

The notion of *lieux de mémoire* builds on Maurice Halbwachs' work on collective memory, and operates particularly well with regards to the cultural production of Nancy and its role in building a regional identity.[1] In the years before the French Revolution, the extensive privileges the king was compelled to grant to many territories—including Lorraine, which remained an independent duchy until 1766—contributed to the pervasive myth afterward that the *ancien régime* had been a golden age of provincial freedoms. In Nancy, which served as Lorraine's capital before its annexation by France, the last duke, former Polish king Stanisław Leszczyński (r. 1736–66), had embellished the city with some of the finest public spaces of the age, including the famed Place Royale (now Place Stanislas), designed by the architect Emmanuel Héré de Corny and the ironworker Jean Lamour (fig. 2).[2] As Nora has posited, the recognition of sites and objects as *lieux de mémoire* requires both the will to remember the past as well as a certain temporal distance from that past; thus, the Place Stanislas, even today, persists for Lorrainers as an index of the province's proud, independent, and refined cultural heritage. These markers often enable people to form their own connections to past experiences that supplement the historiographic reduction of such moments to impersonal, prescribed narratives, attitudes, and understandings. During the nineteenth century, with a growing opposition in the provinces (especially in Nancy) to the centralization of French culture around Paris, these *lieux de mémoire*—and in particular such architectural and spatial ones—helped establish an enduring, distinctive sense of identity among the region's residents based on this collective, shared social memory, much as Halbwachs theorized.[3]

The disaster of the Franco-Prussian War added another layer to the collective memory of Lorrainers that only reinforced their sense of regional identity. While neighboring Alsace was almost fully incorporated into Germany, only the northern third of Lorraine, including the city of Metz, was cut off behind the new frontier. The Germans administered Alsace-Lorraine directly from Berlin as a conquered province, unlike the other states within the Kaiserreich, which enjoyed some autonomy from Prussian domination as ostensibly equal partners in the imperial union. Lorraine residents on both sides of the border deeply resented this arrangement, which essentially reduced German Lorrainers to second-class citizens.[4] This was reinforced by the occupation of French Lorraine until 1874, when the French paid off an indemnity imposed in the Treaty of Frankfurt. Afterward, Nancy became the site of a sizeable, permanent French military garrison, transforming the cityscape in a manner that constantly reminded its citizens of the conflict.[5]

It is not surprising, then, that during the debate in France's National Assembly in 1871 over whether the new Third Republic should accept the Treaty of Frankfurt, Edgar Quinet warned his countrymen that ceding Alsace-Lorraine would mean a "war always latent [and] imminent in the nature of things," implying that in the coming years France would be eagerly looking for an excuse for a war that would allow it to regain the lost provinces and exact revenge for the defeat, a sentiment popularly called *revanche*.[6] This sentiment found resonance among Lorraine residents, who refused to accept that the loss of these areas was permanent. They argued that Alsace-Lorraine was, and always had been, culturally aligned with France, and that the Germans were outsiders who were ruling a people and occupying territory to which they had no connections. The novels of the Lorraine politician Maurice Barrès, such as *Les Marches de l'Est* (1909) and *Au service de l'Allemagne* (1905), portray the Germans as barbarous to an almost unbelievable extent in an attempt to awaken the rest of France to the need to regain the "lost provinces."[7]

But Quinet was only partly right. Arguably, part of the reason that revanche remained so popular in Lorraine was the realization among its citizens that much of the rest of France (except for small pockets of die-hard nationalists), distracted by other concerns, increasingly wanted to forget about the Alsace-Lorraine question. France's chief political issue of the 1870s continued to be whether or not it would remain a republic: although the constitutional laws of the Third Republic were finally promulgated in 1875, two years later the country was rocked by President Patrice MacMahon's failed attempt to seize monarchical power in a coup d'état. In the midst of this turmoil, the government shelved the idea of regaining Alsace-Lorraine indefinitely. An 1897 survey by the popular literary periodical *Mercure de France* asked its readers whether the Franco-Prussian War and the Alsace-Lorraine question remained important issues to them; nearly all replied negatively, and only a few even admitted to having given any thought to the "lost provinces" whatsoever.[8]

Wary, if not fearful of the Germans' military prowess, the French had adopted an official policy by the turn of the century of "unity through peace with progress," within its current borders, attempting to avoid any potential for armed conflict with foreign powers. Memorials for the Franco-Prussian War erected in France, for example, explicitly proscribed any reference to *revanche* and instead focused on the simple commemoration of the sacrifice of soldiers and civilians in service of the nation. The dedication ceremonies in 1875 for the most significant of these French memorials, at the battleground of Mars-la-Tour in Lorraine, near the new frontier, was even strategically delayed from the anniversary of the battle's date to coincide with All Souls' Day to avoid any semblance of anti-German political provocation.[9] As Eugène Florent-Matter summed up the matter in 1908: "Yes, it is necessary to write the history of Alsace-Lorraine over thirty years, and in the margin show the history of French politics for the last thirty years, and we will see thus that hope is the first to die, and then. . .it is possible to forget."[10]

The Arts and the Alsace-Lorraine Question

Most French artists followed this larger pattern of forgetting. While French painters in the 1870s frequently couched the Franco-Prussian War in vignettes of heroism in order to counter the sense that the war was a complete disaster, artists who came of age after 1880 did not know the war firsthand, and to them the conflict seemed less significant; as one French journalist explained in 1897, "the pain of defeat has lost its acuity."[11] Academic history paintings showing heroic French troops in a futile battle of resistance against the Prussian onslaught became rare, especially after 1890. Patriotic French painters and sculptors turned instead toward imagery of Joan of Arc as the timeless protector of the fatherland and Napoléon Bonaparte and the glorious exploits of the Grand Armée.[12]

The issue of Alsace-Lorraine and *revanche* remained a preoccupation for Nancy artists, however, including the multitalented Emile Gallé (1846–1904) and the glassmaker Antonin Daum (1864–1931). Like many of their fellow Lorrainers, Gallé and Daum had fought in the Franco-Prussian War and bitterly resented the imposition of the Treaty of Frankfurt and the

fig. 3
Emile Gallé with Louis Hestaux and Victor Prouvé, *Le Rhin*, carved walnut with inlaid ebony, plum, lemon, holly, rosewood, and pear, 30 x 86 5/8 x 43 in. (76.2 x 220 x 109.2 cm), Nancy, 1889. Photo: Claude Philippot © Musée de l'Ecole de Nancy.

French government's refusal to act on the Alsace-Lorraine question, a frustration they ultimately channeled into their work.[13] Gallé was the unquestioned leader of the artists who burned with desire to see the regions annexed by Germany returned to France. His most famous engagement with the Alsace-Lorraine question was an oak table called *Le Rhin* (The Rhine) that he unveiled at the 1889 Exposition Universelle in Paris (fig. 3).[14] A frieze that spans the tabletop depicts a bearded god representing the Rhine River at its center (fig. 4). This figure clutches a woman, personifying Lorraine, while he wards off an armed group of Germans on the right. A well-equipped cadre of French warriors—to whom Lorraine belongs—stand ready on the left. Inlaid above the scene are the words "The Rhine separates the Gauls [from] all of Germany," borrowed from the Roman historian Tacitus,[15] while among the table's legs, Gallé carved the defiant declaration "I cling to the heart of France."[16] Together, the imagery and text reference a timeless struggle between Germanic and Gallic peoples over Alsace-Lorraine and a claim that the natural border between the two is along the Rhine, the eastern border of Alsace. By implication, Gallé charges that the territory of Alsace-Lorraine must be returned to France, by force if necessary.

Le Rhin's text and figural imagery constitute a political statement in themselves, but the table also includes several other, semiotic references to

fig. 4
Emile Gallé, et al., *Le Rhin*.
Photo: Claude Philippot ©
Musée de l'Ecole de Nancy.

SEPARE
TOVTE LA GERM ANIE
TACITE

figs. 5, 6
Details of fig. 3. Emile Gallé, et al., *Le Rhin*. Photo: Claude Philippot © Musée de l'Ecole de Nancy.

the Alsace-Lorraine question—references to which Gallé and his fellow Lorraine artists returned over the thirty years preceding 1914. One such motif is the thistle, a plant native to the region and featured on the arms of the city of Nancy, which has long served as a symbol of Lorrainers' suspicion of outsiders and their tenacity in repulsing enemy aggression.[17] Positioned in *Le Rhin* just above the words "I cling to the heart of France," the thistle projects menace, as if defending the statement carved underneath (fig. 5). This aspect was not lost on contemporary Parisian observers at the 1889 fair, who linked the imagery with the modern version of Nancy's civic motto, "He who touches me will be pricked."[18]

Bookending the thistle in *Le Rhin* are the table's legs, carved in the shape of eagles,[19] each of which sports on its chest a Lorraine cross, another ancient regional icon of resistance that assumed a new layer of meaning after 1871 (fig. 6). In 1873, the bishops of Metz and Strasbourg led a group of Alsace-Lorrainers to the shrine of Notre-Dame de Sion in French Lorraine, south of Nancy. There they placed a plaque inscribed with the Lorraine cross and the words "Ce name po tojo"—a patois version of the modern French "Ce n'est pas pour toujours," meaning "It is not for forever." This phrase referenced the 1871 partition of Lorraine (and severance of Alsace-Lorraine from France), thus reincarnating the cross as a symbol of resistance to the Germans. In Lorraine, the cross also incorporated a geographic reference, wherein the upper horizontal bar came to indicate Metz, while the lower one was read as Nancy, the two principal cities of the region. Occasionally, the cross would be represented as broken, indicating the separation of Metz (or Alsace-Lorraine) from southern Lorraine (or France).[20] It therefore consecrated every location where it was as a *lieu de mémoire*, reminding all who saw it not only of the geopolitical reality, but also promising the eventual reunification of the "lost provinces" with France. The range of mediums in which Nancy artists used this iconography attests to its resonance throughout Lorraine. By the mid-1880s, Gallé was emblazoning the full range of glasswork from his Nancy factories, including small jars

fig. 7
Emile Gallé, decanter, glass and enamel, 8½ x 5½ in. (21.6 x 14 cm), c. 1885. The Wolfsonian–Florida International University, The Mitchell Wolfson, Jr. Collection, 84.8.31.1.

fig. 8
Emile Gallé, container, glass and enamel, 3 1/4 x 4 1/2 in. (8.3 x 11.4 cm), c. 1885. The Wolfsonian–Florida International University, The Mitchell Wolfson, Jr. Collection, 84.8.31.2.

fig. 9
Daum Brothers, vase, etched cameo glass, height: 12.7 in. (32.3 cm) diameter, Nancy, 1900–05. Photo: courtesy 1stdibs.com.

fig. 10
Daum Brothers, vase, etched glass, 8 x 2 1/2 in. (20.3 x 6.4 cm), Nancy, 1900–05. Photo: courtesy 1stdibs.com.

fig. 11
Lucien Weissenburger, architect, Weissenburger House, Nancy, 1904–06. Detail of dormer with Lorraine cross. Author's photograph.

and decanters, with prickly thistles in full bloom and Lorraine crosses in glittering gold (figs. 7, 8). His fellow glass artists, the Daum Brothers, developed signatures often juxtaposed or entwined with a Lorraine cross, a custom they continued even after the First World War (figs. 9, 10).

The most public of these symbolic gestures, however, appeared in the architectural monuments of Nancy. In 1906, for example, the architect Lucien Weissenburger (1860–1929) built a large speculative apartment house just north of the central business district and included a giant Lorraine cross as the structural members of a dormer, thus exhibiting his staunch commitment to reunification of the region (fig. 11). Meanwhile, his colleagues Emile André (1871–1933) and Paul Charbonnier (1865–1953) crowned the spire of their new bank for Charles Renauld with a huge bronze thistle, whose double meaning combined the motif's revanchist undertones with the institution's dedication to protecting its customers' savings (figs. 12, 13).[21] With the insertion of these regional symbols into the cityscape, the reminders of Lorraine's dismemberment became continuously visible to all of Nancy's citizens, not simply an elite with privileged access to objects of regional identity or a cadre of survivors who personally remembered the fight against the Prussians. If Nancy's built environment had previously functioned as a *lieu de mémoire* that referenced the region's proud independent heritage and produced a relatively straightforward set of collective memories, after 1900 its character became more complicated as it accommodated consciousness of a painful past that, instead of being celebrated, needed to be challenged in the present.

Galvanizing the Nation: The Exposition Internationale de l'Est de la France

Between 1871 and 1911, Nancy's population doubled to nearly 120,000 residents, and prominent industrialists and businessmen, many of whom had relocated from Alsace-Lorraine, exploited the extensive natural resources of the region, making it an industrial powerhouse.[22] For many Nanciens, the mass influx of newcomers was unsettling, but the city's resulting prosperity induced among them a sense of patriotism for a

figs. 12, 13
Emile André and Paul Charbonnier, architects, Renauld Bank, Nancy, 1907–10. Author's photograph.

figs. 14, 15
Postcards, Palace of Liberal Arts and waterslide, from the Exposition Internationale de l'Est de la France, Nancy, Imprimeries Réunies, 1909. Author's collection.

resurgent French nation.[23] The presence of so many natives of the annexed lands also helped reinforce the memories of the war within the minds of Nancy citizens, who could not forget that much of their good fortune at the turn of the century was at least in part due to the misfortunes of their fellow Alsace-Lorrainers.

To celebrate this era of prosperity and to reinforce the links between French Lorraine and surrounding regions (particularly Alsace-Lorraine), Nancy's scions of commerce and industry decided to hold a fair in 1909. Laid out in the Parc Sainte-Marie to the west of downtown, the Exposition Internationale de l'Est de la France, as it was officially called, had all the trappings of a world's fair: white stucco pavilions of axial symmetry that blended baroque and Art Nouveau decor, housing

products of machinery, agriculture, electricity, and the arts, arranged around a court of honor. Individual corporate pavilions, such as those of the great Nancy-based department store Magasins Réunis, occupied a bucolic picturesque setting nearby, intermingled with refreshment stands and amusements, including a waterslide, a miniature railroad, and puppet theaters, among others (figs. 14, 15).[24]

The planners of the exposition, who included not only the leaders of Nancy's Chamber of Commerce and Industry—such as the glassmaker Antonin Daum—but also journalists and municipal officials, conceived of the event as a means to direct the attention of a national audience to the Alsace-Lorraine question by displaying the fruits of their region's labors and their relationship to the annexed territory as vital to the health of the nation. To that end, they commissioned Victor Prouvé (1858–1943), the president of the Ecole de Nancy, the famed association of Art Nouveau decorative artists and architects in Lorraine dedicated to regionalist concerns, to design much of the official branding.[25] The symbols of memory and resistance integral to the Alsace-Lorraine question figure prominently in Prouvé's design for the obverse of most of the fair's commemorative medallions (figs. 16, 17). In the center, a woman personifying Lorraine (dressed in provincial costume) leans on a plow, representing agriculture, while behind her to the left rise the smokestacks of the region's prodigious factories. She is ensconced within a wreath that, at the bottom, consists of a large sprig of thistles, studded with a scroll bearing a Lorraine cross. At the top, the plant forms give way to a banner reading "Lorraine" at the center, surrounded by the legend "Industrie-Science-Arts-Lettres-Commerce," indicating the five fields on display at the fair. The location of the regional iconography at the bottom of the wreath and in front of the personification of Lorraine

fig. 16
Victor Prouvé, *Les Magasins Reunis à la Course Strasbourg-Nancy*, medallion, plated bronze, 1 1/2 in. (3.8 cm) diameter, 1909. The Wolfsonian–Florida International University, The Mitchell Wolfson, Jr. Collection, TD1992.56.

fig. 17
Victor Prouvé, design for medallion, ink, graphite, and paper, 14 1/8 in. (35.9 cm) diameter, 1909. The Wolfsonian–Florida International University, The Mitchell Wolfson, Jr. Collection, TD1992.56.2.

fig. 18
Postcard, Alsatian Village, from the Exposition Internationale de l'Est de la France, Nancy, Imprimeries Réunies, 1909. Author's collection.

indicate that the revival of the Alsace-Lorraine question constitutes a foundational theme of the exposition, promising the eventual reclamation of this territory from Germany.

fig. 19
Postcard, women at work in the Alsatian Village, from the Exposition Internationale de l'Est de la France, Nancy, Imprimeries Réunies, 1909. Author's collection.

The most politically significant part of the exposition was a section near the main entrance called the Alsatian Village (fig. 18), a complex of faux regional structures designed by Nancy architect Emile André arranged around an authentic traditional house imported from Zutzendorf, in the northern part of Alsace, and staged before a mountainous trompe-l'oeil backdrop. Inside many of the buildings of the village were Alsatians dressed in traditional costume performing the everyday tasks of the region's rural residents who thus "reconstituted with a perfect art [and] with authentic materials. . .a little bit of Alsace transported to French territory" (fig. 19).[26] This reconstruction of the Alsatian landscape and architecture implied that French citizens were innately familiar with Alsatian customs and that the region was naturally a part of France, not Germany. For many émigrés from Alsace-Lorraine, the effect was moving:

> Those who enter the old house take off their hats once they cross the threshold. They have serious expressions, and, looking at all these objects, they are reminded of all of them, especially if they are from the lost provinces. Yesterday, an old man came with a young boy. He took a long time touring the house, and, after having visited it, his voice trembling, his eyes filled with tears, said to the boy, "You see, this was just like what we had, which was taken from us, and what I and your mother used to tell you about when you were so young". . . . Then they left for Vienne, from which they had come specifically to see this.[27]

Clearly many individuals who experienced the 1870–71 conflict were filled with the sadness of being forced to leave their homeland afterward to retain French citizenship. This sadness was no doubt mixed with apprehension that Alsace-Lorraine would remain permanently separated from France as the war faded further into history, as well as anger that the French government had not taken steps to reclaim the territory from Germany in the intervening thirty-eight years. But the throngs of visitors who experienced the Alsatian Village from diverse locations throughout France and neighboring countries proved that it served as a *lieu de mémoire* for a truly mass audience, creating what Alison Landsberg has termed "prosthetic memories" for a younger generation of French citizens

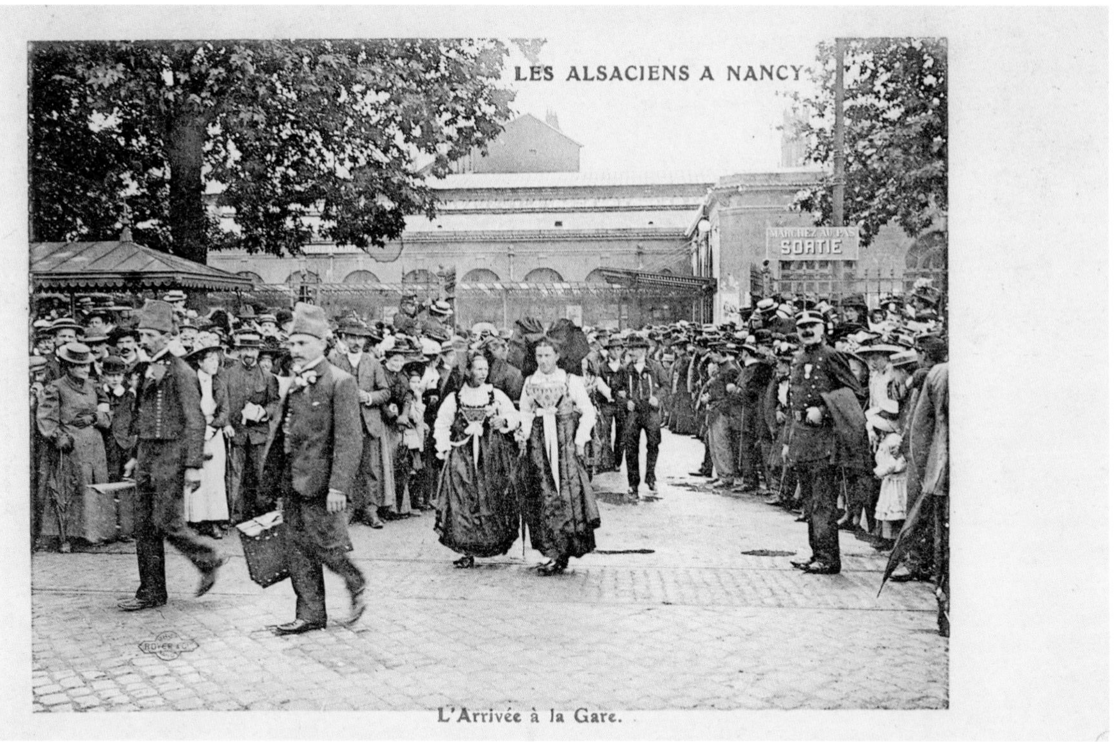

LES ALSACIENS A NANCY
SORTIE
L'Arrivée à la Gare.

fig. 20
Postcard, Alsatian women arriving at Nancy railroad station, Royer & Cie., 1909. Author's collection.

who had no personal memory of the Franco-Prussian War or the loss of Alsace-Lorraine.[28] Indeed, the creation of this contrived architectural space, as Halbwachs might describe it, was the key to engendering a collective memory that linked citizens across the various regions of France with this historical experience, which complemented and blended with established individual and collective memories of the conflict. Its significance is underscored by the fact that the Zutzendorf House was the sole structure at the fair not to be torn down the following year; even today it remains the central monument of the Parc Sainte-Marie in Nancy, thereby continuing to function as a *lieu de mémoire* for several historical moments on civic, regional, and national levels.

Nancy's robust printing industry played a major role in the creation of these prosthetic memories, churning out thousands of postcards showing the Alsatian Village and Alsatian women and girls arriving in Nancy for the fair dressed in traditional costume, in long colored dresses with high waists, white blouses, and large bow-shaped headdresses (fig. 20).[29] Although such images of Alsatian costume were well-known before 1871, after 1909 this archetypal image was nearly always twinned with the peasant girl of Lorraine (as in the model used on Prouvé's medallions), proliferating feminine personifications of the annexed regions.

In the half-decade between the fair and the start of the First World War, this memory industry in Nancy created by an alliance between

44. - Le Souvenir. - Paul Dubois, Nancy
« O Français arrachés tout vivants à la France.
« Nos armes, nos drapeaux, les voyez-vous là-bas ?
« Savez vous vers quel but marche notre espérance
« Et vous souvenez-vous que nous n'oublions pas ? »
Paul Déroulède.

fig. 21
Postcard, *Le Souvenir d'Alsace-Lorraine* by Paul DuBois, c. 1914. The image shows garlands placed around the base by Nancy's municipal cyclist club. Author's collection.

art and printing magnates continued to grow. The year after the fair, the city of Nancy erected in its central business district Paul Dubois's (1829–1905) bronze statue *Le Souvenir d'Alsace-Lorraine* (The Memory of Alsace-Lorraine, fig. 1). It depicts two traditionally-dressed Alsatian and Lorraine women seated on a block of granite from the Vosges Mountains, which formed the post-1871 frontier between France and Germany. The Alsatian figure gazes in the distance at the ridge of the Vosges, waiting patiently for her deliverance by the French fatherland and fervently hoping France has not forgotten about her. The younger woman, representing Lorraine, leans on the Alsatian, her head bowed in sadness. With her left hand, the Alsatian woman clasps the Lorrainer's right in her lap in reassurance. Dubois's work thus provided, like the Zutzendorf House, another *lieu de mémoire* where "faithful Lorrainers. . .[would] come to protest. . .the ever-so-cruel mutilation of their land,"[30] continually reminding Nanciens of the terrible events of the Franco-Prussian War and their dedication to the recapture of the lost provinces.

The power of *Le Souvenir* as a wellspring of collective memory was significantly multiplied once images of the sculpture, with dedicatory mementos scattered around its base, were distributed on postcards (fig. 21). As a pledge to the lost provinces, the cards carry the words of a military call to arms written in 1889 by Paul Déroulède, an extreme nationalist and Franco-Prussian War veteran who spent ten years in exile for plotting to overthrow the republican government precisely because of its passivity in pursuing the Alsace-Lorraine question:

> To all French persons, torn away [from us] yet living for France,
> Do you see our weapons and flags there below?
> Do you know what goal towards which our hope turns
> And do you remember that we do not forget you?[31]

In insisting, as a point of reassurance to the residents of Alsace and Lorraine that France had not forgotten about them and vowed to win them back, by military force if necessary, Déroulède's words belied the reality of the age when he composed them: French indifference to the Alsace-Lorraine question was approaching its peak around 1890. Only some two decades later could his lines—now paired with a powerful symbolic image and disseminated via methods of mass production—begin to play the galvanizing role he had intended.

Mass Production and Cultural Mobilization: The First World War

The mass spectacle of the 1909 exposition and the prodigious industry that propagated its message were attempts to unite the French nation around a set of prosthetic and actual memories of the Franco-Prussian War and the "lost provinces." The efficacy of Lorrainers' efforts stopped short, however, of inculcating the rest of the French nation with a definitive plan—let alone one that required force—for recouping the territorial losses, in consonance with the official diplomatic line of "unity through peace with progress." A German diplomat touring France in 1913 reported that "the wound of 1871 still burns in all French hearts, but no one is disposed to risk his or his sons' necks for the question of Alsace-Lorraine."[32] Historians have documented well that the Alsace-Lorraine question was rarely referenced in the days leading up to the outbreak of war in the summer of 1914, and only on August 1, when Germany declared war on Russia and a German declaration of war on France was imminent, did any French official publicly mention Alsace-Lorraine. Even then, the issue was only referenced as a possible reward in the event of a victory in a defensive war with the Germans that France explicitly had not sought.[33]

If the Alsace-Lorraine question neither prompted French entry into the war nor formed an immediate rallying cry for the nation, it soon emerged as one of the few aims of the First World War upon which France and her allies could agree.[34] As it became clear the conflict would not be a short one and that it would largely consist, on the western front, of a bloody stalemate fought between lines of trenches, French (and British) leaders scrambled to find tangible goals that would convince their increasingly disenchanted citizens that the war was still worth waging. The board game "La Délivrance," issued free to schoolchildren by the city of Paris around 1914, provides a good example (fig. 22). Players move their pieces along the

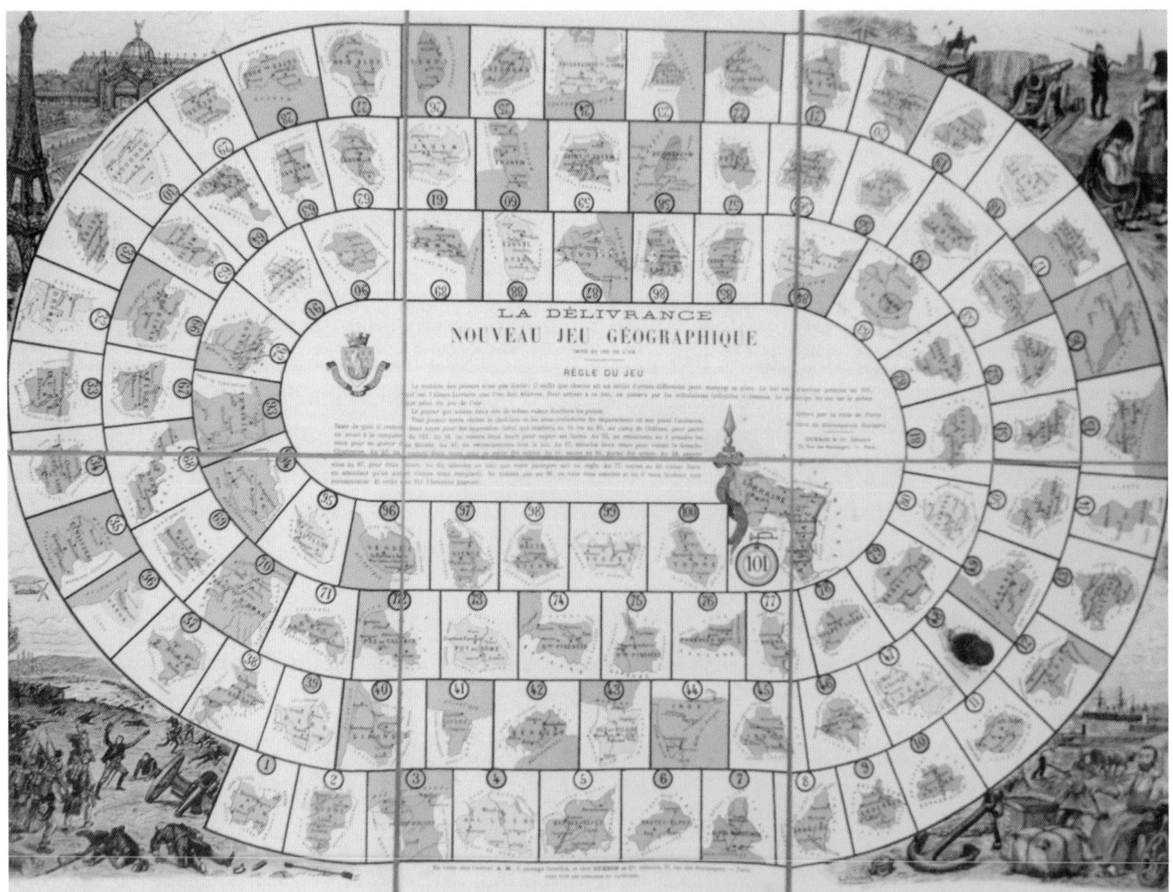

fig. 22
Game, *La Délivrance: Jeu Géographique et Patriotique*, G.Dascher (illustrator). Gustave Guerin & Cie. (publisher), Paris, c. 1914. The Wolfsonian–FIU, The Mitchell Wolfson, Jr. Collection of Decorative and Propaganda Arts, Promised Gift, WC2006.5.7.29.

spiral trail of French *départements*, attempting to become the first to reach the 101st space at the center, representing Alsace-Lorraine; the game's victor is thus assured of a tangible reward for the arduous journey. In this atmosphere, the prewar attempts to construct a prosthetic, collective memory of the "lost provinces" had created fertile ground for propaganda that used the Alsace-Lorraine question as a means of mobilizing the population for total war.

Wartime propagandists could assume that their audiences would be familiar with a repertoire of images that had been propagated by Lorrainers from the 1890s onward in order to assert the identity of their region and of Alsace as indivisible parts of France. Such molding of the minds also extended to the youngest members of French society. In 1917, the publishing house Berger-Levrault—a firm originally from Strasbourg that had relocated to Nancy after 1871 and staunchly supported regionalist politics—released André Hellé's children's book *Alphabet de la Grande Guerre*.[35] The very first page of text reads "A: Alsace" and depicts French soldiers triumphantly entering a town in Alsace in 1914, while a young girl wearing the archetypal regional costume presents them with a welcome wreath (fig. 23). Already the French tricolor flutters from a church spire

ALSACE

Située à l'ouest du Rhin, limite naturelle qui sépare la France de l'Allemagne, l'Alsace fut annexée à l'Empire allemand en 1871. En 1914, après la déclaration de guerre de l'Allemagne, les troupes françaises ont franchi la frontière pour reconquérir l'Alsace.

fig. 23
André Hellé, "A: Alsace," from *Alphabet de la Grande Guerre*, Berger-Levrault, Nancy, c. 1917. The Wolfsonian–Florida International University, The Mitchell Wolfson, Jr. Collection, XC1993.597.

among the structures and landscape that echo the Alsatian Village constructed for the 1909 Exposition Internationale de l'Est de la France.

Even after the Armistice, imagery that evoked the reasons for fighting the war continued to prominently feature the Alsace-Lorraine question. In December 1918, the Galeries Lafayette department store in Paris advertised a New Year's toy sale using posters depicting children at play, a boy outfitted in uniform and a girl donning a bonnet with a patriotic cockade (fig. 24). They excitedly welcome a smartly dressed, beaming American doughboy who presents them with two girl dolls, an Alsatian and a Lorrainer. The poster therefore insists that the triumphal gift to France for the coming year 1919 is the return of the territories to her possession, sure to be formalized in the impending treaty ending the

AUX
GALERIES LAFAYETTE
Georges Redon 18
JOUETS ETRENNES
Pendant toute la durée
DU MOIS DE DÉCEMBRE
MAISON VENDANT LE MEILLEUR MARCHÉ de TOUT PARIS
IMP. MONROCQ. PARIS.

conflict, a feat only accomplished with the aid of American heroism. But the sense of victory is twofold, as the poster evidences the success of the national campaigns of mass cultural mobilization before and during the war, relying on children's prior familiarity with the symbolism of the regional costumes worn by the two dolls. Furthermore, the poster suggests the normalization of these symbolic images into the common experience of French children (and adults, who would be purchasing such toys), for it does not assume a transformative, instructive purpose, but functions in a purely commercial sphere that capitalizes on children's affinity for playtime.

In hindsight, given the official return of Alsace-Lorraine to France in 1919, one could assume that the French had constantly itched since 1871 to reclaim the territories lost to Germany after the Franco-Prussian War. But that was not the case. Hope of recapturing the lost territory could be exploited by propaganda during the First World War only because of the work by artists, architects, fair organizers, and printers from Lorraine before 1914 to ensure that the Alsace-Lorraine question resurfaced and remained on the national agenda. The mass-produced items concerning Alsace-Lorraine disseminated during the war, in turn, emerged themselves as *lieux de mémoire* for an entire generation of French citizens, who would remember the Alsace-Lorraine question as a central issue of the struggle—even if, in truth, it had only been inserted into the cause retroactively. In the years that followed, the recouped territory on the west bank of the Rhine provided a tangible modicum of comfort for a population otherwise exhausted and horribly maimed by the cataclysm.

fig. 24
Georges Reson, *Aux Galeries Lafayette: Jouets Etrennes*, offset lithograph, 1918. The Wolfsonian–FIU, The Mitchell Wolfson, Jr. Collection of Decorative and Propaganda Arts, Promised Gift, WC2006.8.9.2.

NOTES

1. Pierre Nora, "Between Memory and History: *Les Lieux de Memoire*," in *Representations* 26 (Spring 1989): 7–24. Also consult Nora's more comprehensive work on French memory, *Les Lieux de mémoire*, 3 vols. (Paris: Gallimard, 1984–92). The English translations are published as *Realms of Memory*, ed. Lawrence Kritzman, trans. Arthur Goldhammer (New York: Columbia University Press, 1997). Nora's work explores further themes developed by Halbwachs before 1945 in *The Collective Memory*, trans. F. J. Ditter, Jr., and V. Y. Ditter (New York: Harper Colophon, 1980); *On Collective Memory*, trans. Lewis Coser (Chicago: University of Chicago Press, 1992).
2. Wolfgang Braunfels, *Urban Design in Western Europe: Regime and Architecture, 900–1900*, trans. Kenneth Northcutt (Chicago: University of Chicago Press, 1988), 226–29; Pierre Marot, *Emmanuel Héré (1705–1763): biographie du premier architecte du roi Stanislas d'après les notes de Pierre Boye: suivie d'une étude sur la Genèse de la place Royale de Nancy* (Nancy: Berger-Levrault, 1954).
3. Halbwachs, *The Collective Memory*, esp. 128–36. Others, such as Alison Landsberg, have extended this analysis using more modern media such as cinema, calling such developments on an even larger scale "prosthetic memory." See Landsberg, *Prosthetic Memory: The Transformation of American Remembrance in the Age of Mass Culture* (New York: Columbia University Press, 2004), 1–24. The relationship between Paris and the provinces is a complicated one that has been touched on by several scholars. See Alain Corbin, "Paris—Province," in *Realms of Memory*, I, 427–64; Richard Mandell, *Paris 1900: The Great World's Fair* (Toronto: University of Toronto Press, 1967), 40–51.
4. Michael E. Nolan, *The Inverted Mirror: Mythologizing the Enemy in France and Germany, 1898–1914* (New York: Berghahn Books, 2005), 70–71, 84; Frederic H. Seager, "The Alsace-Lorraine Question in France, 1871–1914," in *From the Ancien Régime to the Popular Front: Essays in the History of Modern France in Honor of Shepard B. Clough*, ed. Charles Warner (New York: Columbia University Press, 1969), 114.
5. Pierre Barral, Françoise-Thérèse Charpentier, and Jean-Claude Bonnefant, "La Capitale de la Lorraine Mutilée (1870–1918)," in *Histoire de Nancy*, ed. René Taveneaux (Toulouse: Privat, 1979), 394.
6. Quinet, paraphrased by Charles Hazen in the latter's *Alsace-Lorraine under German Rule* (New York: Henry Holt, 1917), 4.
7. Nolan, *The Inverted Mirror*, 73–80.
8. "L'Alsace-Lorraine et l'état actuel des esprits," in *Mercure de France* 24 (December 1897): 641–815; Seager, "The Alsace-Lorraine Question," 119; Michael Neiberg, *Dance of the Furies: Europe and the Outbreak of World War I* (Cambridge, MA: Belknap Press of Harvard University Press, 2011), 57–60.
9. See Karine Varley, *Under the Shadow of Defeat: The War of 1870–71 in French Memory* (New York: Palgrave Macmillan, 2008), esp. 191–202.
10. Eugène Florent-Matter, *L'Alsace-Lorraine de nos jours* (Paris: Plon-Nourrit, 1908), 82. This was quoted on the frontispiece of Robert Baldy, *L'Alsace-Lorraine et L'Empire Allemand (1871–1911)* (Nancy/Paris: Berger-Levrault, 1912).
11. Declared in the patriotic weekly periodical *L'Alsacien-Lorrain*, September 12, 1897; quoted in Seager, "The Alsace-Lorraine Question," 119.
12. See François Robichon, "Representing the 1870–1871 War, or the Impossible Revanche," trans. Olga Grlic, in *Nationalism and French Visual Culture, 1870–1914*, ed. June Hargrove and Neil McWilliam (Washington, DC: National Gallery of Art; New Haven, CT: Yale University Press, 2005), 82–99; Robert Allen Jay, "Art and Nationalism in France, 1870–1914" (Ph.D. diss., University of Minnesota, 1979), 189–216.
13. See Alain Dusart and François Moulin, *Art Nouveau: l'épopée Lorraine* (Strasbourg: La Nuée Bleue/ Editions de l'Est, 1998), 13–15; Philippe Garner, *Emile Gallé*, rev. and enl. ed. (New York: Rizzoli, 1990), 19–20, 25–26.
14. The table was completed in collaboration with his friends Louis Hestaux and Victor Prouvé.
15. Tacitus, *Germania*, part 1, opens, "The whole of Germany is thus bounded; separated from Gaul, from Rhoetia and Pannonia, by the rivers Rhine and Danube." Translation by Thomas Gordon; online text available at http://www.fordham.edu/halsall/basis/tacitusgermanygord.html.
16. The original inscriptions are in French: on the top, from Tacitus, "*Le Rhin separe des Gauls tout de Germanie*," and among the table legs, "*Je tiens au coeur de France*."
17. This traditional meaning can be traced back at least to the reigns of the Dukes of Lorraine René II (1451–1508) and Antoine the Good (1489–1544). See Pierre Gérard, *La Lorraine...Vivante Réalité Humaine...* (Nancy: Archives Départementales de Meurthe-et-Moselle, 1972), 9; Léon Germain, *Le Chardon Lorrain sous les Ducs René II et Antoine* (Nancy: Berger-Levrault, 1885), 1–32.

18. See Louis Enault, "L'Exposition Universelle de 1889—VII. Les rois de l'Exposition: Emile Gallé," in *La Revue Générale* 7, no. 134 (June 1, 1889): 297; Paul Desjardin, "Chronique de l'Exposition: Les Industries d'art," *Journal des Débats* (September 1, 1889): 2–3.
19. The eagle is also a symbol of Lorraine found on the region's coat of arms and flag.
20. On this, consult Pierre Marot, *Le Symbolisme de la croix de Lorraine* (Nancy: Berger-Levrault, 1948), 38–39; Etienne Thévenin, "Les Lorrains et la Croix de Lorraine," in *Mémoire et lieux de mémoire en Lorraine*, ed. Philippe Martin and François Roth (Sarreguemines, France: Editions Pierron, 2003): 109–17.
21. The studding of architectural monuments with symbolic meaning specific to the city and region was quite common in Nancy during this period. Refer to Peter Clericuzio, "Nancy as a Center of Art Nouveau Architecture, 1895–1914" (Ph.D. diss., University of Pennsylvania, 2011); Francis Roussel, *Nancy Architecture 1900*, 3 vols. (Metz: Serpenoise, 1992).
22. On the émigrés from Alsace-Lorraine to France, see François G. Dreyfus, "Le malaise politique," in *L'Alsace de 1900 à nos jours*, ed. Philippe Dollinger (Toulouse: Edouard Privat, 1979), 99–101; David H. Barry, "The Effect of the Annexation of Alsace-Lorraine on the Development of Nancy" (Ph.D. diss., University of London, 1975), esp. 321–37 and 345–49; Hélène Sicard-Lenattier, *Les Alsaciens-Lorrains à Nancy 1871–1914: Une ardente histoire* (Haroué, France: Gérard Louis, 2002), 116–49.
23. Paul Vidal de la Blache, *La France de l'Est (Lorraine-Alsace)* (Paris: Librarie Colin, 1917), 167. The large numbers of newcomers from Alsace-Lorraine, many of whom would end up competing with established Nancy residents for jobs, must have stimulated some resentment among the local population initially. See Barry, "The Effect of the Annexation of Alsace-Lorraine," 250–56.
24. For more on the fair and its significance, see Peter Clericuzio, "Modernity, Regionalism, and Art Nouveau at the Exposition Internationale de l'Est de la France, 1909," in *Nineteenth-Century Art Worldwide* 10, no. 1 (Spring 2011), http://www.19thc-artworldwide.org/; Béatrice Damamme-Gilbert, "The 1909 Nancy International Exhibition: Showcase for a Vibrant Region and Swansong of the Ecole de Nancy," *Art on the Line* 1, no. 5 (2007): 1–11. In Lorraine, the fair is often referred to as the "1909 World's Fair" ("Exposition Universelle").
25. On the Ecole de Nancy, see Françoise-Thérèse Charpentier, *Art Nouveau: L'Ecole de Nancy* (Metz: Denoël/Serpenoise, 1987); Christian Debize, *Emile Gallé and the "Ecole de Nancy,"* trans. Ruth Atkin-Etienne (Metz: Serpenoise, 1999).
26. Maurice Leudet, "L'Exposition de Nancy," *Le Figaro* 55, no. 172 (June 21, 1909): 3; partially reprinted in "Les Journaux Parisiens et l'Inauguration," *Journal de l'Exposition de Nancy: organe officiel de l'administration* 26 (June 29–30, 1909): 3.
27. Article in *La Petite Gironde*, June 25, 1909, quoted in Pol Simon, "L'Exposition de Nancy et l'Opinion," in Louis Laffitte, *Rapport Général sur l'Exposition Internationale de l'Est de la France – Nancy 1909* (Paris/Nancy: Berger-Levrault, 1912), 830. Vienne is a city in France southwest of Nancy near Lyons.
28. Landsberg, *Prosthetic Memory.*
29. Nancy was perhaps the leading French center for postcard production during the *belle epoque*, due to its burgeoning printing industry, especially the Royer and Bergeret (later the Imprimeries Réunis) firms. See "Numéro Spécial: La Carte Postale Illustré," *Le Figaro Illustré* 22, no. 175 (October 1904): n.p.; Edouard Thiolère, "Imprimeries Réunies de Nancy," "Aux Imprimeries Réunies," and "Monographie Industrielle: Établissements A. Bergeret et Cie, Phototypie d'Art, Nancy," all in *Revue Industrielle de l'Est* 14, nos. 686, 699, and 728 (February 26, May 28, and December 17, 1905): 125–28; 349; and 888, respectively.
30. Emile Badel, "Le Monument du « Souvenir »," *L'Immeuble et la Construction dans l'Est* 28, no. 37 (September 4, 1910): 433. The statue stands in the Place Saint-Jean, now the Place Maginot.
31. From Déroulède, *Réfrains Militaires* (Paris: Calmet Lévy, 1889), 63. The original reads:
   O Français arrachés tout vivant à la France
   Nos armes, nos drapeaux, les voyez-vous la-bas?
   Savez-vous quel but marche notre espérance
   Et vous souvenez-vous que nous n'oublions pas?
32. Quoted in Bernadotte E. Schmitt, *Triple Alliance and Triple Entente* (New York: Henry Holt, 1934), 102.
33. Neiberg, *Dance of the Furies*, 146–47.
34. Ibid.
35. On Berger-Levrault's history, see Jean-Pierre Klein and Bernard Rolling, *Histoire d'un imprimeur: Berger-Levrault 1676–1976* (Nancy: Berger-Levrault, 1976), 98–104.

PROTEAN PROMPT: THE MATCHBOOK AS COMMERCIAL, PRIVATE, AND CULTURAL REMINDER

Anna Jozefacka

Anna Jozefacka is an art historian specializing in modern architecture, art, and design history. She teaches at Hunter College, City University of New York, as well as in Duke University's New York programs. Associate curator of the Leonard A. Lauder Collection, Jozefacka has contributed to the exhibition catalogues *Cubism: The Leonard A. Lauder Collection* (2014) and *The Postcard Age: Selections from the Leonard A. Lauder Collection* (2012). She will begin a post-doctoral fellowship at the Metropolitan Museum of Art in September 2015. She earned her doctorate from the Institute of Fine Arts, New York University, in 2011.

In the early 1950s, Cindy, a young, single white woman, arrives in Washington, DC, from rural North Carolina to attend college. A summer job at the Justice Department turns into five years of living and working in the capital, concluding with a marriage proposal from her future husband. During those five years, she shares an apartment in Georgetown with three roommates, which is thrilling and liberating. Financially independent, without local family ties, she dives into Washington's social scene. She is quick to make friends and enjoys frequent evenings out. Her dating rules are simple: never turn down the adventure of a blind date, and never date two men at the same time. The men she dates tend to be young lawyers on a stint at the Justice Department; settings vary among French restaurants, supper clubs, and hotel bars, with their guarantee of live music. She gets compliments about her resemblance (which she cultivates) to Veronica Lake. She takes up smoking and, after tearing out a match to light a cigarette, mindlessly plays with the matchbook.

figs. 1, 2
DC days matchbook collection. Private collection.

Matchbooks were available everywhere in the 1950s: at corner coffee shops, lunch counters, and upscale restaurants—all places that Cindy frequented. She also encountered them on occasional sightseeing trips to other large cities. Covered with eye-catching advertisements and offered for free, matchbooks were a clever marketing tool in the guise of an everyday accessory. Cindy sometimes left the matchbooks behind on a restaurant table or bar, but more often tossed them into her purse to use later. At some point, she turned the pile amassing at the bottom of her purse, which up until then served as an unwieldy Rolodex or quick source of flame, into a collection. The matchbooks, initially just objects of convenience, came to serve as depositories for her memories of favorite locations and the people with whom she had spent her time.

Cindy, now in her eighties, related this story to me as we picked through the matchbooks that make up what I will call her "DC days" collection, accumulated some six decades prior.[1] Today, the matchbooks help her recall social events and their attendant atmospheres, sounds, smells, and tastes. Commercial taglines printed on the matchbook covers continue to serve as reminders of details from this time. She intended to organize the collected matchbooks one day, perhaps catalog them properly in a matchbook album, but never got around to it. Instead, she kept the matchbooks stashed in an oblong wooden box, without any order (figs. 1, 2). Examining them over the subsequent decades, she found that some matchbooks resonated with powerful memories, while others offered her little. The loosely kept matchbooks, an unwieldy mass of synapses, today interact to create a constellation of narratives as well as dead ends.

fig. 3
Matchbooks, Caruso's Italian Kitchen, Ruby Foo's, and El Mexico, from the DC days collection, 1950s. Private collection.

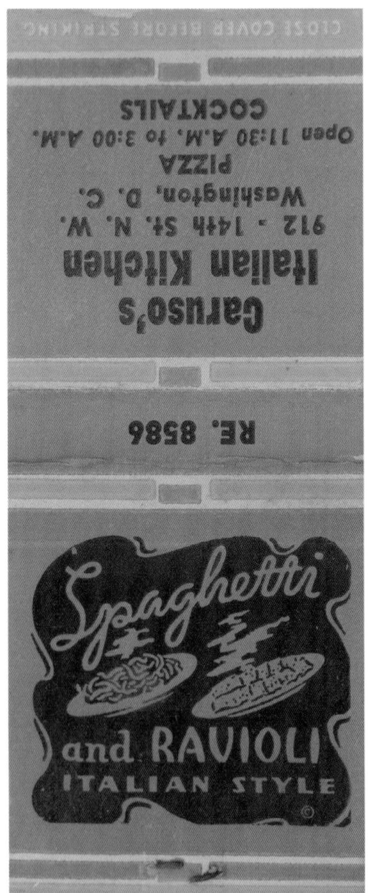

To evaluate the DC days collection is to attempt to categorize an impromptu gathering of objects, intended for short use and then to be thrown away, that has remained intact as a group for over sixty years. Cindy's collection comprises 168 matchbooks dating to the early 1950s, the vast majority commissioned by restaurants and hotels. There are matchbooks from diners, coffee shops, and fine dining restaurants, with cuisines ranging from French, to Italian, Chinese, Mexican, coastal seafood, and barbecue (fig. 3). Matchbooks that advertise cocktail lounges and hotel bars are equally diverse, and include those from large upscale hotels, rural inns, and roadside motels (fig. 4). The bulk of the matchbooks come from Washington, DC, and its vicinity, while a small portion are from destinations such as New York, Chicago, and Miami. A few were issued for noncommercial purposes by embassies or served as personalized wedding party favors. It is easy to dismiss such a collection, hidden in a private home, unorganized, its relevance dependent on a direct connection between the collector and the items it contains. Examining and discussing the matchbooks together with the collector, however, gave me the opportunity to witness how the matchbooks serve as a prompt for Cindy to recall fragmentary personal memories about events that took place in the establishments she frequented, most of which no longer exist, and transmit these to a listener.

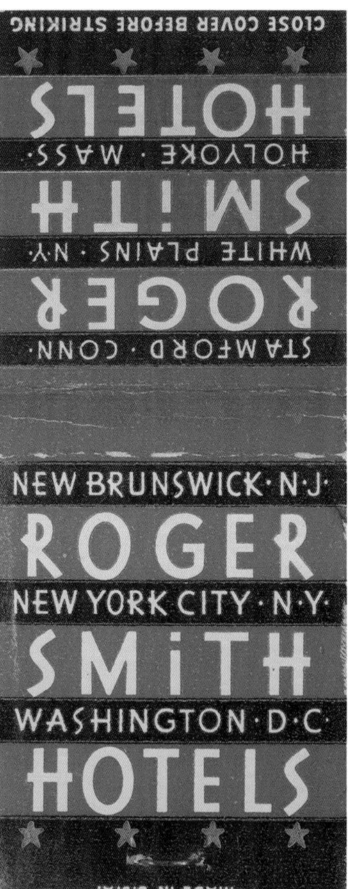

fig. 4
Matchbooks, Bedford Springs Hotel (Bedford, PA), Hotel St. George (Brooklyn, NY), and Roger Smith Hotels, from the DC days collection, 1950s. Private collection.

The matchbook, a common portable lighting device and inexpensive advertising product, had its heyday in the mid-twentieth century, during precisely the period when Cindy was assembling her DC days collection. This essay explores how the form and function of this mass-produced consumer product opened it to appropriation for noncommercial experiences of time and place, and how this secondary layer of significance relates to the matchbook's intended commercial function. Matchbooks have served, in particular, both as vivid tokens of personal experience and as period artifacts—purposes corresponding to contrasting collecting practices. The last part of the essay considers how tangible objects operate within these collecting practices to forge links with either collective or personal experiences of the past.

The Matchbook Industry

By the 1950s, when Cindy began her collection, matchbooks had been in production for six decades. Joshua Pusey, a patent lawyer and avid inventor based in Pennsylvania, filed an application with the United States Patent Office in 1889 for an invention he named the Flexible Match.[2] In the patent statement, Pusey stated that his objective was "to provide a friction-match device which shall be cheap, readily made, convenient in use, and efficient, and which may be handily and safely carried in the pocket."[3] He considered convenience and portability the essential objectives of the Flexible Match, its ready-to-use character underscored by the name itself. A folded strip of thick paper holds and protects the cardboard matches, an improvement on the matchbox and the refillable portable container known as the safe, in existence since the invention of the friction match in the mid-nineteenth century. With a finite lifespan embedded in its design, Pusey's invention anticipated the commonly referenced "throwaway ethic" of the twentieth-century US economy.[4]

Although a paper match can light anything, it was intended to facilitate the habit of smoking. At the time of its invention, the Flexible Match was designed primarily for pipe and cigar lighting, but its appearance coincided with the commercial introduction of the cigarette. The Duke family initiated mass production of machine-rolled cigarettes at the start of the 1880s, and within several years the cigarette was the most popular tobacco product on the market, with such brands as Camel, Lucky Strike, and Chesterfield competing for a rapidly increasing number of consumers. Smoking in public had traditionally been considered a strictly male activity; motivated to expand their pool of customers, tobacco companies directed their advertising campaigns of the 1920s toward women, eventually fostering an environment in which it was acceptable for women to smoke openly in public.[5] By the mid-twentieth century, the habit had penetrated all classes of American society.

fig. 5 (opposite)
Matchbook from Stork Club, New York, from the DC days collection, 1950s. Private collection.

fig. 6
"Mrs. Farrington at the Stork Club (Diners at the Stork Club)," 1949, for *Look Magazine* (unpublished). Photograph by Stanley Kubrick. SK Film Archives/ Museum of the City of New York, X2011.4.11834.8.

The matchbook industry grew apace with the tobacco industry and incorporated its standards. The most widely produced matchbook type, the twenty-striker, held one match for every cigarette found in a standard cigarette pack.[6] The matchbook became a fixture in restaurants and hotel rooms (figs. 5, 6). A wide array of objects, from ashtrays to toilet paper dispensers, was tweaked to offer matchbook-adapted models.[7] Patents include those for a matchbook holder and key ring, a matchbook and compact mirror hybrid, and a matchbook and disposable razor hybrid.[8] There exist at least two patents for a matchbook with emergency ashtray, and combination matchbook and cigarette pack holder.[9] There are also patents for a matchbook as a board game spinner, as place card and cigarette holder, a dual matchbook-toothpick holder, and a combination golf tee and matchbook.[10] Clever and amusing, these hybrids are overshadowed by the matchbook's most commonly encountered yet improvised dual application, namely matchbook and notepad combination. In a pinch, the matchbook's small but sturdy paper surface could be used for writing down street addresses, phone numbers, significant dates, secret codes and messages, ideas that came to mind, and to-do lists.

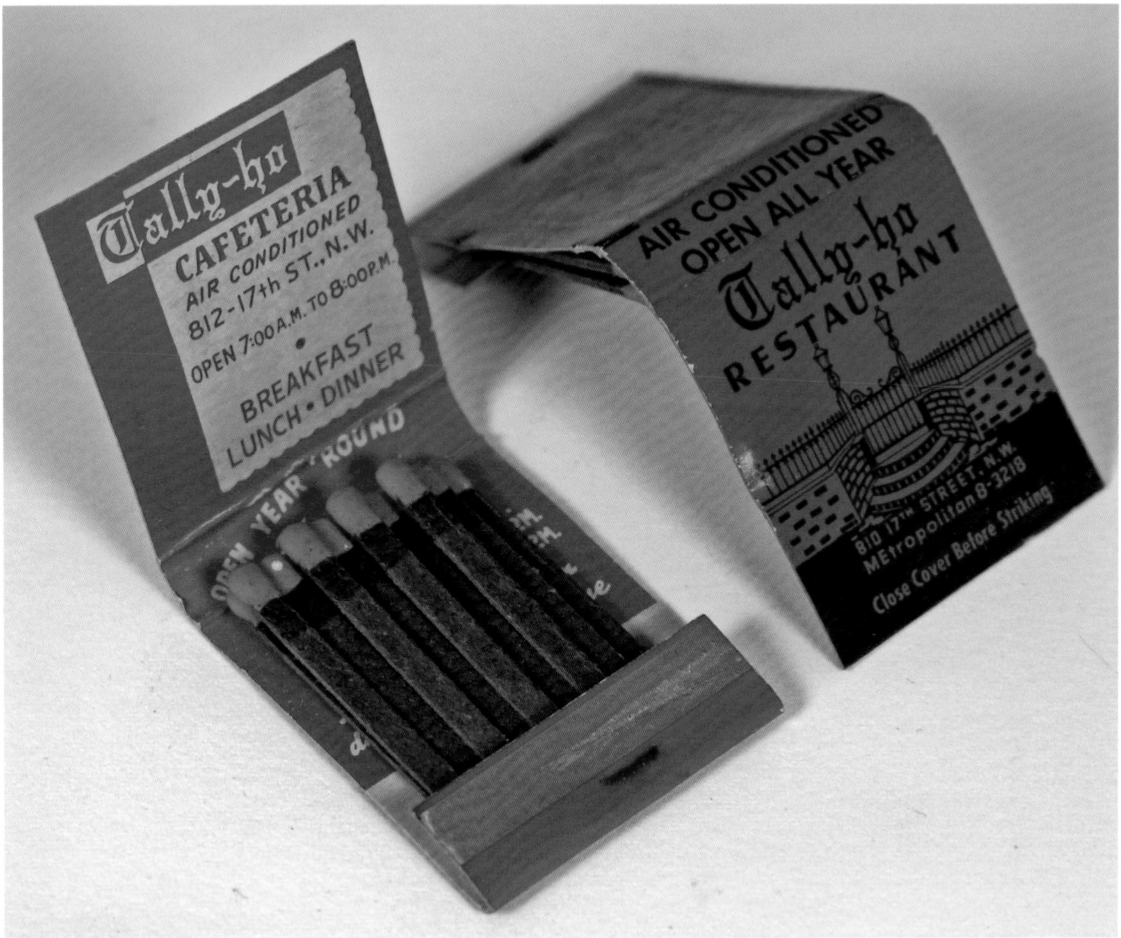

Tally-ho
CAFETERIA
AIR CONDITIONED
812-17th ST., N.W.
OPEN 7:00 A.M. TO 8:00 P.M.
BREAKFAST
LUNCH • DINNER
OPEN YEAR 'ROUND
AIR CONDITIONED
OPEN ALL YEAR
Tally-ho
RESTAURANT
810 17th STREET, N.W.
METropolitan 8-3218
Close Cover Before Striking

Dinner
Luncheon
Breakfast
OPEN FROM
7 A.M. to 9:00 P.M.
WARMUTH'S
RESTAURANT
280 Devonshire St.
BOSTON
CLOSE COVER BEFORE STRIKING

WASHINGTON STREET
SUMMER ST.
DEVONSHIRE ST.
WARMUTH'S
RESTAURANT
ATLANTIC AVENUE
SOUTH
STATION

CLOSE COVER BEFORE STRIKING
hi hat
AMERICA'S
Smartest
BARBECUE
KENMORE 0550
HI-HAT
DELICIOUS FOOD
QUALITY LIQUORS
DANCING
COLUMBUS AT MASS. AVE.
• BOSTON •

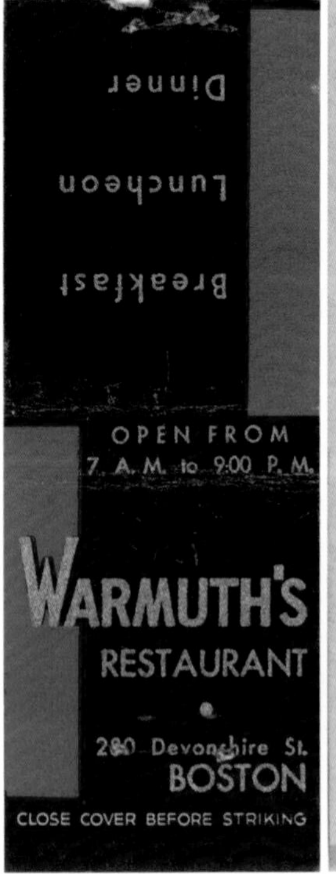

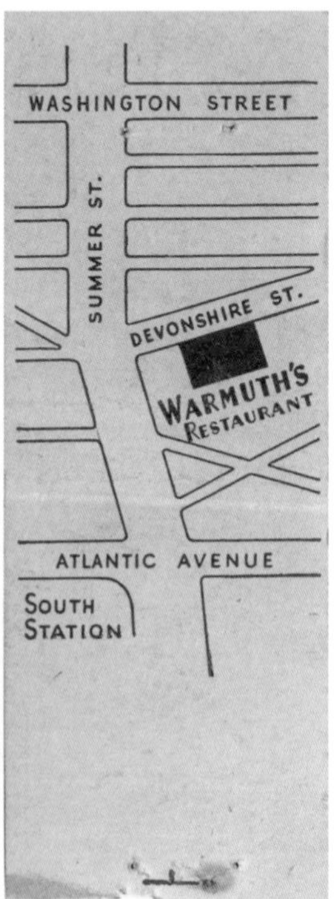

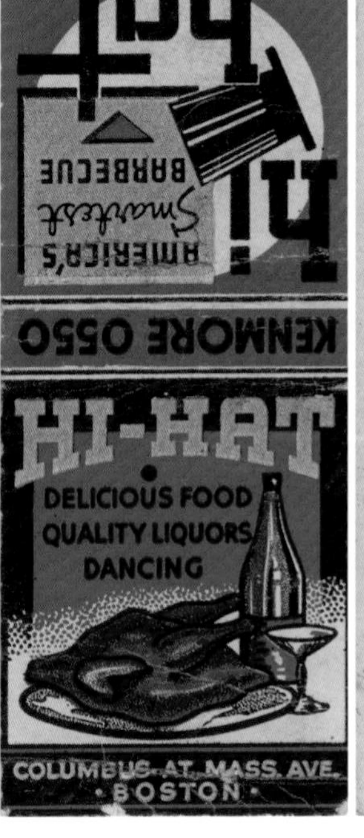

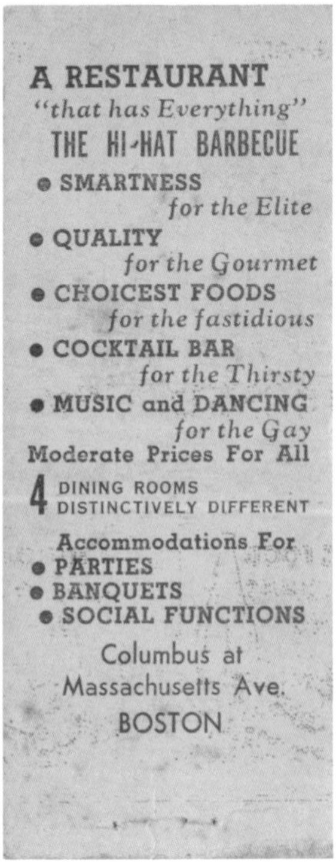

A RESTAURANT
"that has Everything"
THE HI-HAT BARBECUE
• SMARTNESS
for the Elite
• QUALITY
for the Gourmet
• CHOICEST FOODS
for the fastidious
• COCKTAIL BAR
for the Thirsty
• MUSIC and DANCING
for the Gay
Moderate Prices For All
4 DINING ROOMS
DISTINCTIVELY DIFFERENT
Accommodations For
• PARTIES
• BANQUETS
• SOCIAL FUNCTIONS
Columbus at
Massachusetts Ave.
BOSTON

Although Pusey's patent had established the need for a portable lighting device, he had not foreseen the matchbook's advertising potential. That use would develop only after he sold the patent to the Diamond Match Company in 1894. After early failed attempts to sell the matchbook as a straightforward lighting device, the Diamond Match Company began marketing it as a clever and inexpensive advertising product. The idea was propelled by a successful promotional campaign carried out in 1896 by the Mendelssohn Opera Company to advertise its upcoming performances by distributing matchbooks with handwritten information. The real turning point was the Pabst Brewing Company's order, placed with the Diamond Match Company in 1902, for ten million matchbooks sporting the Pabst emblem, which were offered to customers for free.[11]

The matchbook belongs to the robust tradition in twentieth-century advertising of using visual communication to target return business by consumers and circulate the brand. Noncommercial uses for matchbooks included political slogans, social causes, cultural events, and even law enforcement's "Most Wanted" campaigns. The matchbook's particular construction presents several opportunities for designers to fulfill the advertising objective. Although confined to a small surface area, designers have several faces—the exterior cover, the front, back, saddle, and striking surface—on which to work (fig. 7). On the interior, there is the long inside cover face as well as the match stems themselves.

For matchbooks commissioned by the hospitality industry, a requisite was providing factual information, such as location, hours, and services offered, as well as clues about atmosphere or place identity (figs. 8, 9). A commissioning entity, such as a restaurant or hotel interested in matchbook advertising, might hire either a freelance designer or graphic advertising agency to draft its matchbook design. Most American businesses, however, went directly to the matchbook manufacturer to obtain their designs, the result of which was an alloy of preexisting stock images, catchphrases, and taglines, as well as color schemes and surface finishes chosen by the clients from company-issued sales catalogs (figs. 10, 11). Catalogs presented the client with hundreds of options and gave basic instructions as to what to consider when self-designing a commercially successful cover.

fig. 7
Matchbook,Tally-ho Cafeteria, Washington, DC, from the DC days collection, 1950s. Private collection.

figs. 8, 9
Matchbooks, Warmuth's Restaurant and Hi-Hat Barbecue, Boston, 1940s. Boston Public Library.

Restaurant and hotel owners approached matchbook graphics either as a correlate to the overall design program of the establishment, or as augmentation with little regard for decorative continuity. Integrating a matchbook into an establishment's overall graphic and interior design scheme required reproducing building details, matching interior color and design schemes, and incorporating logos. Restaurant chains, such as Howard Johnson's, depended on uniform and integrated design schemes to

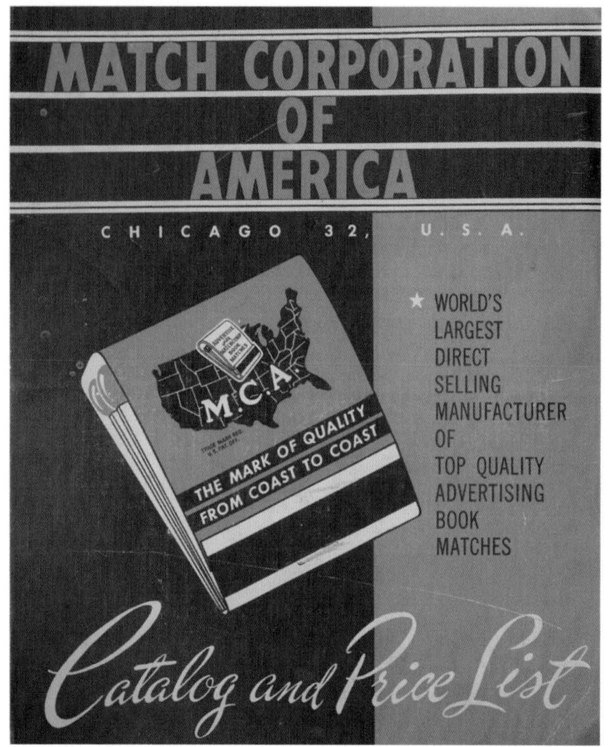

link branches and reinforce brand identity with customers. The exterior covers of Howard Johnson's matchbooks shared many characteristics with the chain's other paper products, such as menus, sugar packets, and place settings: the signature orange and blue color scheme, the logo, as well as the façade of the Howard Johnsons' Colonial Revival building (fig. 12).

Matchbooks produced using stock designs, on the other hand, shared little with the actual appearance of the establishment. Instead, they presented generic images and catchphrases that nevertheless communicated something about the location and its offerings. One restaurant featured in the DC days collection that followed such a strategy is Maxime—a French restaurant once located at 1731 Connecticut Avenue in Washington, DC. The owners selected a stock illustration and paired it with pertinent information about their venture: the name of the restaurant, its address, telephone number, hours of operation, and the fact that it offered music. The stock illustration depicts two silhouetted figures seated across from each other at a table, in an elegant setting, engaged in conversation (fig. 13). Supplementing the matchbook's ambiguity regarding specific décor and palette, Maxime offered its customers postcards featuring a color photograph of the restaurant's interior (fig. 14).

In addition to proffering stock designs and sample options, sales catalogs published by match companies also promoted the advantages of matchbook advertising. A portfolio for Superior Match Company from around 1940 opens with the statement:

> Users of Book Matches know their flexibility; they know there are few—if any—advertising mediums which can produce the same results with such speed and with such economy. Book Matches are used universally; they go into homes, into men's pockets and women's handbags. They are found on bridge tables, on office desks. In short, Book Match Advertising actually REACHES the attention of the ultimate consumer.[12]

figs. 10, 11 (top and opposite) Sales catalog, "Match Corporation of America," c. 1940. Private collection.

Matchbook manufacturers guaranteed that their product would be used and examined many times, in fact up to twenty times—each time a match

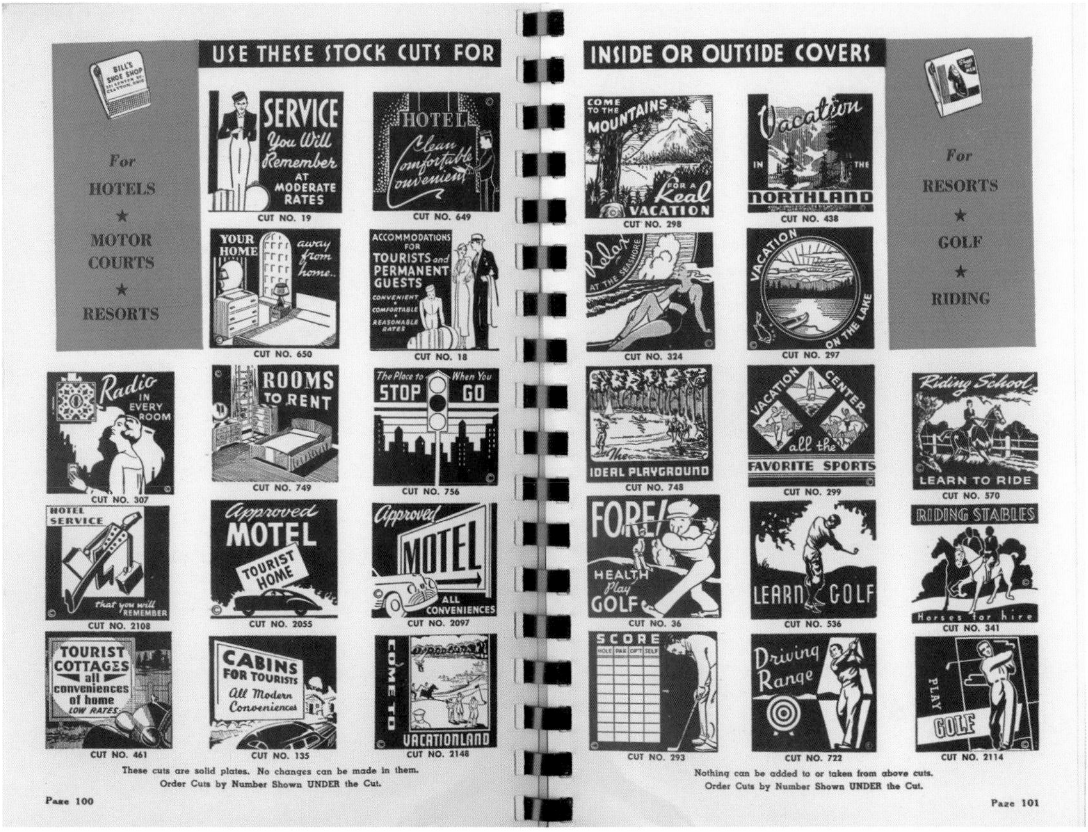

USE THESE STOCK CUTS FOR INSIDE OR OUTSIDE COVERS

For HOTELS ★ MOTOR COURTS ★ RESORTS

CUT NO. 19 · CUT NO. 649 · CUT NO. 650 · CUT NO. 18 · CUT NO. 307 · CUT NO. 749 · CUT NO. 756 · CUT NO. 2108 · CUT NO. 2055 · CUT NO. 2097 · CUT NO. 461 · CUT NO. 135 · CUT NO. 2148

These cuts are solid plates. No changes can be made in them.
Order Cuts by Number Shown UNDER the Cut.

Page 100

For RESORTS ★ GOLF ★ RIDING

CUT NO. 298 · CUT NO. 438 · CUT NO. 324 · CUT NO. 297 · CUT NO. 748 · CUT NO. 299 · CUT NO. 570 · CUT NO. 36 · CUT NO. 536 · CUT NO. 341 · CUT NO. 293 · CUT NO. 722 · CUT NO. 2114

Nothing can be added to or taken from above cuts.
Order Cuts by Number Shown UNDER the Cut.

Page 101

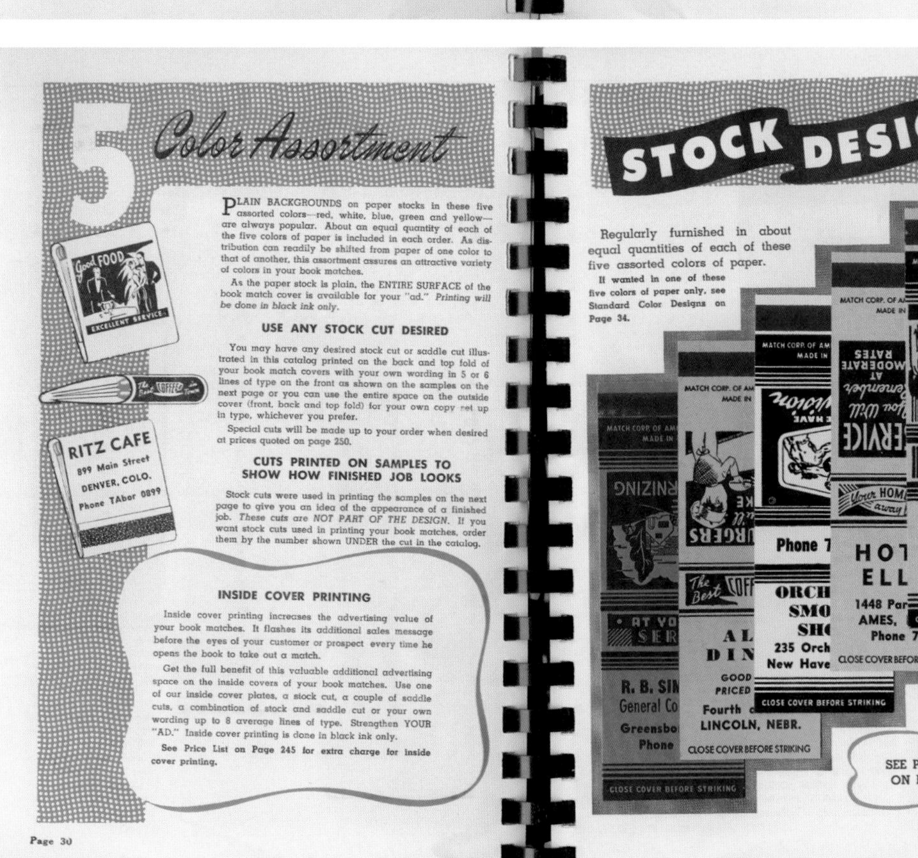

5 Color Assortment

PLAIN BACKGROUNDS on paper stocks in these five assorted colors—red, white, blue, green and yellow—are always popular. About an equal quantity of each of the five colors of paper is included in each order. As distribution can readily be shifted from paper of one color to that of another, this assortment assures an attractive variety of colors in your book matches.

As the paper stock is plain, the ENTIRE SURFACE of the book match cover is available for your "ad." *Printing will be done in black ink only.*

USE ANY STOCK CUT DESIRED

You may have any desired stock cut or saddle cut illustrated in this catalog printed on the back and top fold of your book match covers with your own wording in 5 or 6 lines of type on the front as shown on the samples on the next page or you can use the entire space on the outside cover (front, back and top fold) for your own copy set up in type, whichever you prefer.

Special cuts will be made up to your order when desired at prices quoted on page 250.

CUTS PRINTED ON SAMPLES TO SHOW HOW FINISHED JOB LOOKS

Stock cuts were used in printing the samples on the next page to give you an idea of the appearance of a finished job. *These cuts are NOT PART OF THE DESIGN.* If you want stock cuts used in printing your book matches, order them by the number shown UNDER the cut in the catalog.

INSIDE COVER PRINTING

Inside cover printing increases the advertising value of your book matches. It flashes its additional sales message before the eyes of your customer or prospect every time he opens the book to take out a match.

Get the full benefit of this valuable additional advertising space on the inside covers of your book matches. Use one of our inside cover plates, a stock cut, a couple of saddle cuts, a combination of stock and saddle cut or your own wording up to 8 average lines of type. Strengthen YOUR "AD." Inside cover printing is done in black ink only.

See Price List on Page 245 for extra charge for inside cover printing.

RITZ CAFE
899 Main Street
DENVER, COLO.
Phone TAbor 0899

Page 30

STOCK DESIGNS

Regularly furnished in about equal quantities of each of these five assorted colors of paper.

If wanted in one of these five colors of paper only, see Standard Color Designs on Page 34.

MILLER'S DRY CLEANING
2125 S. 25th St.
Omaha, Nebr.
Phone MA. 9165

SEE PRICE LIST ON PAGE 245

Page 31

fig. 12 (top left)
Matchbook, Howard Johnson's, from the DC days collection, 1950s. Private collection.

fig. 13 (bottom left)
Matchbook, Maxime, Washington DC, from the DC days collection, 1950s. Private collection.

fig. 14 (bottom right)
Postcard, Maxime, Washington, DC, 1950s. Private collection.

fig. 15 (top right)
Howard Johnson's billboard, August 8, 1948. R. C. Maxwell Co. Outdoor Advertising Collection, Item # XXH1724. John W. Hartman Center for Sales, Advertising & Marketing History, Duke University. David M. Rubenstein Rare Book & Manuscript Library.

was struck. The Superior Match Company catalog compared matchbooks to reliable and loyal salesmen, their effectiveness evidenced by their ubiquity. It encouraged clients to examine discarded matchbooks found on the streets to better understand why "seldom if ever will you find a book with even a single match remaining in it," and touted matchbook advertising as less expensive and more effective than poster and newspaper ads. The matchbook cover was "a miniature billboard, doing all that a billboard can do and more, since it is seen by interested people you CAN interest."[13] But in comparison with a large stationary roadside billboard, the diminutive, portable matchbook delivered a far superior advertising result, one catering to repeat rather than incidental customers (fig. 15).

From Disposable Object to Keepsake

Although most matchbooks were used and discarded, as matchbook manufacturers envisioned, a small percentage of matchbooks was saved and kept by customers. Matchbook manufacturers and the companies that advertised through matchbooks explored stratagems to hook or reward repeat customers by printing series or commemorative matchbooks (fig. 16). Working seemingly against the interest of matchbook circulation and repeat usage, restaurants occasionally participated in converting their matchbooks into personal keepsakes destined for treasure troves. At Blue Mirror, a high-end supper club in 1950s Washington, patrons could request photographs of their dates taken and stapled to the club's matchbook, a memento very unlikely to be shared with strangers (figs. 17, 18).

In *Collecting in a Consumer Society*, Russell W. Belk analyzes ties between consumerism and collecting, arguing that modern practices of collecting coincided with the development of consumer culture and thrived in its environment.[14] He points out that the pool of items deemed acceptable collectibles expanded rapidly at the beginning of the twentieth century to include virtually anything, from advertising posters to farm equipment. According to Belk, "mass production, growing world affluence, and the spread of consumer culture have made it possible for collecting to become a truly mass phenomenon."[15] Shorter work hours and greater alienation from work activities also contributed to the development of collecting as a serious activity outside the workplace. In Belk's words: "Because hobbies are often seen as being closer to work than leisure, they provide a guilt-free activity that supports the work ethic and offers more self-control and reward than a corporate or factory career."[16] Belk views collecting in double terms—as a form of consumption as well as a new form of production:

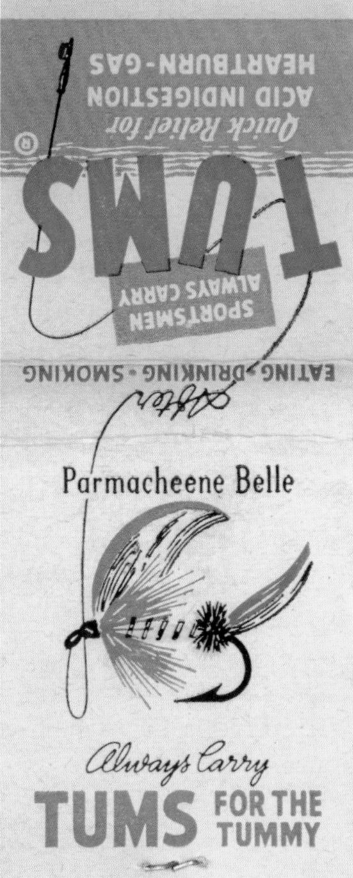

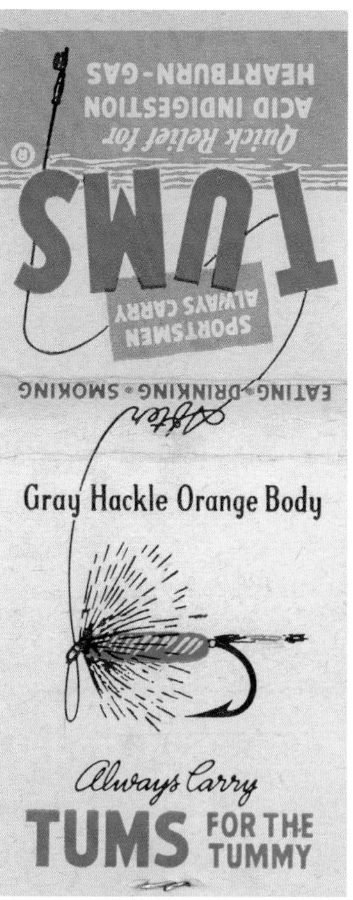

fig. 16
Matchbooks, Tums, Universal Match Corp., St. Louis, 1950s. Private collection.

> Collectors create, combine, classify, and curate the objects they acquire in such a way that a new product, the collection, emerges. In the process they also produce meanings. More precisely, they participate in the process of socially reconstructing shared meanings for the objects they collect.[17]

Belk's observations provide some context for understanding the hobby of matchbook collecting, an activity nearly as old as the matchbook itself, with its own rules, rituals, and vocabulary.[18]

Matchbooks attracted collectors as early as the late 1910s. Evelyn Hovious of California is often mentioned as one of the first hobbyists who actively championed and promoted the activity, as well as demonstrated how absorbing matchbook cover collecting could be. At its peak, Hovious's collection numbered five million items and required the collector to construct a separate dwelling to house it.[19] The first matchbook collectors clubs appeared in the mid-1930s, culminating in the establishment of a national organization, the Rathkamp Matchcover Society (RMS), in 1941. For nearly seventy-five years, the society's annual regional and national conventions have brought members and their collections together, facilitated matchbook trading, and fostered a culture around the hobby (fig. 19).[20]

Members of the matchbook collecting community emphasize the hobby's governing criteria.[21] A matchbook collection may begin as accidental or deliberate, but it must conform to certain established formats reflecting a shared attitude among collectors in order to classify as a "genuine" hobby collection. The hobby collector values matchbooks in mint condition, their strikers intact.[22] Matchbooks that enter a hobbyist's collection go through a radical transformation. The valueless and hazardous matches are removed and thrown away in a process called shucking.[23] The end result is a flattened matchbook cover stored (but not pasted) in an album according to a cataloging system determined by the collector. Within this community of hobbyist collectors, the matchbooks are perceived primarily as ephemera, as advertising products, their value determined mostly by the aesthetic qualities of the cover graphics, subject matter, and their rareness. The collector takes interest in preserving matchbook covers precisely for their fleeting character, their insubstantiality and commonness offering a rich representation of the surface texture of everyday life during the period in which the matchbooks were issued. Considering themselves historians, preservationists, and archivists, they share an ambition to see the collections move from private to public archive, thus partaking in a collective effort to reconstitute and preserve the matchbook's place in the material culture to which it belongs.[24]

Through the process of shucking, the hobby collector decommissions the matchbook, eliminates its original practical purpose, removes it from

fig. 17
Postcard, Blue Mirror Supper Club, Washington, DC, 1950s. Private collection.

fig. 18
Matchbook, Blue Mirror Supper Club, Washington, DC (with photograph of an unidentified man), from the DC days collection, 1950s. Private collection.

fig. 19
Matchbooks, 10th Annual Convention of Matchcover Collectors, Boston, 1950. Boston Public Library.

BLUE MIRROR — 824 FOURTEENTH STREET, N. W. — WASHINGTON, D. C.
5B-H1058

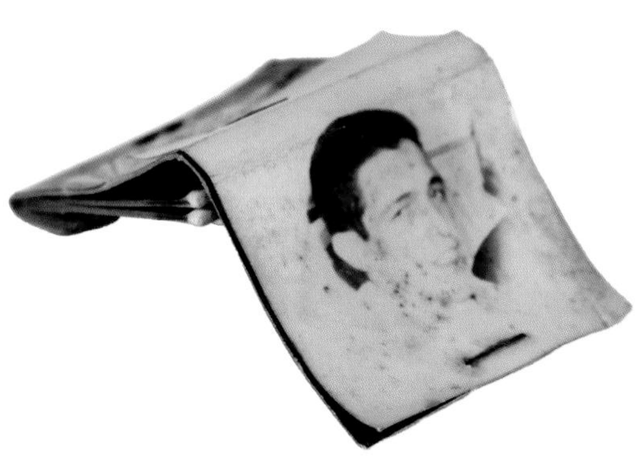

CHICAGO MATCH CO.
Libertyville, Ill., U.S.A.
"Them buckshot 'n four slegs aire from last falls feudin!"
X-RAY
MATCHCOVER FOLIOS
10th Annual Convention Of Matchcover Collectors
HOTEL VENDOME
BOSTON, MASS.
Sept. 8-9-10, 1950
Close Cover for Safety

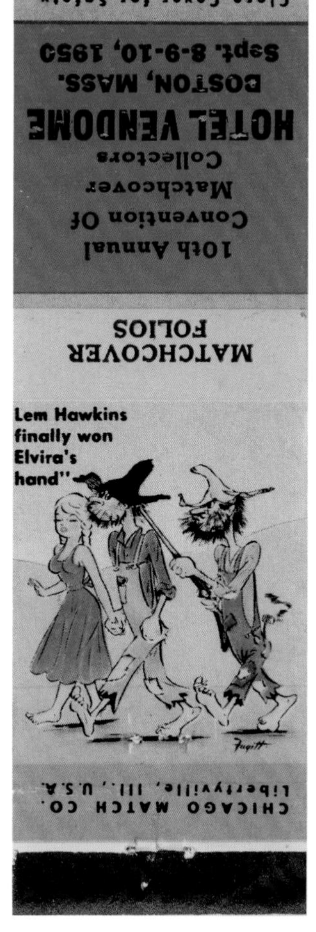
Close Cover for Safety
Sept. 8-9-10, 1950
BOSTON, MASS.
HOTEL VENDOME
10th Annual Convention Of Matchcover Collectors
MATCHCOVER FOLIOS
Lem Hawkins finally won Elvira's hand"
CHICAGO MATCH CO.
Libertyville, Ill., U.S.A.

circulation, and repurposes it as a collectible specifically formatted for the hobby. In Susan Stewart's words, collected objects are "neutralized into the landscape of collection itself."[25] In the case of matchbooks, this happens quite literally as the matchbooks are stripped of their combustible elements. The matchbook cover as collectible still references the places and products advertised on its surfaces, but it is now formally tagged with the collector's term "advertising ephemera," its graphics deemed meaningful according to the qualities they share with those on neighboring covers.

One still occasionally encounters matchbooks as giveaways on restaurant counters and newspaper stands, or discarded on sidewalks. But it is clear that the matchbook today is nearing retirement and has lost its relevance to everyday life. Its demise in the second half of the twentieth century was gradual: first eclipsed by the disposable lighter, then made further obsolete by the decline of smoking thanks to public health campaigns.

Those participating in the hobby of matchbook cover collecting are well aware that the matchbook's heyday, like that of the postcard, is long since past. This is not to say that matchbooks produced during the mid-twentieth century are difficult to come by (although there are rare, much-sought-after items, such as the 1927 matchbook that commemorated a dinner organized in honor of Charles Lindbergh and his first nonstop transatlantic flight). Matchbooks are a staple of today's flea markets and yard sales, pulled from the forgotten corners of parents' homes or sold by those who no longer care about their collections. Online auction sites offer anything from single matchbooks to lots numbering in the thousands. Lots of unsorted matchbooks, often vaguely described as "vintage," can be so large that weight rather than count is used to convey size. One can buy an unused vintage 1950s matchbook for under a dollar.

Online auction sites also demonstrate how readily matchbooks lose their layers of personal relevance when the link between the collector and the collection is broken. Often sellers' broad descriptions of the lots openly disclose a lack of knowledge of the matchbooks offered for sale, providing only vague testimonials to the original owner's past activities and travels as clues to the contents. When preserved and cataloged, such orphaned matchbooks, with memories erased, become physical remnants of the collective past embedded in the consumer culture.

A column that recently appeared in the *Daily Republic*, a paper from Fairfield-Suisun in Solano County, California, offers a case in point about a very different form of matchbook collecting.[26] The author, Murray Bass, was "in the process of making life a little simpler by disposing of things [he] no longer need[ed]," including thousands of matchbooks.[27] But before this purge took place, Bass's son expressed interest in his father's matchbook collection, to which he felt both a sentimental connection and partial authorship, along with his mother. Several thousands of matchbooks collected and preserved in shoeboxes represented Bass family history starting from 1956—marking family trips and places where they had lived. As smokers, the Bass family had maintained the matchbooks unshucked, the matches remaining as practically useful as the printed location names would be helpful for recalling their travels. Examining the matchbooks side-by-side, father and son discovered that they triggered very different memories in each of them, and together weaved a highly layered family history dynamic. Murray Bass ended up shipping the collection to his son.

Similarly, the DC days collection lies outside the hobby of matchbook cover collecting. Nothing about the matchbooks' format, content, or the way they were amassed and stored corresponds to the hobby practice as described above. Whereas hobby collections are in constant flux due to additions, substitutions, and de-accessions, the DC days collection has remained unaltered for nearly six decades. Such dissimilarities underline the different purposes assigned to the collections by their creators. In the DC days collection, the matchbook's ephemeral nature is recognized, but a matchbook is not preserved as an artifact; rather, it remains within its original network of meaning, tangibly linked to non-collecting experiences. Within the personal realm, a matchbook's ephemerality invokes the collector's memories and exists to spark personal stories. Though the prompted narratives both fade in detail over time and overlap unreliably with subsequent experiences, for the owner/collector the matchbooks largely retain their referentiality within the social world from which they originated. They remain within their network of designed functionality, particularly as tools of advertising; for example, the Maxime matchbook still triggers thoughts about the restaurant. In addition, each matchbook's use history can be felt in one's hands, the irreversible cover wear and number of matches remaining attesting not only to the time spent at the site advertised, but also to a prevalent mood, whether anxious or festive.

It seems appropriate to characterize such a personal, non-hobby collection as a trove of mementos destined for an autobiographical scrapbook, which simply never coalesced into an organized whole. The matchbooks were kept not for their pristine condition, nor as a perceived set or series, nor because of their rarity or historical and artistic importance. They were preserved for their link to a cluster of personal experiences and because as a mass they approximate a world within which the collector once thrived and might wish to revisit, reflecting class taste and financial means. Lacking the scrapbook's framework, such collections nevertheless share with the scrapbook a fundamental orientation toward "visual autobiography,"[28] i.e., the period graphics of hotel and restaurant matchbook may be as evocative to the scrapbooker as obsolete snapshot formats and vintage fonts found on old newspaper clippings. Where they diverge is in their refusal of any specific fixed narrative or theme, as they retain the same form and basic condition as possessed on the last day of collecting. Rather than disqualifying the collection or downgrading it to the status of accumulation, this lack of structure opens the possibility for free, unscripted retellings. Moreover, the matchbook that is unattached to an album page and retains its matches remains functional. At any moment, it can potentially return to circulation. One could argue that this preserved functionality and haptic presence allows the collector to maintain a more vivid emotional connection with the amassed objects and, through them, with her past.

When I looked through and held Cindy's matchbooks on my own, their tactility and continuing functionality gave me a sense that the social texture of this period was within my grasp. Seated with Cindy, however, and listening to the memories triggered by individual matchbooks, especially those centering on the intricacies of cocktail bar etiquette and other behavioral codes for young single women in the 1950s, that initial connection vanished. I became aware of my limitations to fully grasp the range of meanings of this collection. It is Cindy's memories that render the collection's format legible, and provide the depth of meaning that is otherwise undetectable to an outsider who is focused on a historical perspective.

The DC days collection's idiosyncrasies, lack of organization, inaccessibility, and dependence on the collector's memory—all required for such collections to retain their full meanings for their owners—are precisely what disqualifies them from entering the public domain. Private memory-based collections in their ramshackle state have little value to archivists and librarians, unlike hobby-type collections, and their lifespans are only slightly extended by their transfer to family and friends. Like the matchbook itself, memory-based collections have a built-in obsolescence. They are mortal. But it was the popularity of matchbook collections as private reminder that has provided the hobbyist collector a large pool of material from which to catalog, completing the circle of public to private and back to public.

NOTES

I would like to thank the editors Marta Zarzycka and Jon Mogul for their constructive and insightful comments that helped me flesh out my ideas during the editing process. I am grateful to Lynda Klich for reading and editing the early draft of the essay and for her continuous support. My deepest gratitude goes to Harold Dean, who was an instrumental part of the writing and thinking process, and whose input greatly influenced my approach toward the matchbook. Finally, I would like to thank Cindy for letting me use her collection as the case study.

1. Although she gave the author full access to the collection and agreed to be interviewed for the purposes of this essay, the collector wishes to remain anonymous.
2. Joshua Pusey, Flexible Match, US Patent 483,166, filed August 6, 1889, renewed March 17, 1892, and issued on September 27, 1892.
3. Ibid.
4. Giles Slade, *Made to Break: Technology and Obsolescence in America* (Cambridge, MA: Harvard University Press, 2007).
5. Charles Goodrum and Helen Dalrymple, *Advertising in America: The First 200 Years* (New York: Abrams, 1990), 191–99.
6. Marisa Wilairat, "Diamond Matchbooks: Development of Advertising and the Corporate Image in Early 20th Century America," *Haverford Journal* 2, no. 1 (February 2006): 74–89.
7. Nicholas Solimine, Combined Toilet Paper Holder, Matchbook Holder and Ash Tray, US Patent D217777, filed November 14, 1968, issued 1970.
8. Julian Holland, Combined Key Ring and Matchbook Holder, US Patent D201016, filed December 23, 1963, issued May 4, 1965; Charles Hill, Matchbook Mirror and Safety Guard, US Patent 2620920, filed November 10, 1948, issued December 9, 1952.
9. William D. Dunn, Cigarette Package and Matchbook, US Patent 2640588, filed September 8, 1950, issued June 2, 1953.
10. Frank W. Ketcham, Match Book Place Card, US Patent 1993845, filed December 30, 1933, issued March 12, 1935; Louis Fried, Combined Match and Toothpick Holder, US Patent 2269196, filed March 29, 1940, issued January 6, 1942.
11. H. Thomas Steele, Jim Heimann, and Rod Dyer, *Close Cover before Striking: The Golden Age of Matchbook Art* (New York: Abbeville Press, 1987), 6–7.
12. Superior Match Company, "Advertise with Superior Union Label Book Matches" (ca. 1940), 1.
13. Ibid.
14. Russell W. Belk, *Collecting In a Consumer Society* (London: Routledge, 1995), 55.
15. Ibid., 53.
16. Ibid., 55.
17. Ibid.
18. Steele, Heimann, and Dyer, *Close Cover before Striking*, 9–11.
19. Ibid., 11. See also Anita Gold, "Custom-made gowns for antique dolls available," in *St. Petersburg Evening Independent* (January 31, 1986): 5B.
20. According to the 2014 RMS convention report, the event took place in St. Louis and had 119 registered participants. Joe De Gennaro, "RMS Convention Report-2014," accessed January 23, 2015, http://www.matchcover.org/Convention%20report.html.
21. A good source for gaining understanding of the world of matchbook cover collecting and its internal discourse is the website the Matchcover Vault: A Resource Site For Matchcover Collectors, owned by Mike Prero. Especially informative is the site's Article Archives, www.matchpro.org.
22. Steele, Heimann, and Dyer, *Close Cover before Striking*, 11.
23. The difficulties of preserving combustible matches in public archives have been outlined by Nora Lackshin in "Off with Their Heads? Matchbooks in Archives," May 2, 2013, Smithsonian Institution Archives blog, accessed January 23, 2015, http://siarchives.si.edu/blog/their-heads-matchbooks-archives.
24. Examples of matchbook cover collections housed in public institutions are the Eleanor Wolpe Matchbook Collection, 1950–1990 and the Elion-Weingarten Matchbook Collection, 1930–1983, both housed at the Archives Center, National Museum of American History, Washington, DC.
25. Susan Stewart, *On Longing: Narratives of the Miniature, the Gigantic, the Souvenir, the Collection* (Durham, NC: Duke University Press, 1993), 156.
26. Murray Bass, "Matchbook covers elicit fond memories of the past," *Daily Republic* (May 18, 2013), accessed October 10, 2013, http://www.dailyrepublic.com/news/locallifestylecolumns/matchbook-covers-elicit-fond-memories-of-the-past/. Additional details about the Bass family's history of collecting matchbooks were supplied by Murray Bass in e-mail correspondence with the author. I would like to thank Mr. Bass for his generous response to my inquiries.
27. Ibid.
28. Jessica Helfand, *Scrapbooks: An American History* (New Haven, CT: Yale University Press, 2008), xvii.

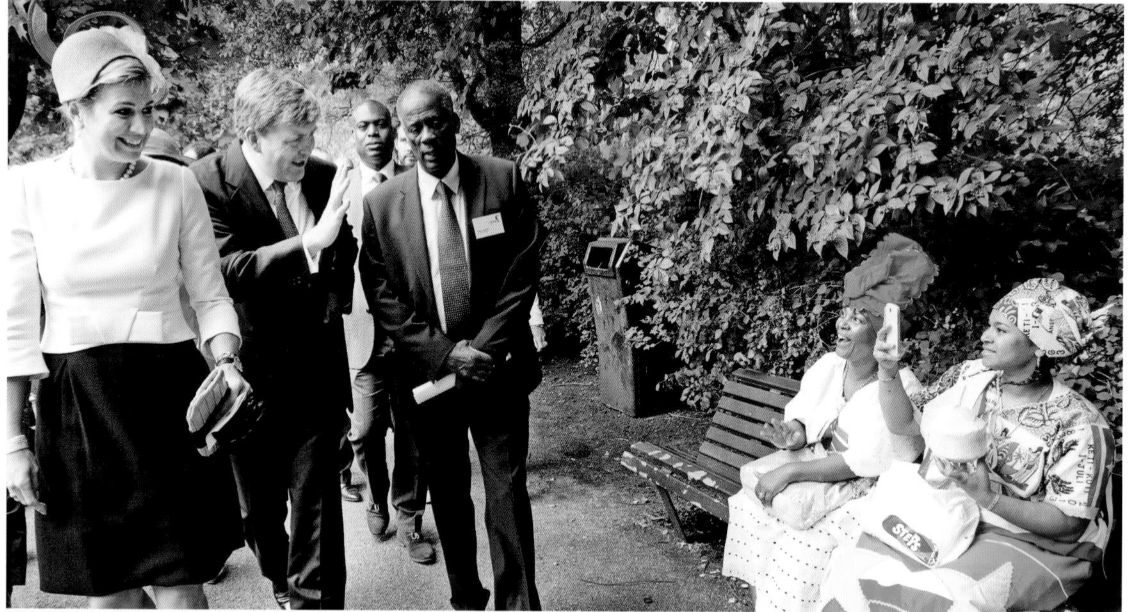

fig. 1
Keti koti celebration in Amsterdam. Photo: Belinda van Dam, 2013. Algemeen Nederlands Persbureau.

fig. 2
Royal couple at the Keti koti celebration. Photo: Robin Utrecht, 2013. Algemeen Nederlands Persbureau.

RE-DRESSING SILENCE: SURINAMESE DUTCH CLOTHING AND THE MEMORY OF SLAVERY IN THE NETHERLANDS

Paul Bijl

Paul Bijl is an assistant professor of modern literature at the University of Amsterdam and an affiliated fellow at KITLV/Royal Netherlands Institute of Southeast Asian and Caribbean Studies. His book *Emerging Memory: Photographs of Colonial Atrocity in Dutch Cultural Remembrance* (2015) is about Dutch colonial memory and forgetting of violence in colonial Indonesia. His current project, funded by NWO/Netherlands Organization for Scientific Research, traces the transnational appropriation of the writings of the Javanese woman Kartini (1879–1904).

Each year on July 1, hundreds of Surinamese and Surinamese Dutch women take part in the annual Keti koti (Broken Chains) festival in Amsterdam's Oosterpark (East Side Park), which commemorates the history of Dutch slavery in the Americas and its abolition in 1863 (figs. 1, 2). Many of these women dress up as *kotomisis*, wearing traditional Surinamese attire that usually includes dresses called *kotos* and folded headscarves called *angisas*.

One of these women, Nancy Wouter, described in a recent interview the shared meaning this clothing has for those who wear it.[1] Wouter, who was visiting the festival with her three daughters, all dressed as *kotomisis*, emphasized the eye-catching qualities of these clothes, with their bright colors, gleaming surfaces, and many rounded and sharp shapes, but also called attention to the way the garments constitute a "tribute" to her ancestors who had resisted slavery. In order to commemorate and honor their ancestors, these twenty-first-century women choose to wear clothes of the type enslaved women in Suriname wore in the nineteenth century. At the end of the interview, Wouter emphasized two things: that Keti koti should become an officially acknowledged, national holiday on which everybody should be able to get a day off work—she had to *take* the day off—and that the history of slavery should be taught in Dutch schools.

This essay argues that the *angisas*, in particular, are tokens of remembrance, as Wouter stated, but that they also serve as a device through which the history of colonialism and slavery can be relived and performed in the context of the present-day Netherlands. It is striking how much emphasis Wouter placed throughout her interview on the oppositional role once played by the clothes she and her daughters were wearing. The bulky *koto*, with its many layers of fabric effectively covering up the shapes of women's bodies, is said by her to have been a necessary invention by female slaves to prevent white slaveholders from "falling in love with them." The *angisa*, she said, made it possible for enslaved women to communicate with one another despite restrictions slaveholders placed on talking among slaves: the patterns on the cloth and the manner in which the *angisa* was folded conveyed coded messages that were intelligible only to other slaves. The Wouters' clothes, in other words, do not only signify a colorful celebration of abolition and of enslaved women's creativity, but also recall the many hardships these women had to go through and their strategies of resistance. Moreover, by offering a critique of the current cultural memory of slavery in the Netherlands—i.e., the ways in which cultural processes and structures shape how memories circulate in a society—Wouter made a connection between enslaved women's resistance and the celebration of Keti koti in the twenty-first-century Netherlands. The *koto* and *angisa* have now become objects that do more than commemorate those women and men who made it possible for Wouter and her daughters to live in freedom today; the garments also restage their resistance against dominant structures in society that would effectively silence the memory of slavery. Rather than solely *display* objects, the clothes are also *performative* objects of remembrance. By putting on these garments, the Wouter family has not only put them on view, but is also performing the forms of resistance practiced by nineteenth-century plantation slaves.

In recent years, authors have analyzed the histories of *angisas* within Surinamese Dutch communities.[2] This scholarship, however, mostly treats *angisas* as museum objects and has not taken into account that women are still wearing them in the Netherlands. In contrast, I position *angisas* within the broader context of the postcolonial Netherlands and analyze the meanings given to them by their wearers as conditioned by Dutch memory and forgetting. The oppositional character of these headscarves that existed during slavery is still operative in the contemporary Dutch context. In order to elucidate the meanings given to their clothes by Wouter and other *kotomisis* in the Netherlands today, I will first discuss how *angisas* work as objects of remembrance and trace the ways in which *kotomisis*, and *angisas* in particular, have been depicted in images and texts since the eighteenth century.

History and Meaning of the *Angisa*

As Nancy Wouter's comments suggest, the meaning that *angisas* have for Surinamese Dutch people today relies on an understanding of what they meant to women in Suriname under slavery and colonialism. Historians

fig. 3
William Blake, *Group of Negros, as Imported to Be Sold for Slaves*, etching, 8 5/8 x 5 1/8 in. (22.2 x 13 cm), 1796. Collection of Robert N. Essick. © 2015 William Blake Archive.

fig. 4
William Blake, *A Surinam Planter in his Morning Dress*, etching, 8 5/8 x 5 1/8 in. (22.2 x 13 cm), 1796. Collection of Robert N. Essick. © 2015 William Blake Archive.

have extensively researched textual and visual materials from Suriname's colonial and postcolonial archives through which the histories of women's clothing, and especially of *kotos* and *angisas*, can be traced.[3] The texts and images found in these archives were mostly written and made by Europeans and reflect the partial and sometimes inaccurate ways in which these writers and artists understood the colonial world, especially Suriname and its enslaved population.

Although historians have pointed out that the practice of communicating nonverbal messages through headscarves was brought to Suriname by enslaved people from West Africa, both textual and visual sources from the seventeenth and eighteenth centuries depict slaves as wearing little clothing. Writings from the time indicate that, except for what they brought themselves from Africa, most slaves were dependent on what their owners gave them—usually just enough to cover the lower parts of their bodies, or even only their waists.[4] An engraving made by William Blake (1757–1827) in 1793 for a book by the Scottish Dutch soldier John Gabriel Stedman (1724–1797) titled *Narrative of a Five Years Expedition against the Revolted Negroes of Surinam* depicts a group of adults and children led to the slave market by a fully dressed European man holding bamboo rattan; the adults are clothed only in loincloths while a child is completely naked (fig. 3).[5] In the other engravings in the book, all based on now-lost watercolors by Stedman, enslaved black men and women have naked upper bodies; in one case, an enslaved woman racialized by Stedman as a "quaderoon" (a person of partially African descent) wears a simple headscarf, though not an *angisa* (fig. 4).

fig. 5
Gerrit Schouten, *Diorama of a Du Party*, paper against a painted background, 17 3/4 x 21 1/4 x 5 1/2 in. (45 x 54 x 14 cm), 1819. National Museum of World Cultures, inv. no. A-6371c.

Stedman wrote a complex, ambiguous book that attacked the most extreme violence of slavery, but not slavery as a system. In the course of the nineteenth century, several artists would depart from Stedman's depiction of slaves in more or less dire situations and develop a more ethnographic approach. It was at the end of the eighteenth century that Surinamese black women started wearing wide skirts, sometimes several on top of one another—an early form of the *koto*. It is not certain whether they were following European fashion, which also favored wide skirts at the time, or going back to African clothing traditions in which multiple cloths were draped around the body, or combining both.[6] The first mention of the word "angisa" occurs in a 1788 dictionary, but there it means handkerchief, not yet headscarf.[7] Evidence of the headscarf as part of enslaved women's dress comes after 1800.

Images of *angisas* can be found in the early nineteenth-century plastic work of Surinamese artist Gerrit Schouten (1779–1839). Schouten made several three-dimensional miniature models from multiple layers of paper against painted backgrounds of situations from life in Suriname. One of the themes Schouten depicted was slave dances, or *dus*, often held to celebrate the new year or around the first of July, already a festive day during slavery. A *du* was a kind of play with music: there were actors, musicians, dancers, and a narrator involved. The Kownu, or king, personifying the Dutch governor of the colony, was a fixed role in these events. A diorama from 1819 depicts such a *du* (fig. 5). The Kownu is right of center, the only figure wearing shoes, which were forbidden to slaves until abolition in 1863; a little to the left of center is the narrator, dressed in a wide skirt, but with naked upper body, and wearing an *angisa*. Clazien Medendorp writes in her study of Schouten's work: "In a *du*, sharp criticism was offered of slavery and plantation life, mixed with ritual dance to honor the gods and ancestors. Whites did not get the deeper meanings of the play."[8] The colonial government made several attempts to forbid these dances, but never fully achieved its goal. Although the first mention of *angisas* having secret meanings did not come until 1835,[9] those depicted in Schouten's diorama are almost certainly playing a role in a subversive performance, even if that role proved hard to read for outsiders like the artist himself.

It may be that the *angisa* first made its appearance in sources from the nineteenth century because it was only then that enslaved women had at their disposal the kinds of fabrics needed to make them. Beginning early in the century, it became a habit for slave owners and their wives to try to distinguish themselves by their elaborately dressed slaves, coinciding with the greater and cheaper availability of fabrics. Some of the women slaves, but certainly only those who were selected to serve in their mistresses' entourage, therefore, had the opportunity to pick up and further develop African ways of wearing headscarves. In the lithographs in the 1839 book *Voyage à Surinam: Description des possessions Néerlandaises dans la Guyane* (Voyage to Suriname: Description of the Netherlands' possessions in Guyana) by the Belgian artist P. J. Benoit (1782–1854), *angisas* can be found on almost every page.[10] Unlike Stedman, whose work he criticized, Benoit chose not to depict the horrors of slavery, but rather created ethnographic scenes of everyday life. Benoit writes about women's clothing in passages on what he calls "missies," creole women who lived with European men in intimate relationships, but officially held the position of housekeepers. In a lithograph from Benoit's book, one such woman is depicted bringing her child to be baptized, preceded and followed by two enslaved girls (fig. 6). Benoit's illustration does emphasize the many variants in which *angisas* came and the many ways in which they could be tied.

fig. 6
P. J. Benoit, *A Missie Bringing Her Child to Be Baptized, Preceded and Followed by a Young Female Slave*, lithograph, 7 3/8 x 5 in. (18.8 X 12.6 cm), 1839. Special Collections, University of Amsterdam, OTM: KF 62-880.

fig. 7
Arnold Borret, *Woman with Angisa from the Side*, watercolor, 2 x 1 5/8 in. (5.5 x 4 cm), 1880. KITLV/Royal Netherlands Institute of Southeast Asian and Caribbean Studies, inv. no. 36B228.

fig. 8
Arnold Borret, *Kotomisi with Orane Twig*, watercolor, 2 3/4 x 4 3/8 in. (7 x 11 cm), 1880. KITLV/Royal Netherlands Institute of Southeast Asian and Caribbean Studies, inv. no. 36A231.

After abolition, formerly enslaved people had more means to buy their own clothes, and they were no longer prohibited from wearing shoes. Between 1863 and 1900, the figure of the *kotomisi* fully emerged. For many former slaves who had not been able to wear the types of rich dresses depicted by Benoit and who often wore nothing more than rags, wearing good (or at least better) clothes of their own choosing was a sign of freedom. When the colonial government prohibited appearing outside one's house bare-breasted in 1879, skirts were lengthened so they could be pulled up above the breasts. Still later, when an undershirt had become a

fig. 9
Julius Muller, *Studio Portrait of a Creole Fish Seller Dressed as Kotomisi*, 11 x 8 5/8 in. (28 x 22.1 cm), 1885–95. National Museum of World Cultures, inv. no. 60012320.

fig. 10
Julius Muller, *A Group of Market Women in Kotomisi during the Parade on the Birthday of Princes Wilhelmina*, 8 3/8 x 10 5/8 in. (21.3 x 27 cm), 1893. National Museum of World Cultures, inv. no. 60006564.

standard part of the dress, an excess of fabric around the waist was turned into another characteristic of what is now considered a classical *kotomisi*: the *kotobere*, a "skirt belly" that encircles the abdomen and inside which women could keep handkerchiefs and money, for instance.[11] Moreover, near the end of the nineteenth century, increasing attention was paid to the ways in which the *angisa* could be tied; it was more and more seen as a medium for communication.[12] As becomes clear here, the communicative function of *angisas* properly developed after abolition, yet is sometimes projected back onto the time of slavery by contemporary wearers of these headscarves. Prototypical examples of late nineteenth-century *kotomisis* can be found in the work of the Dutch jurist and author Arnold Borret (1848–1888) (figs. 7, 8).[13]

The Surinamese photographer Julius Muller (1846–1902) also pictured several *kotomisis* in his studio as well as on the streets of Paramaribo at the end of the nineteenth century, including one showing a group of *kotomisis* parading in Paramaribo in 1893 to celebrate the birthday of Princess Wilhelmina on August 31 (figs. 9, 10). When Muller's photographs were categorized in an 1896 lecture by A. C. Wesenhagen, those of *kotomisis* were grouped under "the lesser population," indicative of the fact that the *kotomisi* was more and more associated with the lower classes in Surinamese society.[14] In the course of the early twentieth century, the *kotomisi* disappeared from the streets of Paramaribo and was relegated to ceremonies and various types of dances. Economic factors played a part, as the amount of fabric necessary for the wide *kotos* and *kotoberes* was difficult to afford. The *koto*, associated more and more with tradition and with the lower classes, appealed less to those Surinamese women who wanted to lead "modern" lives. After the Second World War, however, the *kotomisi*, once rejected as belonging to tradition, became

fig. 11
Surinamese headscarf, made on the occasion of the centenary of the abolition of slavery, polychrome printed cotton, 35 x 32 3/8 in. (89 x 82 cm), 1963. National Museum of World Cultures, inv. no. 3596-1.

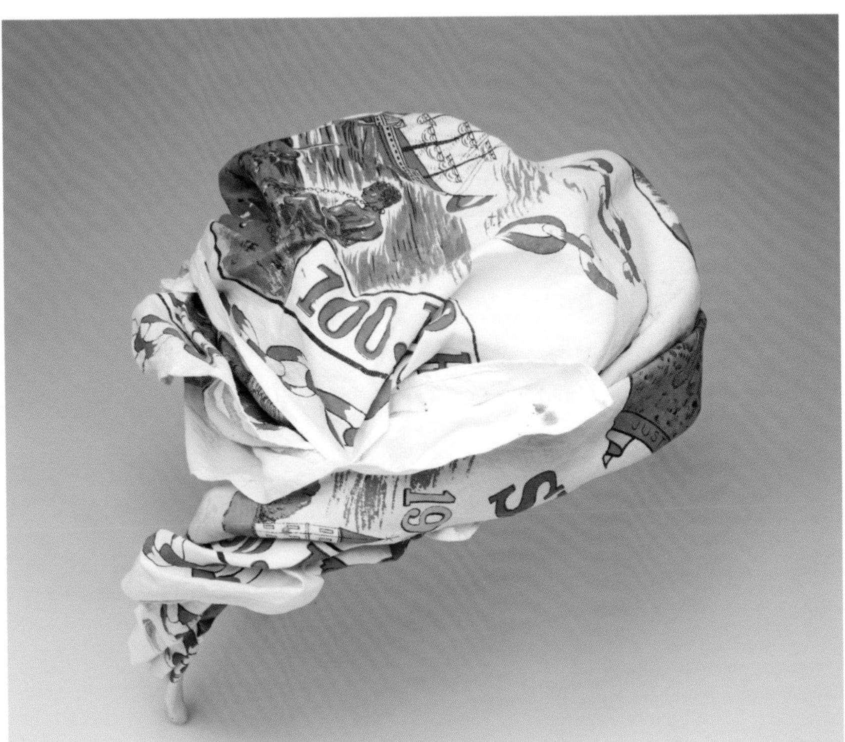

fig. 12
Surinamese headscarf, made on the occasion of the centenary of the abolition of slavery, polychrome printed cotton and pins, 5 x 12 3/8 x 11 5/8 in. (12.5 x 31.5 x 29.5 cm), 1963. National Museum of World Cultures, inv. no. 5332-1.

embraced as part of a national identity that could distinguish Suriname from the Netherlands, from which it gained independence in 1975.[15] This link between the clothing of the *kotomisi* and Surinamese identity can be seen in the headscarves that were made for the celebration of the abolition of slavery: after the Second World War, these commemorative *angisas* no longer depicted Dutch themes as they once had, but now featured broken chains and scenes from slavery (fig. 11, 12).[16]

Two Kinds of Silence: Wearing an *Angisa* in the Netherlands Today

As has become clear, European artists have extensively depicted *angisas* throughout the nineteenth and twentieth centuries, familiarizing European audiences with these headscarves. Yet these objects themselves have also traveled to Europe from the early nineteenth century onward. Already in 1824, the Dutch plantation owner Gaspard van Breugel had a number of dolls dressed as *kotomosis* made for his daughters and nieces in the Netherlands.[17] Over the years, Amsterdam's Museum of the Tropics, where some of these dolls can be found today, has amassed a large collection of *angisas*. After 1945, more and more people from Suriname, who often saw the *angisa* as part of their heritage, migrated to the Netherlands, a high point being the migration of forty thousand Surinamese in 1975, when they were given the choice to become either Surinamese in a new, independent nation, or remain Dutch. These people further developed the shapes and meanings of *angisas* in the Netherlands, drawing from and reworking the historical narrative offered above.

fig. 13
Surinamese headscarf, 13 3/8 x 14 15/16 in. (34 x 38 cm.), undated. National Museum of World Cultures, inv. no. 2884-9.

The basis for a modern-day *angisa* is usually a thirty-five- to forty-inch square piece of pure cotton cloth. These cloths come in many variants, differing from one another in color, pattern, and the signs and texts imprinted on them. A bilingual Dutch and English book on *angisas* published in 2008, *Angisa Tori: The Secret Code of Surinamese Headkerchiefs*, describes how the cloth should be washed, heavily starched, and ironed in preparation for wearing.[18] The *angisa* should be put on and taken off just as easily as a hat, folded into one of the many different shapes that have been developed over time.

An *angisa* gains meaning in part through the pattern on its cloth; in many cases, these cloths carry a name, story, or proverb, with origins in history attached to them. I will provide several examples of *angisas'* contemporary meanings within Surinamese Dutch communities. Several of these headscarves' names and stories are connected to the history of slavery. A cloth with a pattern called *Akuba prat'ati* (Akuba's torn heart) is tied to a story about the female slave Akuba who, after abolition, was finally allowed to marry but was in love with two different men. In addition to the pattern on the cloth, the tying style of the *angisa* also communicates meaning. When the two tips of a knot are pointed upward, for instance, the *angisa* expresses anger or resistance. There are many different tying styles with many different meanings: the Museum of the Tropics (now part of the National Museum of World Cultures) has among its *angisas* one that is folded in a shape called "Kiss me quickly, I belong to someone else," and one in a shape that means "Let it slide" (fig. 13).[19] Nancy Wouter said the *angisas* she and her daughters wear are tied in a style that, through their sharp, upward-pointing shapes denoting anger and defiance, are called "Let them talk." In practice, not all these potential layers of meaning play a role for women wearing *angisas* today. Like Wouter, most of the women interviewed during Keti koti in 2013 only attached a certain meaning to the tying style they had chosen and sometimes to the prints on their headscarves, such as a Surinamese flag or a figurative print of broken chains.

Today in the Netherlands, many women wearing and making *angisas* emphasize the fact that during slavery these headscarves had coded meanings. Mildred Isselt-Dankoor, who offers courses and gives demonstrations in the Netherlands on how to tie *angisas*, spoke about the invention of these headscarves by enslaved women in an interview on Dutch public television in 2011: "People had to work hard and they were not allowed to talk much. This is how this headscarf originated. . . . If you are not allowed to talk you are going to work with your hands and your head. Because they started working with their heads these headscarves came into being. . . . Through them they could nevertheless talk with each other."[20] In the book *Angisa Tori*, the author writes: "This method of communication is not easily understood by a random passer-by; in fact only insiders will understand the essence of the message. So there is a good reason to call this a coded message."[21] In accounts like these, two silences are highlighted: one enforced from the outside, in particular by the slaveholders, and another one produced by the slaves in answer to the first. The difference between the two is that the first silence is imposed to prevent communication and meaning, while the second is a silence that is resounding and meaningful, at least to the privileged and educated observer.

As can be seen from the present tense in the quote from *Angisa Tori*, as well as in Wouter's remarks in her interview, some of the women who wear *angisas* today perceive the subversive meanings of these headscarves to be relevant not only to their great-great-grandmothers, but also to themselves. Especially in the Dutch context, wearers regularly point toward the existence of a silence; this time not imposed by slaveholders to prevent communication among slaves possibly plotting to escape, but maintained by a part of Dutch society on the topic of Dutch slavery and its legacies.[22] Interviewed during Keti koti in Amsterdam in 2013, several women wearing *angisas* expressed concern or discontent about the cultural memory of slavery in the Netherlands. Regina Benescia, for instance, said that slavery has been hushed up in the Netherlands; a woman calling herself Lia pointed out that Dutch people do not know about slavery, as it is not taught in Dutch schools; and according to Claudia Velland, there is still a taboo in the Netherlands on being a descendent from a slave or a slaveholder.[23] Their *angisas*, many women said, were meant to prevent forgetting of the fate of black people under slavery, but also to signal that the past is still in some ways present. A second woman called Regina said, for instance: "[Slavery] is something that has been etched. I was not present back then, but I still live through it on a daily basis at my work because of discrimination."

One reason it is not easy in the Netherlands to talk about the legacy of slavery is the fact that "Dutch" most often means "white." Compound identity markers ("Surinamese Dutch," for instance) are hardly ever used, and nonwhite people are usually referred to according to the nation from which they or one of their ancestors came to the Netherlands ("Surinamese," "Moroccan," or "Turkish"). This practice goes back to nineteenth-century European nationalism, in which race, culture, and nation were imagined to be naturally overlapping entities that could be sharply distinguished into neat containers across the continent.[24] The two Dutch words *allochtoon* (from a strange soil) and *autochtoon* (from the same soil), developed by Dutch policy makers in the 1970s to distinguish first- and second-generation immigrants from people who had been living in the country for a longer time, are used in popular discourse today to denote nonwhite and white people. Even if a black citizen's family has been living in the country for many generations, he or she is still considered an *allochtoon*, not Dutch. If a black Dutch woman wants to speak up about the memory of slavery, she therefore faces at least two challenges: as a black person she cannot speak in the name of Dutch society, and as a Dutch person she cannot talk about slavery. The latter has to do with the specific position of Dutch colonial history in relation to the country's national history.

Cultural memories of colonialism and slavery in the Netherlands are diverse, and often at odds with one another. Different histories, moreover, exist within different mnemonic frames. Elsewhere I have argued that, with respect to violence in the Dutch East Indies, the contemporary Republic of Indonesia, most Dutch live in a state of what Ann Laura Stoler has called "cultural aphasia."[25] Unable to see the hundreds of thousands of Indonesian and thousands of Dutch deaths during the many colonial wars, as well as many other episodes of violence in the Dutch East Indies, as part of national history, the Dutch have periodically rediscovered their colonial past over the last century without giving it a meaningful position in national frames of remembrance. These regularly "emerging memories," as I have called them, always submerge again only to reemerge at a later moment, after which the cycle repeats itself.[26]

The cultural memory of slavery in the Americas has a rather different status at the moment, but a no less problematic one. In the Netherlands, spokespersons or "memory brokers" for this history are present and vocal, whereas Indonesian voices are seldom heard within the Dutch public sphere.[27] One outcome of the difference in cultural memory of slavery (in the West) and colonialism (in the East) is that, while the victims of the latter are never recalled in the public sphere outside of the moments when they emerge and briefly haunt the nation, the slaves who were transported to the Americas are commemorated each year during a ceremony at the National Slavery Monument in the Amsterdam Oosterpark, in the presence of Dutch cabinet members and sometimes the Queen or King (fig. 2).

Nevertheless there are widespread attempts to compartmentalize this history and bracket it off from national history.[28] Guno Jones has recently distinguished two discourses in the Netherlands with respect to the memory of slavery, namely a "Dutch postcolonial discourse" that has partly broken public silence about slavery in the Netherlands, and an "ethno-nationalist discourse" that attempts to distinguish national history from the history of slavery and rejects the renewed interest in slavery in recent years.[29] Evidence of the Dutch postcolonial discourse can be found not only in the aforementioned monument, but also in the establishment in 2003 of a National Institute for the Study and Documentation of Slavery and its Legacy.

Still, the ethnonationalist discourse has gathered momentum in recent years, as the right-wing Freedom Party made electoral gains and in 2010 became a de facto part of the Dutch government. This last fact led to the closing of the institute and to the slashing of budgets for various other postcolonial research institutes, such as the Royal Netherlands Institute for Southeast Asian and Caribbean Studies and the Royal Tropical Institute. Even before 2010, Hero Brinkman, a member of parliament for the Freedom Party, said, regarding politicians from the Dutch Antilles bringing up the history of Dutch slavery, "it's about money for them." He stated: "The Dutch were the slave drivers and today we are supposed to feel guilty about this and buy off this feeling with a big bag of money: total nonsense. I don't have to feel guilty at all about what our ancestors did hundreds of years ago."[30] In 2011, Eric Lucassen of the same party told the government of Sint Maarten—a country in the Caribbean within the Kingdom of the Netherlands—to "quit those pathetic stories about slavery."[31] The history and memory of slavery are strongly contested terrains in the Netherlands, leading to active attempts to silence those who wish to put them on the public and scholarly agenda. It is in this politically charged context that *angisas* have gained renewed meaning.

That slavery is still a highly contested part of the past in the Netherlands could again be seen only six months after Keti koti 2013. In the winter of 2013–2014, Amsterdam residents regularly encountered a poster with an image that has often returned to the Dutch public sphere as an icon of slavery. This engraving by William Blake, from Stedman's *Narrative*, is titled *Flagellation of a Female Samboe Slave*. In it, a young black woman is depicted, in Stedman's words, "tied up with both Arms to a tree . . . as naked as she came to the World, and lacerated in such a shocking Condition by the Whips of two Negro Drivers, that she was, from her neck to her Ankles literally died [sic] over with blood."[32] This image has gained various meanings over the course of the last two centuries. In the book by Stedman, who was not in favor of the abolition of slavery, the image depicted the kind of brutal treatment of slaves his writings opposed, whereas abolitionists in the nineteenth century used his texts and images to promote their cause.[33]

In Amsterdam in 2014, however, large font letters were printed across the woman's body, stating "Stop Talking about Slavery Already" (fig. 14). Paradoxically, the poster was meant to draw people to an exhibition about the legacy of slavery in the Netherlands at the Museum of the Tropics and thus to make them *start* talking about slavery. Yet there are many in the Netherlands who believe that it is time to *stop* talking about slavery. Nancy Wouter and her daughters, as well as many others during Keti koti, wear their *angisas* as display and performance objects to prevent precisely that from happening. From interviews like Wouter's, it becomes clear that it is not only the silence that has changed character, but so too has the language spoken by the *angisas*—from concrete messages communicated between slaves through certain tying styles and patterns, to an act that signals a still-relevant past that should not be forgotten. *Angisas*, in short, have retained their subversive connotations for many of their wearers, because they commemorate a past that cannot always be talked about aloud within the current order of discourse in the Netherlands.

fig. 14
Museum of the Tropics, exhibition poster for *Black & White: Stop Talking about Slavery Already*, 46 7/8 × 33 1/2 in. (119 × 85.3 cm), 2013. National Museum of World Cultures, inv. no. 5877-247.

Tropenmuseum
HOU NOU
EENS OP OVER
SLAVERNIJ
ZWART&WIT
TENTOONSTELLING & EVENEMENTEN
1 NOV. 2013 / 1 JULI 2014

M

SNS REAAL FONDS

AFK amsterdams fonds voor de kunst

JANIVO

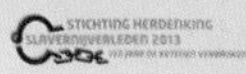
Prins Bernhard Cultuurfonds

kfHein,fonds
BankGiro Loterij

NOTES

1. Nancy Wouter, interview by Maria Platteeuw, "Eerbetoon aan mijn voorouders," Amsterdam Museum, http://hart.amsterdammuseum.nl/66281/nl/eerbetoon-aan-mijn-voorouders. A photograph of Wouter and her daughters was published to accompany the text; however neither the museum nor the author were able to reach Wouter to obtain permission to print the photograph here.
2. See Ilse Henar-Hewitt, *Surinaamse koto's en angisa's* (Paramaribo: Westfort, 1987); Laddy van Putten and Janny Zantinge, *Let them talk: de historische ontwikkeling van de kleding van de creoolse vrouw* (Paramaribo: Stichting Surinaams Museum, 1988); Helen Wijngaarde, "De kracht van klederdracht," *OSO: tijdschrift voor Surinaamse taalkunde, letterkunde en geschiedenis* 26 (2007): 290–305; Christine van Russell-Henar, *Angisa Tori: The Secret Code of Surinamese Headkerchiefs* (Paramaribo: Fu Memre Wi Afo, 2008); Marjon Meurs, "Veel om het lijf: de Kotomisi als beladen cultureel erfgoed" (master's thesis, Utrecht University, 2010); Markus Balkenhol, "De kotomisi en haar kinderen: slavernij en erfgoed nieuwe stijl in Nederland," *OSO: tijdschrift voor Surinaamse t aalkunde, letterkunde en geschiedenis* 31 (2012): 55–71.
3. See especially Van Putten and Zantinge, *Let them talk*.
4. Ibid., 19.
5. John Gabriel Stedman, *Narrative of a Five Years Expedition against the Revolted Negroes in Surinam*, ed. Richard Price and Sally Price (Baltimore: Johns Hopkins University Press, 1988).
6. Van Putten and Zantinge, *Let them talk*, 22–23.
7. Ibid., 57.
8. Clazien Medendorp, *Kijkkasten uit Suriname: de diorama's van Gerrit Schouten* (Amsterdam: KIT, 2008), 74.
9. Van Putten and Zantinge, *Let them talk*, 57.
10. Pierre Jacques Benoit, *Voyage à Surinam: descriptions des possessions Néerlandaises dans la Guyane* (Brussels: Société des Beaux-Arts, 1839).
11. Van Putten and Zantinge, *Let them talk*, 45.
12. Ibid., 38.
13. Rosemarijn Hoefte and Clazien Medendorp, *Suriname: gezichten, typen en costumen naar de natuur getekend door A. Borret* (Leiden: KITLV, 2003), 37–38.
14. Steven Vink, *Suriname door het oog van Julius Muller: Fotografie 1882–1902* (Amsterdam: KIT; Paramaribo: Stichting Surinaams Museum, 1997), 33.
15. Van Putten and Zantinge, *Let them talk*, 47.
16. Ibid., 47–48.
17. Susan Legêne, *De bagage van Blomhoff en Van Breugel: Japan, Java, Tripoli en Suriname in de negentiende-eeuwse Nederlandse cultuur van het imperialisme* (Amsterdam: Koninklijk Instituut voor de Tropen, 1998), 242–43.
18. Van Russel-Henar, *Angisa Tori*, 129–31.
19. Ibid., 38, 68.
20. Mildred Isselt-Dankoor, interview, "Mildred and Martijn," *Aanpakkers*, NTR, December 16, 2011.
21. Van Russell-Henar, *Angisa Tori*, 129.
22. See Alex van Stipriaan, et al., *Op zoek naar de stilte: sporen van het slavernijverleden in Nederland* (Leiden: KITLV; Amsterdam: NiNsee, 2007).
23. These and other interviews can be found on the website of the Amsterdam Museum, http://hart.amsterdammuseum.nl.
24. See Benedict Anderson, *Imagined Communities: Reflections on the Origin and Spread of Nationalism* (London: Verso, 1983).
25. Ann Laura Stoler, "Colonial Aphasia: Race and Disabled Histories in France," *Public Culture* 23 (2011): 121–57; Paul Bijl, "Colonial Memory and Forgetting in the Netherlands and Indonesia," *Journal of Genocide Research* 14, nos. 3–4 (2012): 441–61.
26. Paul Bijl, *Emerging Memory: Photographs of Colonial Atrocity in Dutch Cultural Remembrance* (Amsterdam: Amsterdam University Press, 2015).
27. On the notion of "memory brokers," see Lori Holyfield and Clifford Beacham, "Memory Brokers, Shameful Pasts, and Civil War Commemoration," *Journal of Black Studies* 42, no. 3 (2011): 436–56.
28. See Andrew Goss, "From *Tong Tong* to Tempo Doeloe: Eurasian Memory Work and the Bracketing of Dutch Colonial History, 1957–1961," *Indonesia* 70 (2000): 9–36.
29. Guno Jones, "*De Slavernij* is *onze* geschiedenis niet: over de discursieve strijd om de betekenis van de NTR-televisieserie 'De Slavernij'," *BMGN Low Countries Historical Review* 127, no. 4 (2012): 56–82.

30. *Kamerstukken II* 2008–09, 15-1052, http://www.tweedekamer.nl/kamerstukken.
31. *Kamerstukken II* 2010–11, 32 500 IV, nr. 41, 14, http://www.tweedekamer.nl/kamerstukken.
32. Stedman, *Narrative of a Five Years Expedition*, 264.
33. Elmer Kolfin, *Van de slavenzweep en de muze: Twee eeuwen verbeelding van de slavernij in Suriname* (Leiden: KITLV, 1997), 44.